T0339971

Management and the Sustainability Paradox

Management and the Sustainability Paradox is about how humans became disconnected from their ecological environment throughout evolutionary history, beginning with the premise that people have competing innate, natural drives linked to survival. Survival can be thought of in the context of long-term genetic propagation of a species, but it also involves overcoming of immediate adversities. Because of a diverse set of survival challenges facing our ancestors, natural selection often favored short-term solutions that, by consequence, muted the motivations associated with longer-range sustainability values.

Managerial decisions and choices mostly adopt a moral calculus of costs versus benefits. Managers invoke economic and corporate growth to justify virtually any action. It is this moral calculus underlying corporate behavior that needs critical examination and reformation. At the heart of it lie deep moral questions that we examine in this book, with the goal of proposing ethical solutions to the paradox. *Management and the Sustainability Paradox* examines the issue that there appears to be an inherent paradox between what some businesses view as "a need for progress" and "a concern for sustainability." In business, we often see a collision between ideas of progress and sustainability, which shapes corporate actions and managerial decisions. Typical corporate views of progress involve the creation of wealth, jobs, innovative products, and social philanthropic projects. On the basis of these "progressive" actions they justify their inequitable distribution of surpluses by paying low wages and exploiting ecological resources. It is not difficult to see the antagonistic interplay between technological and social innovation with our values for social and environmental well-being and a dualism that needs to be overcome.

This book is intended to broadly appeal to an academic and policy maker audience in the sustainability and management fields and will be of vital reading for managers seeking to reconnect our human chain with the natural environment in the cause of sustainable business.

David M. Wasieleski is Albert Paul Viragh Professor of Business Ethics, Duquesne University, USA, and Affiliate Research Professor, ICN Business School, Nancy, France.

Sandra Waddock is Galligan Chair of Strategy, Carroll School Scholar of Corporate Responsibility, and Professor of Management at Boston College's Carroll School of Management.

Paul Shrivastava is Chief Sustainability Officer and Professor of Management, Pennsylvania State University.

Routledge Studies in Management, Organizations and Society

This series presents innovative work grounded in new realities, addressing issues crucial to an understanding of the contemporary world. This is the world of organised societies, where boundaries between formal and informal, public and private, local and global organizations have been displaced or have vanished, along with other nineteenth century dichotomies and oppositions. Management, apart from becoming a specialized profession for a growing number of people, is an everyday activity for most members of modern societies.

Similarly, at the level of enquiry, culture and technology, and literature and economics, can no longer be conceived as isolated intellectual fields; conventional canons and established mainstreams are contested. **Management, Organizations and Society** addresses these contemporary dynamics of transformation in a manner that transcends disciplinary boundaries, with books that will appeal to researchers, student and practitioners alike.

Recent titles in this series include:

For a full list of titles in this series, please visit www.routledge.com

Management and the Sustainability Paradox

Reconnecting the Human Chain

David M. Wasieleski, Sandra Waddock, and Paul Shrivastava

Routledge
Taylor & Francis Group

NEW YORK AND LONDON

First published 2021
by Routledge
605 Third Avenue, New York, NY 10017

and by Routledge
2 Park Square, Milton Park, Abingdon, Oxon, OX14 4RN

First issued in paperback 2022

Routledge is an imprint of the Taylor & Francis Group, an informa business

Publisher's Note
The publisher has gone to great lengths to ensure the quality of this reprint but points out that some imperfections in the original copies may be apparent.

Library of Congress Cataloging-in-Publication Data
A catalog record for this book has been requested

ISBN 13: 978-0-367-50561-5 (pbk)
ISBN 13: 978-1-138-20478-2 (hbk)
ISBN 13: 978-1-315-46877-8 (ebk)

DOI: 10.4324/9781315468778

Typeset in Sabon
by Apex CoVantage, LLC

Contents

Prologue

As between clear blue and cloud,
Between haystack and sunset sky,
Between oak tree and slated roof,
I had my existence. I was there.
Me in place and the place in me.

Nobel Prize–Winning Poet Seamus Heaney, *Human Chain*

Throughout our evolutionary history, humans have always been in search of a better world, a utopia. We constantly redefine and remake our environment in an unending quest for a better, more comfortable life. With technological advances, we shape our living space to reflect our needs and ways of life. Through our efforts, our cities are transformed into visions of human prowess. Ironically, this has contributed to our separation from nature.

Jane Jacobs

Urban studies author and activist Jane Jacobs influenced urban design and renewal in major cities around the world in the postcolonial era.[1] She advocated the duality of 'thinking globally and acting locally' in order to make cityscapes livable and vibrant for all residents, encouraging diversity of activities and uses to make cityscapes accessible.[2] Jacobs encouraged city planners to take a street-level view of their cities when redesigning them. Her vision involved building low- to mid-rise buildings in self-contained, mixed-income, densely populated neighborhoods that would serve the needs of their inhabitants. To her, regeneration of postcolonial cities like London, New York, Melbourne, Toronto, among others means giving the residents a voice in creating livable, workable, and vibrant neighborhoods. For cities to thrive, they need diversity of cultures and of thought. They should exist independently of political life surrounding them.[3] Thus, she promoted *connection and independence* for the people inhabiting a particular locale.

Jacobs called Toronto, Ontario, Canada, her home. Here she was active in shaping the civic agenda of the city as it expanded at an exponential rate in the last half of the 20th century. Looking at Toronto today, it does not take one long to notice that the architects of the fourth largest city in North America did not always listen to her. While she vociferously argued for cities to spread out low to the ground so residents could interact with one another, and keep their "eyes on the street," Toronto politicians decided to build up. In April of 2014, the Canadian Broadcasting Company reported that there were 147 high-rise cranes currently under operation in the downtown core of Toronto, building sky-rise condominiums, luxury hotels, and lavish corporate headquarters for both Bay Street and foreign capitalists.[4] To give you some perspective, that is over 90% of the world's high-rise cranes operating in a single city at one time. With each additional story stacked onto these cement-and-glass towers, dwellers are removed further and further from the ground.

Yet, perhaps one has to question Jacobs's philosophies. Toronto is widely touted as a "world class" city. The Canadian news daily the *Globe and Mail* published research from the Reputation Institute in 2013 that listed Toronto as the Number 1 place to work and the Number 2 place to live in the world.[5] These rankings are based on the extent to which the city has an advanced economy, an effective government, and an appealing cultural environment. In 2014, *Forbes Magazine* ranked Toronto as one of the most influential cities in the world,[6] and in 2018, it was considered the 13th most "reputable" city by Forbes.[7] The magazine rooted its influential city rankings on the amount of foreign direct investment cities have attracted, the concentration of corporate headquarters in the city, the number of particular business niches those headquarters dominate, ease of travel to other global cities, strength of producer services, financial services, technology and media power, and racial diversity. The reputable cities ranking criteria were being "well-developed," offering appealing environments and positive experiences. *Notice the imprint of business in this list of criteria.* According to Princeton University, Toronto has the highest percentage of non-native-born residents (approximately 49% of the population were born outside Canada). As a result, the city is recognized by UNESCO as the most ethnically diverse city in the world.[8] The city's residents are historically considered to be hardwired to be open to the outside world.[9] The *London Telegraph* also declared Toronto's skyline one of the most beautiful in the entire world, a distinction voted on by its worldwide readership.

For those of you who have ever been to Toronto, you can attest to its stunning, futuristic skyline, its beautiful relationship with Lake Ontario, and its multifaceted neighborhoods with cuisine from virtually anywhere in the world. If one can look past the city's high cost of living, one can see a city with endless possibilities. The downtown financial district core is renowned for its underground city, affectionately known as the "PATH." The idea of the PATH has redefined life in northern cities. When the weather is cold, wet, windy, or icy, residents and visitors alike are greeted to a luxury troglodyte existence. Each skyscraper in the central corridor has access to this underground world of lavish shopping, fine dining, organic gardens, award-winning architecture, public transportation, and its own social sphere.

Sergio's Story

Let us tell you the story of Sergio. Sergio recently moved to Toronto from a metropolis in a warmer climate. He loves the city for many of the reasons we describe above. Initially, though, the more severe weather worried him until . . . he embraced the PATH! Yes, the PATH has become a new way of life. Sergio wanted to live a healthy and well-connected lifestyle. Like many newcomers to the city, he wanted to live close to his workplace, shopping centers, banks, restaurants, dry cleaners, and a local watering hole, where he could share a glass of cheer with friends. Ideally, he would live in close enough proximity to all these conveniences of life, that he could walk everywhere. Well, the Queen City did not disappoint. He rents a one-bedroom apartment in a high-rise condo building off of Bloor Street, adjacent to the Yorkville area of town, just north of the main corporate district. His office is in a different high-rise tower on Wellington Street in the financial core.

On a typical winter weekday morning, Sergio's day goes something like this:

He wakes up around 5:30 in the morning and immediately takes the elevator down 30 floors to the in-house gym and exercise area. Normally he tries to jog 15 kilometers on the treadmill before doing a couple of laps in the indoor, chlorinated swimming pool. When finished with his workout, he proceeds to take a shower underneath his flow-control faucet. While getting dressed, he likes to admire the aerial view of the city from his apartment while drinking a cup of fair trade coffee. Then he proceeds down to the PATH, which is accessible from the lobby of his building. He walks down a half-flight of stairs and heads two blocks west to grab the University subway line. He takes the subway for four stops, gets out, and walks another two blocks underground to his office building, where he emerges from the labyrinth below into the main atrium, where only a couple of the blurry faces looks familiar.

Sergio's office looks over Lake Ontario. He can see Toronto Island from his desk if he stretches his head. In the summer, he occasionally catches a glimpse of the ferries running from the lakeshore to the island. But it is winter. Temperatures have not been above freezing for almost three weeks. Although the climate has definitely become more moderate in recent years, this is the year of the Polar Vortex, which has had her talons in Toronto for much of the season. At the moment, the lake is frozen in between the Queens Quay Harbourfront and the island. (Ironically, ice skaters do not attempt to skate on the lake but rather on a man-made rink overlooking the lake.) Despite the extreme cold, Sergio still does not own a winter coat. In fact, he did not even pack one today (–20C at daybreak). Instead, he wore a smart argyle sweater that he had to take off part of the day because his office feels like a terrarium in the afternoon sunlight.

His day proceeds uneventfully. He has several mind-numbing meetings sprinkled throughout the afternoon, causing him to question his professional choices and career. As his colleague from the London office (whom he's never met before today) gases on, ad nauseam, about cutting costs this quarter so the boss "can make his targets," Sergio temporarily escapes his immediate world and gazes out the window, dreaming of hiking along the promontories of Georgian Bay and diving into the water to cool off. His visions of the lower Lake Huron mainly come from the art of the Canadian "Group of Seven" painters,[10] of which he has several reproductions hanging on his office walls.

At lunchtime, Sergio heads back downstairs and does a little shopping for some organic fruits and vegetables for his home in the Loblaws grocery store closest to his building. He knows he wants to buy organic, but he does not pay attention to the territory from which they come. Luckily, the lines move quickly and he is able to squeeze in a bite to eat. He is in a hurry so he grabs a sandwich from a shop that claims to only serve locally raised meats, although Sergio has no idea where that may be. Without any time to dwell on such things, he races back to the office, eats his sandwich, and goes back to the conference room.

During the afternoon meetings, he is told that tomorrow he has to take the train to Montreal. Though it will be even colder in Quebec, the VIA Rail station is located only a few blocks from his business meeting location. So he can walk underneath rue St. Catherine through the shops without having to go outside. He will not have to feel the biting wind off the St. Lawrence. Frankly, he does not know—or want to know—what –30C feels like. Thankfully, the main train station in Toronto, Union Station, can also be accessed via the PATH.

Eventually the meetings end and our friend has put in a full day. Afterward, he agrees to meet his new acquaintances for a drink to decompress from the day of computer screens, spreadsheets, and triple bottom lines. His colleagues suggest a place in the Entertainment District with a beautiful atrium filled with tropical plants and trees and completely enclosed and shut off from the frigid Southern Ontario air.

After a couple of well-nursed drinks, Sergio grabs his belongings and trots to the nearest subway stop through the PATH, which serves as his

Oregon Trail each day. He gets home late for a weekday. He is exhausted. Before going to bed, he tries to relax. Without ever looking again out the window at the view from his unit, he clicks an MP3 file on his computer to play sounds of a babbling brook, climbs into bed, shuts his eyes, and dreams of Georgian Bay again.

Broken Human Chain

Sergio's story is not unusual. It illustrates a paradox of modern life—the desire for a sustainable, even flourishing, lifestyle while being completely disconnected from nature itself. Charles de Gaulle lamented in 1968, "The age we are living is marked by the acceleration of scientific and technological progress demanding a vast regeneration both within ourselves and in our relations with others . . . the problem is to accomplish this without France ceasing to be France." In this context, de Gaulle was speaking about France losing her identity through the increased loss of the agricultural lifestyle that was once so prominent in his country. Even back then, the president perceived a technology-driven separation between the farmers and their craft. France's is not an isolated case. Due, in part, to the social and technological acceleration of reality, we have become unlinked with nature; we are cognitively and emotionally isolated from our ecological environment.

This book attempts to elucidate the paradox of the human condition. While we are born out of nature and often have primal urges to be reconnected with it, as a global society, we have progressively built up physical and psychological walls around us that completely separate us from our natural environment. Think about Sergio. He loves being outdoors, in natural beauty, and has a real concern for sustainability issues. But his actual daily life does not realize these deeply embedded desires. Not once during his day did Sergio's skin ever touch the outdoor air. Not once did his feet actually come into contact with the natural ground. His feet were encased in rubber and canvas. His shoes only stepped on the concrete and asphalt of the PATH and manufactured flooring of his office building. Even at home, his bare feet only touched carpeting and ceramic tile.

Let us be clear, however. We think Toronto is a great city, and Sergio's life is not too shabby. There are so many wonderful benefits and amenities in modern life. It is difficult to imagine what life would be like without climatically controlled hallways and technologically sophisticated subterranean malls. Humans have cleverly redefined their daily environments to emphasize comfort, convenience, and safety. We do not want to lose or slow down technological advancements. In fact, we hope and expect the world to offer even more inventions to make our lives more economical and luxurious. Never in this book do we argue to "undo" any of these fabulous developments in favor of a return to a time when "Man" [*sic*] was intimately intertwined and *one* with nature. Rather, we ask . . . is it possible to have *both*? If so, how can that be done?

Have you ever longed for those peaceful moments at the beach or on top of a mountain where you can hear nothing but sounds of the water, wind, and birds? Or, have you ever been truly moved by a landscape painting or stopped in your tracks when you catch a glimpse of a sunset? Why are those Corona ads so successful? It is common to want to "find your beach"—a place where our skin actually touches the air, and the ground, where we are not quarantined from nature. The sense is present in us already. It is natural. Regardless of where you come from—no matter what part of the world—people from <u>all</u> cultures around the globe have the same natural drives. Sadly, our connections to these natural states have often been reduced to a sort of nostalgia for what once was or what still could be in isolated instances.

We argue in the chapters that follow that numerous tensions, even paradoxes, limit the perspectives of many people today. In the developed or industrialized world, we live in a world dominated by values of what scholar Bill Frederick called economizing, which are supplemented by power-aggrandizing and technological values.[11] Yet our longing to be in nature puts us deeply in touch with another set of values that we argue are much needed today—values of ecologizing[12] and civilizing,[13] to bring balance back into the relationship between us humans and the natural environment from which we come and to which we are integrally related.

Reconnecting the Human Chain

The inspiration behind this book comes from the poetry of Nobel Laureate Seamus Heaney. His last published collection of poems is titled, *Human Chain*, from which we base our own subtitle, and a brief excerpt of which opens this prologue. We intend our book to be, in part, a tribute to his *oeuvre*, which collectively offers a deep understanding of the human condition. Throughout his illustrious career, Heaney spoke about continuities of human interaction but at the same time recognized the transmission from one social and psychological state to another.[14] He exquisitely describes how humans struggle with drives for both cultivation and destruction in terms of our relationships with each other and our surroundings. These tensions and even paradoxes are the dualities of life. In the chapters to follow, we will explore some of these paradoxes and the ways in which they have shaped today's dominant "modern" culture, especially in the industrialized (Northern and Western) world. We humans, in Heaney's terms, have both the ability and the motivation to cultivate *and* destroy. This book attempts to address a whole cascade of human dualities and dualisms to see if there can be a synthesis that allows us to transcend the limitations of today's perspectives and enable movement toward a world where all, including all living and human beings, can flourish.

To frame our efforts, we use as a metaphor the symbol of an interlocking chain with individual links represented by different paradoxes, dualisms, and dualities outlined in the initial chapters. In describing what we see to be fundamental <u>tensions</u> from human history, we outline competing sets of natural survival drives that helped *cause* a break in the chain between humans and nature. Then, using that same links in the chain, we show how the opposing drives can actually be reimagined for resolving the conflict.

Humans have been alienated from nature by cultural and social pressures over time. In this book, we address this separation from nature by individuals and modern organizations in different types of economies. Namely, the produce and consume model as bolstered by modern industrial capitalism disconnects societal members from nature, leading to an eventual disregard for and separation from nature. By the end of this book, we lay out pragmatic ways to re-accentuate our lost ecological values and create a new sustainability ethic.

About This Book

In this book, we explore the following questions:

- Can individuals, business organizations, and societal legislative bodies strive toward social innovations that do not mute our natural environmentally oriented values?
- Can we innovate to reconnect (linkage value) with nature?

<u>The book's thesis</u>: *There exists a universal sustainability ethic rooted in the naturally derived environmental values embedded into the cognitive algorithms of all human brains, but that cultural adaptations through evolutionary time have gradually created a synapse—an adaptation gap—in terms of the activation of these algorithms. Survival pressures and a changing environment presented numerous challenges to humans from the Pleistocene Era to the present moment. Humans innovated and developed technological tools through natural selection in response to these survival pressures, but our awareness and activation of our environmental values and drives has been muted by cultural influences.*

An additional component to this analysis involves the possibility that social and technological acceleration contributes to the formation, interpretation, and governance of sustainability ethics.[15] Included in this social category are the laws that societies/cultures develop to control our sustainable behaviors. Critical theories of modernity highlight the increasingly fast-paced development of social conventions and technological tools available to individuals. In this book we acknowledge the temporal variables associated with the maintenance and development of behavioral norms for the protection of our ecosystems.

Finally, we will also examine other natural human tendencies for the maintenance of group norms that have evolved through natural selection. Strong reciprocity[16] and an aesthetic instinct[17] are appropriate areas for exploration in terms of how sustainability ethics formed and how they can be maintained.

Ultimately, we propose contours of an ethical system based on an ecological—ecologizing—foundation that would be suited to honoring the lives of future generations and that have a long-term focus. These features of this approach will allow us humans to create global governance over the global commons, deal with intergenerational equity issues, and foster holistic development of human potential in ways that today's approach of "economizing," as we will explain later, does not.

Our intent in the chapters ahead is to offer strategies for reconnecting the human "chain" and thereby re-establishing our links with nature, both emotionally and cognitively. Through our research and the work of many great scholars, we have discovered quite a bit of evidence that most people would like to feel and experience a greater bond with nature. When we drift off at night or daydream during a boring meeting, our thoughts often float to a serene, remote spot where no manmade device can bother us. We often desire a disconnection from our concrete and plastic society and to (at least temporarily) spend time in an organic, more primitive environment.

But, we also recognize that there exists a moral imperative to *live with, in, and of* nature rather than project a dominion *over* it. Thus, our book seeks to resolve our natural human paradox as a normative necessity. We believe that no matter one's political inclination or viewpoint on sustainability issues, there lies beneath a natural sensitivity to preserving our ecological environment. Over *Homo sapiens'* evolutionary history, this sensitivity has been suppressed by a dominant set of values that do not *value* their opposite and that in fact are much more linear in their orientation. Our muted values for sustainability were, from this perspective, an unavoidable evolutionary consequence to survival pressures throughout time. Yet, the countervailing values that embed and value paradox in our thinking and actions still exist and can, we argue, reemerge through creative human intervention. If we can transcend and include today's economizing and technologizing values[18] into a more broadly defined set of values, for example, ecologizing and civilizing values, then we believe there is hope for a better future for humans—and all of life's creations. It is possible to move from *Homo faber* ("Man" the creator) *to Homo sustinens* ("Man" the cooperator with nature).[19]

Our outlook in this book, then, is filled with hope. While we identify these essential links of the chain as dualisms of human nature, each exacerbating the gap between people and the ecological environment, we ultimately see real, pragmatic opportunities for flipping the dualism into a duality, where we can restore a <u>balance</u> among our natural drives, while simultaneously recognizing the both/and of paradoxes in our world. Our goal is certainly not to suppress our motivations for economizing efficiency and technological progress. On the contrary, we look for solutions for establishing more of an equilibrium between humans' short-term survival motives and our more enduring sustainability needs.

It may surprise some of you that one of the sources for the solutions we seek for restoring this balance and re-soldering our chain together lies with business organizations. (!) Yes. Through our own doing, corporations have become the most prominent and important institutions in all of society.[20] Business is such an integral member of society that we often personify corporations and think of them as individual entities. We even treat them as persons when it comes to the law. Without business, much that we experience in daily life would not exist. Business makes it possible to accomplish feats that would otherwise not be achievable on our own. But businesses are only one, albeit very important, piece of a very complex puzzle of actors whose perspectives need to shift from dominance to partnership or collaboration, as we will discuss later, and from economizing toward ecologizing as core values that drive our own actions and attitudes as people, and the institutions that we create.

All are but parts of one stupendous whole, whose body nature is, and God the soul.

–Alexander Pope

Notes

1. Jacobs, J. (1961). *The death and life of great American cities*. New York: Vintage.
2. http://www.urbancentre.utoronto.ca/pdfs/researchbulletins/CUCSRB30-WellmanJaneJ.pdf
3. Jacobs, Jane. (1961). *The death and life of great American cities*. New York: Random House.
4. http://www.cbc.ca/news/canada/rob-ford-s-cranes-in-the-sky-line-examined-by-economists-1.2607440
5. http://www.theglobeandmail.com/news/toronto/is-toronto-world-class/article14937799/
6. http://www.forbes.com/sites/joelkotkin/2014/08/14/the-most-influential-cities-in-the-world/
7. Strauss, K. (2017, October 3). The world's most reputable cities in 2017, *Forbes*. https://www.forbes.com/sites/karstenstrauss/2017/10/03/the-worlds-most-reputable-cities-in-2017/#17284b0e6dcf
8. https://www.princeton.edu/~achaney/tmve/wiki100k/docs/Toronto.html
9. Levine, Allan. (2014). *Toronto: Biography of a city*. Toronto: Douglas & McIntyre.
10. Group of Seven (artists). Wikipedia, https://en.wikipedia.org/wiki/Group_of_Seven_(artists).
11. Frederick, W. C. (1995). *Values, nature, and culture in the American corporation*. Oxford, UK: Oxford University Press.

12. Frederick, W. C. (1995). cited above.
13. Waddock, S. (2002). *Leading corporate citizens: Vision, values, value-added.* New York: McGraw-Hill.
14. Heaney, Seamus. (2010). *Human chain.* New York: Farrar, Straus and Giroux.
15. Rosa, H. (2010). *Alienation and Acceleration.* NSU Press: Helsinki; Adams, 2009; Lubbe, 2009.
16. Fehr, E., & Fischbacher, U. (2003). The nature of human altruism. *Nature,* 42(5), 696–785.
17. Dutton, Denis. (2009). *The art instinct: Beauty, pleasure and human evolution.* New York: Bloomsbury.
18. As we will explore in depth in later changes, these values were forcefully articulated by William C. Frederick in his pathbreaking book *Values, nature, and culture in the American corporation.* Oxford, UK: Oxford University Press, 1995.
19. Munasinghe, Mohan, and Swart, Rob. (2000). *Primer on climate change and sustainable development: Facts, policy analysis and applications.* Cambridge: Cambridge University Press.
20. Micklethwait, John, and Wooldridge, Adrian. (2005). *The company: A short history of a revolutionary idea.* New York: Modern Library.

Section I

Tensions in Values Have Created Today's Problematic World

As the Prologue makes clear, for many people today there is a split in our consciousness that directly relates to how we humans connect with nature—or, in far too many instances, do not connect with nature. That disconnect has resulted in a dominant set of societal values that largely govern today's world and that disconnect those of us who live in the developed West/North from the natural forces and dynamics that created our existence in the first place. That disconnect has significant consequences, as we hope to demonstrate throughout *Human Chain*.

The fundamental argument that we make in this book is that we humans need to once again recognize, understand, and act upon knowledge that integrates us internally and intimately with nature. We need, that is, to instill in our human social and economic systems an ecologizing set of values that complement and expand today's dominant economizing and technologizing values, which we explore more deeply in Chapter 4. We need to connect more closely with the beautiful blue planet or what astronauts call the "blue marble"—Earth viewed from space—that is our only home and from which we draw everything we are and need. In other words, to be better in tune with nature's capacities, resources, and limitations, humanity has to move from values of economizing, power aggrandizing, and technologizing—to use Frederick's terms[1]—to ecologizing and civilizing values that honor and understand the world around us much more completely.

In this first section of *Human Chain*, we will emphasize the deep connectedness of humanity to nature that arises from many cultures' origin stories, not to mention the way the members of these cultures live their lives. Then we will look at how the set of origin stories in the Western/Northern world have been misunderstood—some might say perverted—towards a set of values in which we humans are somehow meant to dominate over nature rather than live in harmony with her. This important disconnect has resulted in numerous tensions and dualisms in values and human experiences over the "chain" of human development that further reify—or make real—this disconnect to the point where Sergio's story in the Prologue has become the story for far too many of us.

As the discussion of the tensions will illustrate, we in the "developed" world need to reintegrate these dualisms, tensions and seeming paradoxes so that we can reorient our minds to the realities that humans and other living beings face on the planet today. Those realities include increasing recognition that human activities, along with business and other institutional models that set out to "dominate" nature are no longer feasible. Human activities—particularly economic and business activities combined with population growth, which has grown exponentially since the Industrial Era began—have now reached a point at which civilizational and ecological collapse resulting from overuse of ecological resources, climate change, and growing inequality are entirely possible. Values of dominance, materialism, and continual growth have the outcome of producing ever-greater material and financial wealth for the few, with the many being left further and further behind. The societal implications of that growing gap could mean ever-greater divisiveness and social unrest, unless something changes dramatically. And, of course, this values orientation to economizing, manifested today in neoliberal economics, has also produced a massively unsustainable set of human institutions, practices, and population pressures that put the future of our civilization at risk.

In this fraught context, we humans, at least in the "developed" world, need a relatively dramatic shift of mind—or what systems thinker Donella Meadows called mindset change.[2] In important ways, we need to reintegrate ourselves with nature and close the gaps in thinking and practice that some of the dualisms and gaps we will explore have created. Towards that end, we believe that an ecologizing set of values combined with civilizing values can both include and transcend the economizing, power aggrandizing, and technological values, so that they are moderated as needed in what observers now call a "full" (as opposed to empty) world and that have gotten us into this mess. The implications of the dominance of ecologizing values include what the "instrumentalization" of nature, that is, the use of nature as a solely human resource, a perspective that is not consonant with long-term flourishing for all on the planet, something we explore in Section 1.

The dominance of humans over nature arises from what we label the split minds, split worldviews in Chapter 3. There we explore the distinctions between the left and right brain and the implications of that split for today's perspectives on the nature and purpose of the economy and the businesses that comprise it, along with the assumptions that support today's dominant economic and societal paradigms. These ideas will set us up for a discussion in Section II on the paradoxes that the splits and differences in values have engendered.

Notes

1. Frederick, W. C. (1995). *Values, nature, and culture in the American corporation*. Oxford: Oxford University Press.
2. Meadows, D. (1999). *Leverage points: Places to intervene in a system*. Harland, VT: The Sustainability Institute. Retrieved from: http://donellameadows.org/archives/leverage-points-places-to-intervene-in-a-system/.

1   The Sustainability Paradox

There is a widening adaptive gap that can be understood in terms of sensory, cognitive, and emotional responsiveness to our environment. In order to promote and support individual and group survival, humans have created and developed elaborate structures of organization at multiple levels, from small community-based organizations to huge global transnational corporations and from local tribes and communities to societies in the context of nations to, from some perspectives, a global community. Paradoxically, individual and cultural inventions that aided in human survival actually have, in many cases, increased our distance to our ecological environs. Thus, the main tension we wish to explore in this book is between the culturally driven economic lives and our ecological context.

Over many thousands of generations any connection with nature that humans experienced and felt became muted and suppressed by these cultural and symbolic messages, leading to behaviors that had little regard for our ecosystem. We argue that short-term survival pressures through evolutionary time generated cultural responses that gradually led to the disintegration of the relationship between "man" [sic] and the natural world (forming an adaptation gap). It is our view that we need a combination of re-purposed businesses oriented towards the greater good and well-functioning governments combined with a (now largely voluntary) global governance system that sets and maintains high standards and values for various institutions. Combined with the support of powerful democratically based civil society organizations, all are needed to ensure the appropriate balance between human interests and the interests of other living entities on the planet.

Paradoxes and Business

The core identified problem that serves as the impetus for this book is that there appears to be an inherent paradox between what some businesses, which are by default today's most powerful institutions, view as "a need for progress" and "a concern for sustainability" that manifests in much weaker civil society and ecological institutions today. As stated by Thorstein Veblen, "The accustomed ways of doing and thinking not only become an habitual matter of course, but they come likewise to be sanctioned by social convention, and so become right and proper and give rise to principles of conduct."[1] In business, we often see a collision between ideas of progress and sustainability, which shapes corporate actions and managerial decisions. Typical corporate views of progress involve the creation of wealth, jobs, innovative products, and social philanthropic projects. On the basis of these "progressive" actions they justify their inequitable distribution of surpluses by paying low wages and exploiting ecological resources without worrying about replenishment or renewal (land, water, forests, etc.). It is not difficult to see the antagonistic interplay between technological and social innovation with our values for social and environmental well-being. It is a dualism that needs to be overcome.

Managerial decisions and choices mostly adopt a moral calculus of costs versus benefits, that is, a utilitarian values orientation. Managers invoke economic and corporate growth to justify virtually any action, in part because today's dominant narrative of neoliberalism, as we will discuss later, justifies and celebrates continual growth and expansion with little regard for the social or ecological costs. If long-term sustainability enters into this thinking at all, it does so in a superficial morally challenged framework that emphasizes the short-term benefits over long-term risks. It is this moral calculus underlying corporate behavior that needs critical examination and reformation as we consider how businesses might be re-purposed around socio-ecological benefit and the greater good for all. At the heart of this paradox lie deep moral questions that we examine in this book, with the goal of proposing integrated solutions to co-existing paradoxes or dualities. Symbolically, we favor an evolution of sorts from *Homo faber*, the idea that humans control the environment through technologies,[2] to *Homo sustinens*, referring to humans who work to sustain their ecological environment. The former view of "man" favors "dominion *over* nature" in a Baconian sense. The latter emphasizes "reconnecting *with* nature" to achieve a sustainable co-existence.

Nature, Evolution, and Human Beings

The starting point for this adventure through time is with natural science and evolutionary descriptions of human behavior. We contend that there are naturally derived values, developed through natural selection over evolutionary time, that are universally "human." In other words, there exists a set of values that are hardwired into the human brain for governing the fair and proper use of environmental resources—a care for the ecological environment. These values are predominantly found today in Indigenous, Eastern, and Southern cultures, rather than the Western cultures with which readers are more likely to be familiar, as we discuss in the next chapter. But there also exists a competing set of drives that promote the immediate protection and well-being of our genetic material so that it can be passed onto future generations.

For example, Hunter–Gatherers had a challenge of finding food within limits of human energy/effort, limited mobility, lack of tools, and lack of organizations as we know them. This challenge gave rise to an ethics of taking <u>what was needed</u> yet not over-exploiting natural resources.[3] Among settled agriculturalists it was necessary to determine <u>fair boundaries</u> (and property rights) for food production and the rules of consumption and storage[4] in order to remain in right relation to the ecological environment. In industrial societies, the main challenges are <u>over-consumption</u>, excessive extraction of natural resources, and pollution. This behavior overwhelms natural ecosystems in the wake of new, competing economic models (capitalism, socialism, communism).[5] The goal is to change the institutions in place that propagate the existing "ways of seeing."[6]

Evolutionary psychologists argue that our brains took their present form in the Pleistocene Era of *Homo sapiens* development (between about 2.6 million years ago until about 12,000 years ago).[7] Since then there has not been enough evolutionary time for humans' brains to have changed/evolved substantially. The algorithms and neural modules in our modern brains have the same form to satisfy functional challenges facing our ancestors at that time. Although the underlying principles may be embedded into the human cognitive architecture, the context of humans' relationship with nature has changed substantially throughout evolutionary history. We argue that the links with nature in the human chain have been severed at different points in human history as a natural way of *coping* with new, unfamiliar challenges and situations. This disconnect has caused human beings to have developed the capacity to reshape their environments in significant ways.

Simply stated, the ecological challenges facing modern-day individuals and corporations were not experienced by our hominid ancestors. Human societies were much smaller then, and their ecological impacts were limited, even when they shifted from roving nomadic tribes to more settled agricultural villages. This different context may be in part a reason for current society's struggle to motivate sustainable behaviors across the world. Our brains experience an intrinsic dissonance when navigating environments that do not resemble ancestral ones. Our collective ability to make "sense" of our current ecological challenges[8] is muted by the superseding focus on short-term competing survival demands. The emotional and cognitive drivers in our brains, however, have the capacity to adapt to modern situations.[9] Although the same algorithms that were formed in the distant past are still being activated at present, they are used for different purposes. Thus, the manifestation of ecological and individual values has evolved over time in response to changing cultural demands on societies.

These two orientations for the ecological surroundings and the immediate familial needs are not far-fetched, nor are they new to the human condition. For instance, the whole idea of property rights has its origins in the natural, deeply embedded need to cohabitate with each other, but within the boundaries of our natural environment.[10] The "rules" may have become socially constructed and have taken the form of various symbols to communicate the intended norms, but the underlying motivation to live in a community exists independently of its cultural manifestation and indeed has evolutionary value. In an Aristotelian sense, we are born out of the earth (Eros); we are a part of nature and cannot be separated or distinguished from the natural world. In short, we have an unavoidable <u>connection</u> with nature. We *are* nature, but we are separated from it. Why was that integral sense of connection lost and how do we get it back? That is the fundamental question of this book. We begin by looking back at some of the myths and narratives our ancestors used to cope with an uncertain world.

Notes

1. Veblen, T. (1914). *The instinct of workmanship and the state of the industrial arts*. New York: Macmillan.
2. Arendt, H. (1958). *Human condition: Place of publication not identified*. Chicago: University of Chicago Press.
3. Bonner, J. T. (1980). *The evolution of culture in animals*. Princeton, NJ: Princeton University Press.
4. Diamond, J. M. (1999, August). *Review of Diamond, Jared, Guns, Germs and Steel: The fates of human societies*. Retrieved from: www.h-net.org/reviews/showrev.php?id=3298.
5. Davis, C. (2009). *The monstrosity of Christ: Paradox or dialectic?* Boston: MIT Press.
6. Berger, J. (1972). *Ways of seeing: A book made by John Berger*. New York: British Broadcasting Corporation and Penguin Books.
7. Berger, J. (1972). *Ways of seeing: A book made by John Berger*. New York: British Broadcasting Corporation and Penguin Books.
8. Weick, K. E. (1995). *Sensemaking in organizations* (Vol. 3). Thousand Oaks, CA: Sage.
9. Pinker, S. (2002). *The blank slate: The modern denial of human nature*. New York: Penguin.
10. Greene, J. (2013). *Moral tribes*. New York: Penguin.

2 Sustainability's Roots in Primitive Societies

Creation myths or origin stories are the myths that different cultures use to tell how the world and humans' place in the world began. These stories are interesting in that they all speak of the fantastical origins of our human identity. Notably, common to most creation stories is that nature is the root or raw material of humans, integrally and inextricably connecting us humans to Earth and other living beings. The Hopi tale of four creations below illustrates our main point: in the beginning there was nature and humans were "of" it. And, we will argue, we still are "of" nature.

Creation Myths

Our largely modern and Western consciousness of humans as separate and distinct from and superior to nature is in some ways the starting point of this journey, as we explore below. First, let us explore several creation myths, starting with the Hopi tale of four creations.

> At first the world was eternal space. The Creator, Taiowa, was all that existed. There was no life, no shape, no time, no one. Taiowa created the finite in Sotuknang as his agent to establish nine universes—the nine solid worlds. Sotuknang was instructed to gather the waters from the space to make land and sea. He then gathered air to make winds and breezes, and life as Spider Woman. He empowered her to create life. Spider Woman mixed earth and with saliva with the Creation Song to make two beings—Poqanghoya solidified the earth. Palongawhoya sent out sound to resonate vibrating energy through the earth. The two were then sent to the poles of the earth to keep it rotating.
>
> Spider Woman made all the plants, the flowers, the bushes, and the trees, the birds and animals, using earth and the Creation Song. She made human beings by mixing her saliva with yellow, red, white, and black earth. She made four men and four women in her own form. She left a soft spot in their foreheads to hear the voice of Sotuknang and their Creator. Sotuknang gave them four languages. His only instructions—respect the Creator and live in harmony with him.[1]

Many other myths frame human origins in nature, including the Norse mythologist Snorri Sturluson's Edda, as translated by Anthony Faulkes describes origins of humans as follows:

> *In the beginning was time. There was nothing, no sand, nor sea, nor cool waves, no heaven, no earth. Niflheim was made before the earth. There a spring gave rise to twelve rivers. Surt the giant with a flaming sword guarded the hot and bright Muspell in the south. The north was frigid frozen ice rivers of Ginnungagap. The sparks and warm winds of Muspell thawed the frigid edge of Ginnungagap, into drips that thickened into the form of a man. He was Ymir. Ancestor of the frost-giants. More ice drips formed a cow. From her teats flowed four rivers of milk. The cow licked on the salt of the rime ice. A man's head began to emerge. By the third day of licking, the whole man had emerged. He was Buri. He had a son named Bor, who married Bestla, a daughter of the giants. Bor and Bestla had three sons, one of whom was Odin, the most powerful of the gods.*[2]

Another origin story that highlights how humans evolved from nature, this one from a First Peoples perspective, is the Cherokee Story of Corn and Medicine:

> *Before earth was Galúnlati, a stone vault with just water and darkness in the sky. Only animals were in Galúnlati. Galúnlati became overcrowded and the animals needed more room. To scout for land they sent down the Water-beetle to explore. Water-beetle dove below the water and returned with mud from below. That mud grew into earth. The island of earth is suspended at its four corners, from ropes that hang down from the sky. Someday the ropes will break and sink the earth back into the water.*
>
> *The new earth was very soft. Many birds flew down to explore the new land. It was too wet for them to stay. A buzzard flew down and searched. He became tired. His wings flapped against the ground digging valleys where they hit the ground. They formed mountains where they pulled away. This was the rugged Cherokee country.*
>
> *Eventually the earth dried and the animals moved down. There was no light. The animals set the sun passing from east to west. The sun close and hot, some animals were burned, the crawfish became crimson. Animals raised the sun repeatedly, until it was high enough that all could survive. The plants and animals were told to stay awake for seven nights in the Cherokee medicine ceremony. The animals all stayed awake the first night, and many stayed awake the next few nights. Only the owl and the panther and a couple of others stayed awake all seven nights. They were given the ability to see at night. They hunt at night when the others are asleep. The same thing*

happened among the trees, and only the cedar, pine, spruce, holly, and laurel stayed awake all seven nights. They can stay green all year round.

Humans came after the animals. The first woman give birth every seven days. They multiplied rapidly. There were so many of them that it seemed they all might not survive. So women were made to have just one child each year. Among these early people were a man and a woman name Kanáti ("The Lucky Hunter") and Selu ("Corn"). Kanáti would hunt each day and return with game. Selu would prepare the game by the stream near their home. She would return home with baskets of corn. She pounded the corn into flour for bread.

Asian cultures are known for their communitarian perspectives, in which family and relationships, holistic views, are dominant culturally, as opposed to more Anglo-Saxon orientations towards individualism.[3] The Pangu origin myth of China, which like many creation stories has multiple variants—as do many stories from Indigenous cultures—demonstrates how humans come from (interestingly, parasites in) nature:

In the beginning the universe was nothing but chaos, and the heavens and the earth were intermingled—a big black egg being commonly used as an analogy. Pangu was born inside of this egg and slept for 18,000 years, during which time the Yin and Yang balanced as he grew. When he awoke, he realized he was trapped within it. He cracked the egg and began to push it apart, essentially splitting the Yin and Yang. The upper half of the shell became the sky above him, and the lower half became the earth. The longer he held them apart, the thicker they grew and the taller he became, thus pushing them further apart—by precisely 10 feet per day. Here versions begin to change. Some claim that a turtle, a qilin, phoenix, and a dragon assisted him in this task. After another 18,000 years Pangu died, his body forming the various parts of the earth, and the parasites on his body forming humans. Another version states that he formed the earth with a chisel and hammer, while yet another version states that a goddess who later inhabited the earth formed humans.[4]

Obviously, we could explore many other creation myths; however, this short collection of creation myths from around the world illustrates the variety of stories that bind cultures together. Simultaneously, it demonstrates the fundamental idea that from the perspective of many cultures, we humans are inextricably a part of that creation story, having arisen from some natural source. Thus, humans are in and of nature in these stories from different places around the world. Creation myths are stories or narratives that explain how the world began and how people came to inhabit that world. Such myths are important because they help to frame what anthropologists call the cultural mythology that helps the community and individuals within it understand their place in the world.[5] As the sampling of creation myths above show, creation myths tend to be stories of the sacred and are frequently the basis of religious beliefs and influence whole cultures. In most of these tellings, humans are but one part of a vast array of creatures and elements.

Western Creation Myths

These creation tales are stories we now read to children to inspire awe about the mystery of our origins. They also carry the seeds of our understanding about how the world becomes intelligible to humans. These narratives squarely anchor human origins in nature. We understand the world by mechanisms of experiences, language, and eventually codified knowledge systems (religions, sciences, laws). Understanding the world is essential to survive in it, to sustain ourselves. Yet something has gone array in humans' understanding of their place in and of nature in much of the Western understanding.

"Modern" and Western conceptions of human beings' place in the world are strongly influenced by the world's dominant three religions, Christianity, Judaism, and Islam. The Bible's and Qur'an's stories of Genesis strongly influence Islamic, Christian, and Jewish mythologies and have had a dramatic impact on how people in the developed and industrialized world view human beings' place in the world. Each presents a dominant creation myth that has strongly influenced how Western civilization has developed, though they appear to draw from similar sources and tell much the same story in the end. The Bible's Genesis story is representative:

> *In the beginning when God created the heavens and the earth, the earth was a formless voice and darkness covered the face of the deep, while a wind from God swept over the face of the waters. Then God said, "Let there be light" and there was light. And God saw that the light was good, and God separated the light from the darkness. . . . And over the course of six days God created night and day, evening and morning, the sky that hovers over the waters, the dry land called Earth, the vegetation and plants that yielded seed, the sun, moon, and stars, swarms of living creatures of every kind, including winged birds that flew over the dome or sky. God blessed them, saying, "Be fruitful and multiply and fill the waters in the seas, and let birds multiply on earth."*
>
> *Then God said, "Let us make humankind in our image, according to our likeness, and let them have dominion over the fish of the sea, and over the birds of the air, and over the cattle, and over all the wild animals of the earth, and over every creeping thing that creeps upon the earth."*

So God created humankind in his image . . . male and female he created them . . . and said to them, "Be fruitful and multiply, and fill the earth and subdue it; and have dominion over the fish of the sea and over the birds of the air and over every living thing that moves upon the earth.[6]

Notably, in another version of the biblical creation story, God created Adam, man, out of dust, and Eve, woman, from the rib of Adam, situating both of them firmly in nature. The Qur'an states that Adam and Eve were created by Allah with souls and conscience, knowledge, and free will. Allah created Adam, "we created man from sounding clay, from mud molded into shape" (15:26).[7] As in the Old Testament in the Bible, which informs both Christianity and Judaism, the Qur'an is clear that "God is the Creator of all things and He is the Guardian over all things" (39:62).[8]

Broken Chain: Domination Versus Ecologizing

Unlike the Eastern and Indigenous origin stories cited above, the origin stories of the Old Testament of the Bible and the Qur'an emphasize the power of a single—male—god to create all of life's creations from nothing. Interestingly, the biblical creation story has long been interpreted to mean that humans are meant to have "dominion" or dominance and power over Earth and its creatures. Biblical scholar Justin Holcomb has pointed out that this interpretation means that Christians—and arguably Western culture in general, influenced as it is by the Bible—have been "particularly weak in dealing with ecological issues and the deterioration of the natural environment," in part because the word "dominion" is generally misconstrued. Holcomb claims strongly that "Dominion does not mean destruction, but responsibility. It is important to avoid flawed convictions about the right and power of humankind in relation to the rest of the natural world."[9] The Hebrew word translated as dominion is *radah*, which has connotations of having power over, ruling, even subduing[10] other living beings. This notion of dominion stands in contrast to ideas about stewardship that place humans into a quite different relationship with nature. In contrast, the word for human in Hebrew is *adam*, which connotes to "ground" or "earth." Related to Genesis, Adam came from the earth and will return to the soil, ultimately. *Humus*, also from Hebrew, refers to "humility." More specifically, it is the state of being close to the soil. According to David Abram, this suggests that ancient humans were in a humble relation to the environment. With the development of the dominion ideal, we have subdued this value.[11] In Chapter 5, we will revisit this cultural ideal of dominion by examining its natural counterpart, power-aggrandizing values.

Dualisms Versus Dualities

As we will see throughout this book, the idea of humans having power *over* nature has shaped many of the tensions we will articulate in the coming chapters. The tension between masculine and feminine values or, in the Chinese tradition, yin and yang, the split between mind and body, the tension between atomization and fragmentation and holism, the tension between empiricism and intuition or consciousness, to name just a few. In the Western world, these tensions manifest as positivism, dominance of "male" values, and in our economic, business, and other institutional systems. They are what scholar William C. Frederick called "economizing" values, which are supported by power aggrandizing values, over other values associated with what he termed "ecologizing"[12] and also "civilizing" values[13] that fit with many of these ancient traditions, bringing a more holistic perspective.

For many of us, making sense of the world, making it intelligible, is a story of separation from nature. It is also a separation of mind from body, which springs from Descartes's famous phrase, "I think, therefore I am." These ideas have resulted in emphasis on positivist science, empiricism, and values of economizing. As we experience and better understand the world, we also have in far too many instances separated ourselves further from nature, distancing it, objectifying it, dominating it, and inadvertently destroying it.

This dualism of separation and survival seems hardwired into the human brain—the bicameral brain,[14] or the right and left hemispheres.[15] As we will discuss below, the two hemispheres of the brain are different in structure and function. They vary in attention and flexibility, in what is implicit to them, and what is explicit. They identify different things as the unique, as personal, as body, as time, as depth. They shape higher-level brain functions of language and metaphor, music and aesthetics, empathy and morality, certainty and the conception of the self. Most importantly, they jointly facilitate the separation of self from nature and from others when, as McGilchrist argues, the left brain's detail orientation dominates right brain holism. Language emerged not to serve the human drive to think or communicate (although it aided these greatly), but the drive to act, change things around us, manipulate the world we occupied, that is for purposes of using tools and weapons, for hunting, for defense, and to build what Stein calls a theory of mind, as well as for mating purposes.[16]

Split Minds

Rooted in the human brain structure are deep cultural and social concepts, belief systems that have emerged to make sense of the world. One of these core concepts is that of values. Philosophers have been concerned with values for a long time. Aristotle, Socrates, Kant, and others discussed values in their treatises on ethics and aesthetics. Plato, Hobbes, and Rousseau deliberated over the problems of government and citizen responsibility. While no general theory of values has emerged, the notion that humans are driven by them seems well ensconced among both Eastern and Western thinkers. Values motivate behavior. Humans act to fulfill needs and desires and codify these motivations as values. So understanding values and their connection to survival is critical.

As McGilchrist has argued in his masterpiece *The Master and His Emissary*, the detail-oriented left brain, which he labels the "emissary," has come to dominate the more holistically oriented right brain in Western civilization. That domination shapes the disconnect that too many of us have from nature and even from our "whole" selves,[17] and in many ways frames the disconnect between economizing and ecologizing values that we use to frame the ideas in this book.

As we briefly saw, many Indigenous and Eastern creation stories gave credence to value systems that see us humans as part of nature. In contrast, the biblical stories of Genesis and the Qur'an separate humans from nature, particularly in Western traditions, and place us somehow superior to it, placing "man" (males) in dominant power positions. From that perspective, Nature is ours to control and manipulate. In contrast with many Indigenous[18] and Eastern mythologies, Western religious, economic, social and legal frameworks are undergirded by the idea that human beings are apart from, superior to, in "dominion" or dominating over nature. It is a perspective that, when embedded into a set of economic assumptions, that is, economizing assumptions, that as we will see do not even recognize business and economic impacts on nature or society, is creating a good deal of havoc with the Earth's capacity to support human civilization.

A psychological perspective on the evolution of human self-consciousness is embedded in the works of researchers such as Gregory Bateson,[19] Julian Jaynes,[20] Iain McGilchrist,[21] and many others. They propose that the human mind evolved in response to survival needs into two unique and separate bicameral chambers. An "ego" consciousness (personhood) evolved to separate us from nature and others or our species. This ego consciousness involved a separation of man from God in Christianity (with concomitant loss of divinity, sacredness) and separation from Nature in other traditions. It also is evident, as we will show in chapters to come, in the many paradoxes and tensions that it generated— from separation of masculine and feminine, mind and body, to "man" from nature, among others. The lack of integration of paradoxical or seemingly opposite tendencies and ways of being over the long-term creates an untenable situation, because from a systems perspective, all of these paradoxical or tension-filled dualities exist simultaneously. At some point, they need to be reconciled into an integrated perspective on how we humans can live in balance and harmony with the world around us.

That is, they need to guide us, we believe, towards values of ecologizing that transcend, yet include, economizing and related values that dominate today.

Over time, economizing (or left-brain) values have become increasingly important in personal, social, and cultural formations of our "modern" worldview. At the same time, "survival" the mother of all values, is still with us in the form of "sustainability." The 1987 United Nations report, "Our Common Future," often called the Brundtland Report, provided what has probably become the most common definition of sustainable development. The Brundtland Report says sustainable development is "development that meets the needs of the present without compromising the ability of future generations to meet their own needs."[22] While we might argue that continued "development," particularly along today's path, is problematic, the idea of sustainability is meant to get us to a flourishing world of dignity and wellbeing for all.

Our disconnectedness from nature, from the "environment," as if we could somehow live without it, creates a sort of blindness in some people to the impacts of many of today's systems and practices on the world around us. Humans survived in early days through instrumental use of nature, the "taming" of fire, and manufacture of tools, domestication of animals, and development of agriculture, with increasing and progressive instrumentalization of nature. When human populations were relatively low (in prior centuries), instrumental exploitation of nature was not a significant problem. Nomadic societies had developed foraging patterns and migrating temporary settlements that allowed nature to recuperate seasonally or over time from excessive use and even abuse by humans. Moreover, the total use of resources then was small compared to nature's ability to regenerate them.

Settled agricultural societies evolved farming and animal husbandry practices that expanded further instrumentalization of nature as a resource. These developments involved bringing vast swathes of land under agricultural use, including domesticating many species of animals for farm work and human consumption. Yes, there was ecological destruction as a result, but it was mitigated to some extent in many cultures by an ethos of stewardship of resources, and farming in consonance with natural cycles of resource regeneration. The underlying anthropocentric values—dominion over nature—were institutionalized and justified by the desire and need to feed growing populations.

Humans, in their self-perception of being distinct from nature and superior to it, have thus arrogated rights to themselves to instrumentally use nature to fulfill their desires. This separation of human and nature is the institutionalization of "man's" desire for dominion over women, humans desire for dominion over nature, creating some of the tensions that we will explore in more depth in the next few chapters.

The Emerging Need for Ecologizing

It was the industrialization and technologization of agriculture, coupled with vast expansion of population in the 19th and 20th centuries, that caused the large-scale collapse of ecosystems and species, such as through overfishing and overhunting of some species. Further, human population has more than quadrupled on the planet since 1900 and is continuing to grow rapidly. With the advent of industrialization and use of fossil fuels drawn from the ground, there is no real expectation of significant population growth slowdown for decades to come (unless, of course, dire predictions about the impact of climate change on human civilization come true in their worst form). Pressures caused by today's economizing values and the accompanying dominant narrative of neoliberalism have resulted in a growth-at-all-costs economic system. With its underlying materialism, the attitude and values that nature is there for exploitation by humans and has infinite resources and renewal capacity, have created an unsustainable and destructive "presence" for humans on the planet. In a sense, we truly have become the "parasites" envisioned by the Chinese Pangu origin myth discussed earlier. The unsustainable development of the last century manifested the truly destructive capacity of the instrumentalization-of-nature value.

One conclusion we want to make is that survival, a commonly accepted central value, even considered as a human (or any living being's) instinct, is better seen as a double-edged sword. It allows us to institutionalize mechanisms that help survival in the short and medium terms. But some of these mechanisms may turn against our own long-term survival. Developing a sustainability ethic that is effective over longtime horizons of multiple generations of humans, and natural process cycles is the challenge of our time. We discuss this temporal tension more in the next chapter.

It is the tension between today's dominant values of economizing over values of ecologizing that we believe has created many of the crises that humanity now faces. Donella Meadows told us that the most important lever for system transformation is changing—and ultimately—transcending mindsets.[23] That is exactly the task that faces humanity now in overcoming the economizing, power aggrandizing, and technological values that impede us from recognizing our inexorable connection to—and dependence on—nature, that is, moving towards ecologizing values. We will discuss the inevitable tensions these apparent paradoxes create in upcoming chapters.

Notes

1. Creation Stories. Fourth Edition (2000, July). "Creation stories from around the world: Encapsulations of some traditional stories explaining the origin of the Earth, its life, and its peoples." November 17, 2011.

2. Sturluson, S. (2006). *The Prose Edda: Norse mythology.* London: Penguin Classics.
3. Lodge, G. C., & Vogel, E. F. (Eds.). (1987). *Ideology and national competitiveness: An analysis of nine countries.* Cambridge, MA: Harvard Business Press.
4. Pangu and the Chinese Creation Story. *Ancient origins: Reconstructing the story of humanity's past.* Retrieved from: www.ancient-origins.net/human-origins-folklore/pangu-and-chinese-creation-myth-00347.
5. Dow, J. (1986). Universal aspects of symbolic healing: A theoretical synthesis. *American Anthropologist, 88*(1), 56–69.
6. *The Bible*, The book of genesis, chapter 1. Retrieved from: www.vatican.va/archive/bible/genesis/documents/bible_genesis_en.html.
7. Islam Creation Story. Retrieved from: http://www2.nau.edu/~gaud/bio301/content/iscrst.htm.
8. Cited at, *Story of creation (Part 1 of 2), the religion of Islam.* Retrieved from: www.islamreligion.com/articles/11041/story-of-creation-part-1/.
9. Holcomb, J. Why it's wrong for Christians to mistreat creation. *Christianity.com.* Retrieved from: www.christianity.com/christian-life/political-and-social-issues/why-it-s-wrong-for-christians-to-mistreat-creation.html.
10. Welchel, H. (2012, December 3). *A biblical view of dominion: Stewardship, theology 101.* Retrieved from: https://tifwe.org/a-biblical-view-of-dominion-stewardship/.
11. Abram, D. (2012). On being human in a more-than human world. Center for Humans & Nature. Retrieved from: www.humansandnature.org/to-be-human-david-abram.
12. Frederick, W. C. (1995). *Values, nature, and culture in the American corporation.* Oxford: Oxford University Press.
13. Waddock, S. (2002). *Leading corporate citizens: Vision, values, value-added.* New York: McGraw-Hill.
14. Jaynes, J. (2000). *The origin of consciousness in the breakdown of the bicameral mind.* New York: Houghton Mifflin Harcourt.
15. McGilchrist, I. (2009). *The master and his emissary: The divided brain and the making of the western world.* New Haven: Yale University Press.
16. Stein, J. F. (2003, November). Why did language develop? In *International congress series* (Vol. 1254, pp. 207–213). New York: Elsevier.
17. McGilchrist, I. (2009). *The master and his emissary: The divided brain and the making of the western world.* New Haven: Yale University Press.
18. Arrows, F. (2016). *Point of departure: Returning to our more authentic worldview for education and survival.* Charlotte, NC: IAP.
19. Bateson, G. (1979). *Mind and nature: A necessary unity* (Vol. 255). New York: Bantam Books.
20. Jaynes, J. (2000). *The origin of consciousness in the breakdown of the bicameral mind.* Boston: Houghton Mifflin Harcourt.
21. McGilchrist, I. (2009). *The master and his emissary: The divided brain and the making of the western world.* New Haven: Yale University Press.
22. Brundtland, G. H. (1987). *Our common future: World commission on environmental development.* Oxford: The Brundtland-Report Oxford University Press.
23. Meadows, D. (1999). *Leverage points: Places to intervene in a system.* Harland, VT: The Sustainability Institute. Retrieved from: http://donellameadows.org/archives/leverage-points-places-to-intervene-in-a-system/.

3 Breaking the Chain

Paradoxical Tensions Between Business and Sustainability

In this chapter, we begin to argue that the human chain with nature is broken in part because of some chronic tensions between business and sustainability. We label these tensions as dualisms, where the current world in which we live is composed of a series of competing principles that exist at the same time. Paradoxes are phenomena that are false only if they are true and true only if they are false. We contend that sustainability is one of these paradoxes, but we start with the idea that some concepts related to sustainability are "double." It is useful for our arguments to demonstrate some of these dualisms within the management field in order to understand more clearly the existing tensions that are severing our human chain.

We see in the management literature that social, environmental and ethical issues continue to grow in importance. Stakeholders are now expecting that businesses address these issues as part of their responsibilities.[1] Social and environmental sustainability management and business ethics, however, have developed as academic fields concurrently, but separately. Despite the fact that sustainability related issues have implicit ethical implications, these two areas of inquiry operate in their own silos. This separation can even be seen at the Academy of Management, where the Organizations and Natural Environment Division (ONE) separated from the Social Issues in Management Division (SIM) in the 1990s. At one time they were in the same division and intimately linked. Now, although there is much overlap in the research emanating from each division and there have been efforts to integrate the two, they are treated separately.[2] We do see corporate social responsibility and sustainability integrated to an extent, especially in the sense of measuring corporate social responsibility (CSR) and sustainability outcomes.[3] But ethics remains less embedded into the theoretical development of sustainability, providing more evidence of a broken chain.

In definitions of corporate sustainability, an organization's activities should include concerns from both social and environmental stakeholders through the normal business operations of the firm.[4] The concerns are to be addressed and balanced at the same time, but in reality, they are mainly treated separately and in opposition.[5] Moreover an integrated definition provides a business case for sustainability, where sustainable organizational activities are strategically oriented. Absent too often are the underlying ethical concerns that could drive business behavior towards sustainability. Nor, because it emphasizes companies, does the term corporate sustainability acknowledge particularly well the broader issue of ecological sustainability—or, in our terms, flourishing and well-being for all needed at the planetary level. The "standard conception of human nature given by neoclassical economics . . . is a significant obstacle to an accurate conception of ethics and how this limits consideration of sustainability."[6]

Beyond the widespread recognition of the triple bottom line (People, Profit and Planet),[7] introduced in 1997 by John Elkington and later withdrawn because of its narrow application, management scholars firmly remain embedded in their disciplinary fields of research.,[8],[9] Such disciplinary silos represent yet another type of fragmentation and atomization that has resulted from the split mind phenomenon. As we will discuss later, this perspective is firmly (and sometimes unconsciously) embedded in the tenets of neoliberalism. Today's dominant economic theories—most typically neoliberal in orientation—generally focus heavily on profit, the link between profit and people, or both. Growth and profit, however, do not necessarily lead to happiness and fulfilment.[10] What is needed is more advanced theorizing about sustainability[11] that incorporates ethics, as well as science, spirituality, humanities, the arts, and politics, to name only a few disciplines now operating in their separate silos. Thus, there exists a dualism between sustainability and ethics that contributes to humans' disconnectedness from nature. Missing is the connection between People and Planet, the human chain.

Paradoxes in management refer to "contradictory yet interrelated elements—elements that seem logical in isolation but absurd and irrational when appearing simultaneously."[12] But the broad range of possibilities in which dualisms exist needs to be laid out. Moreover, efforts are required in management research to resolve paradoxical tensions in scholarly discourse.[13] "Paradox is an old concept. Its roots lie in ancient teachings across Eastern and Western thought, apparent in such works such as the Tao Te Ching and the Judeo-Christian Bible."[14] Our approach argues that a paradigmatic shift in Western thinking is needed about ethics and sustainability and human beings' relationships with themselves, with others, and with nature, one that draws on more holistic Eastern and Indigenous perspectives and integrates Western traditions. We will revisit the East–West divide later in this chapter.

As we have contended, there is an observable dualism in the business ethics literature between ethics and sustainability.[15] The dualism is that these two concepts are generally perceived in the management literature as being incompatible and mutually exclusive. Business ethics and sustainability both need a broader, more unified or integrated approach that is able to address newly developing themes in a fast-changing global environment.[16] A reframed approach to business ethics can overcome this dualism and reduce the white space. We advocate redressing the relationship between ethics and sustainability by reconceiving it as a *duality*. Duality "denotes the twofold character of an object of study without separation."[17] As we will suggest later, we believe that drawing from William Frederick's ideas about today's dominant values of economizing and power aggrandizing can helpfully be supplemented by a shift towards "ecologizing" values[18] that help to bridge some of these dualities.

Building on our discussion in the previous chapter, a dualistic perspective normally works with "clear-cut and decisive contrast, a well-defined boundary. This boundary often becomes synonymous with opposition and potential conflict."[19] Such a perspective is not able to explain sufficiently how organizations manage in the real world to reconcile stability and change. In Frederick's terms, economizing and ecologizing need to be reconciled, as we will elaborate, in order to survive and to prosper, following objectives that he designates explicitly as "imperatives."[20]

Our position is to change the point of view and adopt the perspective of *duality*. This perspective "resembles dualism in that it retains the idea of two essential elements, but it views them as interdependent, rather than separate and opposed." This idea of dualism is sort of like the intertwined double helix of DNA or the intertwined snakes of the medical symbol of the caduceus (also the Greek symbol of the god Hermes), which cannot be teased apart and retain their integrity or identity.[21] By adopting this viewpoint, management scholars and professionals can accept the conceptual distinctions but are not obligated to promote the existence of the separation.

Paradoxes and Sustainability

Paradoxes constitute an attempt to reduce reality to polarized "distinctions that mask complex interrelationships,"[22] as well as blur the simultaneous nature of truths that may conflict between two elements.[23] A paradox refers to the "simultaneous existence of two inconsistent states . . . a duality of coexisting tensions,"[24] both of which are real and exist simultaneously. It is with this tension between interconnected concepts of business ethics and sustainability that we wish to generate new insights and realize the potential for new understandings.[25] With paradoxical tensions, the tendency is for people to emphasize distinctions rather than search for interdependencies[26] or holistic integrity, partly because of the Western tendency to fragment and atomize wholes into their component parts in a left-brain way of thinking. This tendency can lead to the stifling of learning about how integrally related elements can inform each other and provide a more complete understanding of a situation or of reality. Paradoxical tensions change over time and the interaction of both elements causes a constant influencing of one another.[27]

Alone, dualities are not the same as paradoxes. Duality could be composed of elements that are complementary in nature. "However, they can become paradoxical when framed as oppositional tendencies."[28,29] Thus, a duality is embedded within paradox. Through a duality approach, a more comprehensive understanding of these tensions may enable synergies between the elements and potentially more theoretical insights.[30,31] This duality way of re-thinking about management and sustainability can give managers and scholars the freedom to adopt a more liberating framework for addressing sustainability; one that does not view it as contradictory to business. This new conceptualization can enable managers to understand how these competing conceptions can actually be mutually enabling.[32,33] To elucidate the paradoxical tensions that exist in dualities, a dialectical approach is necessary.[34] We introduce the idea of new narratives reshaping mindsets as part of this approach in Chapter 8.

Ethicist Kenneth Goodpaster initially introduced the idea of the "separation thesis" in his explanation that ethics and business are incompatible.[35] Business ethics scholars ever since have been studying how to treat ethics and business as a duality, where they are not mutually exclusive. Otherwise, they are committing what stakeholder scholar Ed Freeman calls the separation fallacy—separating ethics out from business actions.[36] Freeman argues that, in essence, they are a duality (like the DNA molecule) that cannot retain integrity (wholeness) when tackled separately. Goodpaster (2007) studied organizational cultures and argued that ethical cultures develop in part as a result of efforts to change people's mindsets. He claims that one dominant mindset in business organizations today is one of teleopathy, which is the unbalanced pursuit of purpose by individuals or organizations, a mindset fostered by today's dominant narrative of neoliberalism as we will see in Chapter 4. In business today, "purpose" tends to be narrowly confined to the maximization of profits for the welfare (financial wealth) of shareholders, rather than being a more holistic concept about the welfare—or well-being—of all.

To counter a focus on such narrowly defined outcomes, Ardichvili advocates a mindset of corporate compassion that emphasizes the wide range of stakeholders who are engaged in or affected by the activities of firms—or, for that matter, other types of organizations.[37] An unwavering respect for all stakeholders' rights and needs, rather than simply those of shareholders, implies that a level of compassion and dignity for all is both relevant and important. Equally important is to gain perspective on the embeddedness of businesses, including large corporations, in their broader societies, which in turn are embedded in the context of the natural environment.

Towards that end, it is vitally important to reconsider how the purpose of companies, particularly corporations, is defined, both in the law and in business practice. As noted, today many people believe that the purpose of the firm is to continually increase profits so as to "maximize shareholder wealth," in the lingo of neoclassical economics (or neoliberalism), which we discuss in depth in Chapter 8 and in the famous phraseology of Milton Friedman.[38] Yet there are many other important constituents (stakeholders) in companies (and any other type of organization as well), beyond investors or shareholders, who contribute to its overall effectiveness and who are deeply affected by its activities. These stakeholders include employees, clients, or customers, suppliers and distributors, governments, and communities where the enterprise operates, among others.[39] Indeed, some of these stakeholders are equally as important as, if not more important than, investors. For example, consider how a business's operations would be limited were there no employees or customers. Consider also that although investors make a financial investment in firms in return for financial rewards, employees too are making an investment (albeit, yes, getting paid), putting in sweat equity, loyalty, and commitment to their work that deserves recognition as well. To define company purpose, in such a systemic context, as favoring only one of multiple stakeholders is not only committing another kind of separation fallacy but creating an unnecessary (and more complex) kind of dualism that privileges one set of investments over others.

One effort to overcome the inherent dualism in shareholder wealth maximization type of thinking has been undertaken by scholars Thomas Donaldson and James Walsh. In a seminal paper that attempts to develop a theory of businesses, they propose a much more "embedded" perspective on the purpose of business, and argue that the real purpose of business is to create what they term "collective value" absent any (human) dignity violations.[40] The idea of collective value places businesses into their broader context, for businesses and other types of organizations like governments and civil society enterprises are part of large collectives of communities, regions, and nations. Businesses cannot be separated from these broader contexts and retain their integrity and identity any more than the DNA molecule can be torn apart and retain its nature.

Ambicultural Blending

Conceptual models rooted in dualism, including the shareholder perspective just discussed, are guided by extreme polarized dichotomies, like success and failure, competition and cooperation, good and bad,[41] right and left, or male and female, and so on. These dualisms create the very tensions that we discuss in the next chapter that need to be integrated as we attempt to reconnect the broken human chain. When one of the premises of a theory presented as a dualism involves ends of a spectrum, typical responses tend to focus on single, pragmatically oriented solutions. Finding the optimal, ideal decision is an approach that is deeply rooted in Western models of management, including business ethics.[42] These dichotomies are overemphasized and need to be overcome in favor of more holistic or integrated approaches like the stakeholder perspective or other systemic approaches as we will be discussing more as we go along. Thus, we propose one possible way of thinking about these tensions in a productive way.

One approach for resolving the dichotomies in management theory and practice is ambiculturalism. By integrating common opposites through extolling qualities from each concept, ambiculturalism provides a new way of seeing those concepts. In effect, it closes the space between the two extremes. It is a form of what is known as third-way thinking, which advocates a synthesis of extreme positions to find a new less extreme and more central, shared position—or a wholly new, more integrated perspective. With an emphasis on duality and interdependence, this approach respects the relation between perspectives. Although the Western social sciences focus on standardizing processes for optimal outcomes, Eastern philosophy favors an examination of the whole experience.[43] Quantifiable metrics and measures drive the Western paradigm. Thus, what is quantifiable tends to be valued more. Things that are not readily measurable, from that perspective, either do not exist or are unimportant. In the East, not everything that is valued is viewed as quantifiable and the qualitative aspects of life are often considered to be more important than empirically quantifiable outcomes—things like family and relationships, and respect, for example. We need an ambicultural blending of these two different perspectives so we can expand what businesses and other institutions might value and include items that are not always readily quantifiable, that is, that are qualitative yet valuable. Such a perspective might help bridge the gap between today's business practice and the need for ecological sustainability and regenerative business practice.

Extended beyond business to other human institutions, including families, governments at many levels, local communities, educational, health care, and social institutions of all sorts, and religious bodies, we can see that the narrowness of identifying business purpose solely with financial and profitability (or maximized shareholder wealth) outcomes is another separation fallacy. No human institution worth participating in has only one value or important set of norms, or even purposes. Human institutions are inherently complex, with multiple different goals and objectives, some of which are not readily quantifiable. So, one of the imperatives we face in repairing the broken human chain is to somehow integrate these multiple purposes and goals more holistically.

Ambiculturalism allows us to productively critique the dominant Western assumptions and open our minds to the traditions of other cultures.[44] It recommends that we reorient our minds towards 'balance' and calls for the integration of the self and the other, as well as a reintegration of human beings with nature, and hence provides an important clue to understanding the current paradox of sustainability, as evidenced by the broken links in our human chain.

Among the most important issues facing the world in the coming years is sustainability, which as we discussed above still needs to be integrated with the field of ethics.[45] Like the physical sciences, which tend to operate separately from the social sciences, business ethics and sustainability too often find themselves often operating in different silos, when what is needed is a way of bridging across these disciplines in a transdisciplinary or more integrated manner. For years, for example, business ethics has been considered by management scholars to be its own field.[46] We view this *paradoxically* as both good and bad. It is positive that business ethics as a discipline has developed enough to produce meaningful empirical research and a strong theoretical base. However, it is problematic that business ethics sits isolated from fields like management and sustainability, which could benefit from an integration so as not to commit the separation fallacy. It is even more problematic that it seems unlinked, as is much of management theory, in fact, to the natural sciences, to the humanities, to the arts (though some inroads have been made in that domain), and to the human spirit (though again, some inroads are beginning to evolve there, too).

It is possible that one of the reasons for the separation of research in sustainability, management, and ethics is a developmental issue for the field—and others like it—in terms of the paradigm shifts that Thomas Kuhn spoke about in his important book, *The Structure of Scientific Revolution*,[47] the business ethics field is still in the emergence stage.[48] The more obvious reality from our perspective is that of the dualistic nature of Western thinking. Western approaches to ethics, for example, are not equipped to foster integration across fields that have staked out disciplinary expertise, even when doing so is an imperative. Although Western scholars have promoted an agenda for incorporating ethics into business organizations (overcoming the original separation fallacy) as a solution to sustainability, this task would be more easily accomplished through an Eastern or even Indigenous perspective (described in subsequent sections)[49] that allows for the simultaneous existence of dualities—opposites paradoxically integrated into the same phenomenon.

The problem with addressing sustainability as part of a more integrated and holistic perspective that encompasses ethics, all aspects of management, and an understanding of the socio-ecological contexts in which organizations exists in part because of how the West defines sustainability. The UN World Commission on Environment and Development (1987) promoted sustainability through the adoption of an Anthropocentric, or human-centered, view of the term. "This view . . . prioritizes a human bias . . . and places" "human needs and wants . . . above the survival and development of other species."[50] For the "planet" aspect of the triple bottom line to have increased prominence in business and other institutional decisions, it needs to be viewed as having moral legitimacy.[51] For example, to date, many observers conclude that must be an interaction between sustainability and ethics to create a moral justification for sustainability issues.[52] From the perspective of (living) human beings born of a living planet, as author and global thinker David Korten phrases it,[53] and the presumably near universal desire for survival, however, there could be no more fundamental ethical issue than that of sustainability, at least from the human perspective.

Arguably, sustainability issues have been handled mostly using an approach that assumes a discount rate of costs and benefits in a linear fashion. This approach separates the purported "value" of the natural environment away from any sense of integral value, that is, value simply because it is. In other words, because of the division thought accruing from the left-right brain dichotomy and the disconnect of humans from nature, we in the west tend to see the natural environment only as something valuable when humans can exploit it for financial gain. Unlike for many Indigenous people, for whom nature has inherent worth—a dignity even, worthy of being treated as sacred—Western views tend to place value only on the material benefits provided by nature. Hence recent efforts to put human prices on so-called natural capital, without regard for its intrinsic worth—or the intrinsic dignity of the other living beings that inhabit nature. What a difference it might make if we valued nature for its own sake and accorded, as many native peoples do, dignity to all living beings.[54]

Business ethicists repeatedly call for an integrative approach to guide the field; one that overrides the restrictive assumptions of economic rationality.[55] Yet these calls are also rooted firmly in the Western paradigm and do not reach beyond the hemisphere or the industrialized North. For example, there has been a stated need for a more functional ethics that considers the needs of different stakeholders. This "functionalism," however, sits in the shadow of an overarching strategic goal of increasing shareholder value, that is, as part of the neoliberal paradigm that dominates today's thinking (see Chapter 4 for elaboration), without questioning the validity or consequences to other stakeholders or of the planet itself of that objective.

Business organizations have attempted a similar Western-thinking influenced integration of ethical and responsible business practices and sustainable enterprises in recent years so as to generate greater "value" for the organization.[56] The whole extended debate on whether it is possible for businesses to be responsible and profitable at the same time, or whether greater attention to responsibility results in more or less profits, is a reflection of such dualistic or fragmented thinking. Indeed, the widespread adoption of Porter and Kramer's conception of "shared value," argues that companies should pursue strategies and opportunities that have both profit and social/sustainability benefits, as opposed to engaging in charity or CSR efforts.[57] This conception of shared value neatly restricts companies' responsibilities to what we shall see in the next chapter are the tenets of neoclassical economics—the idea of profit making that benefits shareholders. It embeds them ever more firmly in business as usual, with all of the now known consequences to long-term human and planetary flourishing. In a sense, shared value pretends to foster a shift in thinking when in reality it simply provides another way for firms and their leaders to continue exploiting nature and human beings without real regard for the long-term consequences of doing so.

Tension Between Vital and Ideal

Andreas Weber, author of *Enlivenment*, asks, "What is life, and what role do we play in it?" in order to generate a fundamental shift in our understanding of the concepts of nature and culture.[58] Taking an ecological perspective (or what we label ecologizing), he underlines our lack of comprehension regarding what constitutes life and argues that society moves beyond the Enlightenment's rationalistic, empirically driven ideals. As an alternative, he offers the concept of "enlivenment" (discussed in Chapter 8). In the West, society is embedded in the institution of Logos (and the use of Indo-European language). In management, scholars are less inclined to embrace the idea of the "more-than human" world, as defined by cultural ecologist, David Abram.[59] Abram acknowledges that the world is composed of many life forms beyond human beings, including animals, plants, and landforms. Rather, Western scholars are more rooted in a firm anthropocentrism.[60]

Earlier in this chapter, we discussed the idea of duality. In Chinese thought, duality is illustrated through the integration of the "self" and the "other."[61] In the West, notions of the self and the other are treated as dichotomous entities. But in Chinese philosophy, they are viewed as interdependent and complementary.[62] An example of this type of integration is the well-known circular yin/yang symbol, in which two opposites exist within a circle, each morphing and blending with the other. Underlying yin and yang in Taoism (Daoism) is the principle that all objects that exist possess characteristics that are inseparable yet opposite. So, opposite forms are contained within the "other." The symbol can be taken to represent apparent opposites in nature.

This continuous, integrated perspective from the Chinese yin/yang symbol does not illustrate the opposition, but rather, the oneness of the entity, the duality of its form. Together, both elements, are necessary to complete the whole. So, oft-conceived opposites like light and dark, masculine and feminine (discussed later in this book), empty and full, or whatever other dichotomy, are combined to realize the full nature of the entity. The conception of the separation of either/or is a Western thought propelled by our languages. Thinking of two extremes as part of the same totality is a Chinese perspective that could inform business ethics and sustainability.[63] We promote the goal of making management theories, the reintegration of the broken human chain, and our mindsets in pursuing ambicultural ideas as a way of overcoming dualisms in thought.

In contrast, Greek philosophy saw the world as being separated into two parts: sensibility and immanence on one pole and intelligence and transcendence on the other, with the latter being promoted as being preferable to the former. Relating back to our notion of "split minds," this separation was reinforced by Descartes during the Enlightenment 16th with his famous maxim, "I think, therefore I am." This notion suggests a separation of the body and the brain. French sinologist and philosopher Francois Jullien, who spends much of his career disseminating Chinese thought, challenges Western thinkers to reconceptualize the way we think about "life" and "living"; to revise our conceptions with insights from the East.[64] Jullien suggests that Western philosophers have largely de-emphasized the actual experiencing of life, favoring the creation of conceptual and objective questions about meaning.[65] He proposes that we consider living as a continuous, fluid process of vital nourishment. From this perspective, the question becomes not so much how to understand and fragment meanings about life, but rather to actually live it, to feed and nourish it as a slowed down process that is more holistically oriented.

We agree with David Abram,[66] who in his remarkable book *The Spell of the Sensuous: Perception and Language in a More-Than-Human World*, argues that Western perspectives, including those on sustainability, need "a rejuvenation of our carnal, sensorial empathy with the living land that sustains us." Beyond the illusion of separation, how can one discover inclusion?[67] How could humans perceive or feel at the vital level, beyond figures and words (and associated contracts), their forgotten entanglement between themselves and their environment? These questions open a door to enter the space between People and Planet and place us on a path beyond the dominant Western point of view. We can thus move towards a less fragmented and more holistic perspective in which we begin to envision ourselves and all of our human institutions, including businesses and other organizations, as integrally embedded in nature and interdependent with her.

Integrative Social Contracts Theory as Possible Means to Balance Tensions

In this section, we explore another tension we see existing in discussions surrounding sustainability, the separation between different levels of social contracts in societies, another fracture in the human chain. One of the most promising recent attempts at tackling global ethics issues is the Integrative Social Contracts Theory (ISCT).[68] The goal of ISCT is to provide a framework to make managerial decision-making more in line with the expectations and impacts of relevant communities affected by business decisions. The ISCT framework examines social contracts from a practical perspective where local agreements can be aligned and balanced with macro-level contracts without violating overarching ethical norms that govern global society.

Social contract theory is derived from the political philosophy of the 17th and 18th centuries. John Locke led the movement for theories of consent and political obligation (1690) through which he identified reciprocal obligations of members of society and the government. Social contract theories originating at that time form the basis of modern-day social contract theory in business ethics. There are three elements that characterize social contract theory which hold relevance to our purposes in this book: "1) Consent of the individual, 2) agreement among moral agents, and 3) a device or method by which an agreement . . . is obtained."[69]

Integrative Social Contracts Theory Background

Tom Donaldson constructed a moral foundation of the corporation through social contract theory. Social contracts serve the role of granting legitimacy to organizations through the consent of business operations by those affected stakeholders. Business and other types of organizations exist by rite of the cooperation and affirmation by society. Donaldson acknowledges, however, that consent among stakeholders is not universal: that a problem with a contractarian approach to business is that some stakeholder groups' interests may conflict.[70] "Contractarians approach rights on the basis of trying to discern which rights logically, or defensibly, can be seen to be those, which the members of society would agree to in principle and divorced from their own personal circumstances."[71] Thus, the main problems with using social contract approaches in business relate to competing stakeholder perceptions of what is acceptable and varying cultural perceptions of ethical desirability. Norms or principles that supersede all cultural contexts are seemingly necessary.

In response to the need to create a framework for sorting through competing agreements in society about what rules are acceptable for business, Donaldson and Tom Dunfee proposed their Integrative Social Contracts Theory.[72] This contractarian theory "offers a theoretical account of what makes actions, decisions, policies, and practices morally right in the context of commercial life."[73] ISCT has as its basis two kinds of contracts. The first social contract, macro-social contracts, "are hypothetical agreements about a broad normative framework designed to guide all economic arrangements."[74] These contracts, according to the theory, create "moral free space" among different groups of rational contractors. Thus, these agreements create enough flexibility with which to allow certain groups of individuals form their own specific norms, unique to their context. This leeway takes the form of micro-social contracts, which are defined by specific local economic communities in terms of the norms designed to govern behavior. These types of contracts are integrated into a framework for business ethics. This latter type of contract is based on "authentic" norms of the community, which are indicated by the widespread acceptance within a single community. The normative foundation of micro-social contracts is developed "freely" by agents in that community.

In order to prevent an overreliance on relative norms of behavior within a business community, ISCT assumes that each authentic norm within a particular community is tested by a set of universal principles that guide individuals across societies and cultures. Thus, the "moral free space" described above is held in check by these overarching principles for behavior or hypernorms. Hypernorms are "principles so fundamental to human existence that . . . we would expect them to be reflected in a convergence of religious, philosophical, and cultural beliefs."[75] They represent the highest order of normative guidance in social contract contexts. These hypernorms supersede all locally developed norms and are intended to be absolute, definitive guides for behavior. Hypernorms are "fundamental conceptions of the right and the good"; so ingrained in what it means to be human that they serve as general heuristics for ethical behavior. To the extent that they exist, hypernorms can become important and resonant memes shared widely across different cultures and, hence, important elements of any new narratives or stories that support a move to an ecologizing mindset. That is why, for example, Haidt's foundational values of care, fairness/justice, authority/respect, loyalty/ingroup, and sanctity/purity[76] are so important to thinking about new narratives and stories—because they represent relatively universal values. We will build on these ideas in the last chapter of this book.

Through social contracting fostered by the ISCT framework, a compatibility across levels of social contract can be achieved. Social contracts are broken into macro- and micro-level agreements governed by prevailing hypernorms. ISCT presents us with a potential framework that allows us to move away from the ideal vision (absolutes) of social exchanges to a more "living" approach. We use this Western ethics theory as a mere example of how a theoretical blending may be achieved and as a forum within which our attempt at fostering a duality between sustainability and ethics may be realized.

We now refer back to our arguments earlier in this chapter on the quest for the ideal versus the vital, from Chinese thinking. We find that the main concrete consequence of the partnership between economic development and philosophic thinking is manifested in the quest for happiness, which is often focused on individual happiness, often thought to be gained through material means as evidenced in the dominance of neoliberalism in Western thought. The traditional Chinese notion of happiness is different; it is more oriented to health and well-being with a general preference for the collective or the good of the whole community. The current quest for happiness, as we know it, has been made in the West, though it is becoming somewhat more prevalent as a result of globalization. The quest for "happiness" as expressed in much of Western culture is based on consumption and focuses on the market for personal (individual) growth and stimulation at a time where traditional bearings (anchored in politics and/or religion) have been somewhat lost.[77] Related to hypernorms, the popularity of this notion of what happiness means, however, does not mean that it has universal value.

In a globalized society, it is necessary to recognize alternative ways of thinking, some of which might help us reconnect the broken human chain. Importantly, Eastern societies possess cultural orientations very different from the ones that have dominated in the West over millennia, as we can see in the origin stories presented in Chapter 2. Although rooted traditions are transformed and adapted over time (ontologies), along with their ways of knowing (epistemologies), Eastern philosophies can arguably constructively inform business and more general notions of ethics differently from the ontologies and epistemologies of the West.

Avoiding the Separation Between Vital and Ideal

Management scholars and many others are hardly able to embrace the "more-than human" world, as defined by Abram in *The Spell of the Sensuous*.[78] That world of other beings, nature's abundance, and "spirit" beyond what can be empirically evidenced, however, may be a key to healing the disconnect that we call the broken human chain. Despite the potential power of broadened perspective, many Western thinkers are still deeply embedded in anthropocentrism, that is, a human-centered perspective, that is common especially when addressing business ethics.[79]

The separation of the observable and the transcendent from Greek philosophy does not exist in the traditional Chinese view. In terms of what gives enlivenment to our human enterprises at all levels, the shift proposed by Jullien, with which we concur, is to reconsider the process of living as involving vital nourishment.[80] This goes beyond our typical understanding of the European conception of life.[81] Jullien's philosophy of living can be key to address the challenges of quality of life and to favor sustainability through an interdisciplinary lens that can help fix the broken chain, and heal our disconnect from nature. To accomplish this healing, we advocate integrating the vital *and* the ideal into a duality that can help to inform global thinking, not just Western or Eastern. We further argue that this duality can exist within sustainability.

This integration of the "vital" and the "ideal" questions solely "evidence-based management," which is promoted in the West and is used in international research.[82] Moreover, cross-cultural management thinking typically uses an outside view and is driven by theory.[83] Instead of focusing on a comparative approach, it is propelled by contextual factors motivates a dialogue across cultures. Historically, the search for happiness and the governance of people have been hand in hand under Western ideology because they are linked to the platonic utopia of the Republic. "This idea of happiness, constantly in need of renovation, was the price—the heavy price—that had to be paid in order for the political to emerge as a separate order, favourable to autonomy."[84]

In the following chapters, we break down these tensions by level of analysis. We start in Chapter 4 with an examination of individual-level tensions that have helped facilitate breaks in the human chain with the natural environment.

Notes

1. Herremans, I. M., Nazari, J. A., & Mahmoudian, F. (2016). Stakeholder relationships, engagement, and sustainability reporting. *Journal of Business Ethics, 138*(3), 417–435.
2. Klewitz, J., & Hansen, E. G. (2014). Sustainability-oriented innovation of SMEs: A systematic review. *Journal of Cleaner Production, 65*, 57–75.
3. Romero, K. C. C., & Lamadrid, R. L. (2014). Rethinking corporate social responsibility within the sustainability agenda: Issues and challenges for Asian-based companies. *Journal of Global Responsibility, 5*(2), 180–202. https://doi.org/10.1108/JGR-06-2014-0023.
4. van Marrewijk, M., & Werre, M. (2003). *Journal of Business Ethics, 44*, 107. https://doi.org/10.1023/A:1023383229086p-107.
5. Gao, J., & Bansal, P. (2013). Instrumental and integrative logics in business sustainability. *Journal of Business Ethics, 112*(2), 241–255.
6. Friedland, J. (2012). Beyond empiricism: Realizing the ethical mission of management. *Business and Society Review, 117*(3), 329. doi:10. 1111/j.1467-8594.2012.00409.x.
7. Elkington, J. (1997). *Cannibals with forks–Triple bottom line of 21st century business.* Stoney Creek, CT: New Society Publishers.
8. Becher, T., & Trowler, P. (2001). *Academic tribes and territories: Intellectual enquiry and the cultures of disciplines.* Buckingham: Open University Press.
9. Schoolman, E. D., Guest, J. S, Bush, K. F., & Bell, A. R. (2012). How interdisciplinary is sustainability research? Analyzing the structure of an emerging scientific field. *Sustainability Science, 7*(1), 67–80.
10. Layard, R. (2011). *Measuring the subjective well-being of nations: National accounts of time use and well-being: Well-being measurement and public policy.* NBER Book Chapters.
11. Hahn, T., Pinkse, J., Preuss, L., & Figge, F. (2014). Tensions in corporate sustainability: Towards an integrative framework. *Journal of Business Ethics, 127*(2), 297–316. doi:10.1007/s10551-014-2047-5.
12. Lewis, M. W. (2000). Exploring paradox: Toward a more comprehensive guide. *Academy of Management Review, 25*(4), 760.
13. Klang, D., Wallnöfer, M., & Hacklin, F. (2014). The business model paradox: A systematic review and exploration of antecedents. *International Journal of Management Reviews, 16*(4), 454–478. doi:10.1111/ijmr.12030.

14. Smith, W. K., & Lewis, M. W. (2011). Toward a theory of paradox: A dynamic equilibrium model of organizing. *Academy of Management Review*, 10(1), 5–64.
15. Holland, D., & Albrecht, C. (2013). The worldwide academic field of business ethics: Scholars' perceptions of the most important issues. *Journal of Business Ethics*, 117. doi:10.1007/s10551-013-1718-y.
16. van Liedekerke, L., & Dubbink, W. (2008). Twenty years of European business ethics–past developments and future concerns. *Journal of Business Ethics*, 82, 273–280. doi:10.1007/s10551-008-9886-x.
17. Farjoun, M. (2010). Beyond dualism: Stability and change as a duality. *The Academy of Management Review*, 35(2), 203. Retrieved from: www.jstor.org/stable/25682409.
18. Frederick, W. C. (1995). *Values, nature, and culture in the American corporation.* Oxford: Oxford University Press.
19. Farjoun, M. (2010). Beyond dualism: Stability and change as a duality. *Academy of Management Review*, 35, 203.
20. Farjoun, M. (2010). Beyond dualism: Stability and change as a duality. *Academy of Management Review*, 35, 202.
21. E.g. Elias (1991); Giddens, A. (1984). *The constitution of society.* Berkeley, CA: University of California University Press.
22. Klang, D., Wallnöfer, M., & Hacklin, F. (2014). The business model paradox: A systematic review and exploration of antecedents. *International Journal of Management Reviews*, 16(4), 457. doi:10.1111/ijmr.12030.
23. Lewis, M. W. (2000). Exploring paradox: Toward a more comprehensive guide. *Academy of Management Review*, 25(4), 760–776.
24. Eisenhardt, K. M. (2000). Paradox, spirals, ambivalence: The new language of change and pluralism. *Academy of Management Review*, 25(4), 703.
25. Eisenhardt, K. M., & Westcott, B. J. (1988). Paradoxical demands and the creation of excellence: The case of just-in-time manufacturing. In R. E. Quinn & K. S. Cameron (Eds.), *Paradox and transformation: Toward a theory of change in organization and management* (pp. 169–193). Cambridge, MA: Ballinge.
26. Sundaramurthy, C., & Lewis, M. (2003). Control and collaboration: Paradoxes of governance. *Academy of Management Review*, 28(3), 397–415.
27. Smith, W. K., & Lewis, M. W. (2011). Toward a theory of paradox: A dynamic equilibrium model of organizing. *Academy of Management Review*, 36(2), 381–403.
28. Stoltzfus, K., Stohl, C., & Seibold, D. R. (2011). Managing organizational change: Paradoxical problems, solutions, and consequences. *Journal of Organizational Change Management*, 24(3), 349–367, p. 352.
29. Fairhurst, G. T., & Putnam, L. L. (2012). Paradox, contradictions, dialectics, and dualities, working paper. *Human Relations*.
30. Graetz, F., & Smith, A. (2008). The role of dualities in arbitrating continuity and change in forms of organizing. *International Journal of Management Reviews*, 1(3), 265–280.
31. Sutherland, F., & Smith, A. (2011). Duality theory and the management of the change-stability paradox. *Journal of Management & Organization*, 17(4), 534–547.
32. Farjoun, M. (2010). Beyond dualism: Stability and change as a duality. *Academy of Management Review*, 35(2), 202–225.
33. Smith, W. K., Erez, M., Jarvenpaa, S., Lewis, M. W., & Tracey, P. (2017). Adding complexity to theories of paradox, tensions, and dualities of innovation and change: Introduction to organization studies special issue on

paradox, tensions, and dualities of innovation and change. *Organization Studies, 38*(3–4), 303–317. https://doi.org/10.1177/0170840617693560.

34. Ford, J. D., & Backoff, R. W. (1988). Organizational change in and out of dualities and paradox. In R. E. Quinn & K. S. Cameron (Eds.), *Ballinger series on innovation and organizational change. Paradox and transformation: Toward a theory of change in organization and management* (pp. 81–121). New York, NY: Ballinger Publishing Co and Harper & Row Publishers.

35. Goodpaster, K. (1991). Business ethics and stakeholder analysis. *Business Ethics Quarterly, 1*(1), 53–73.

36. Freeman, R. E. (1994). The politics of stakeholder theory: Some future directions. *Business Ethics Quarterly*, 409–421.

37. Ardichvili, A. (2013). The role of HRD in CSR, sustainability, and ethics: A relational model. *Human Resource Development Review, 12*(4), 456–473.

38. Friedman, M. (1970, September 13). The social responsibility of a business is to increase its profits. *The New York Times Magazine*, pp. 122–124.

39. These ideas were articulated formally in Freeman, R. E. (1984). *Strategic management: A stakeholder approach*. Boston: Pitman.

40. Donaldson, T., & Walsh, J. P. (2015). Toward a theory of business. *Research in Organizational Behavior, 35*, 181–207.

41. March, J. G. (1991). How decisions happen in organizations. *Human-Computer Interaction, 6*(2), 95–117.

42. Feldman, M. S., & Pentland, B. T. (2003). Reconceptualizing organizational routines as a source of flexibility and change. *Administrative Science Quarterly, 48*(1), 94–118.

43. Chen, E., & Miller, G. E. (2013). Socioeconomic status and health: Mediating and moderating factors. *Annual Review of Clinical Psychology, 9*, 723–749.

44. Chen, M. J. (2014). Becoming ambicultural. *Academy of Management Review, 39*, 119–137.

45. Holland, D., & Albrecht, C. (2013). The worldwide academic field of business ethics: Scholars' perceptions of the most important issues. *Journal of Business Ethics, 117*. doi:10.1007/s10551-013-1718-y.

46. Enderle, G. (1996). Focus: A comparison of business ethics in north America and continental Europe. *Business Ethics, 5*(1), 33–46.

47. Kuhn, T. S. (2012). *The structure of scientific revolutions*. Chicago: University of Chicago Press.

48. Holland, D., & Albrecht, C. (2013). The worldwide academic field of business ethics: Scholars' perceptions of the most important issues. *Journal of Business Ethics, 117*. doi:10.1007/s10551-013-1718-y.

49. Bernal, E., & Edgar, D. (2012). The development of a model of sustainability management, based on biological ethics. *International Journal of Management, 29*(3), 177–188.

50. Borland, H., & Lindgreen, A. (2013). Sustainability, epistemology, ecocentric business, and marketing strategy: Ideology, reality, and vision. *Journal of Business Ethics, 117*(1), 173.

51. Mena, S., & Palazzo, G. (2012). Input and output legitimacy of multistakeholder initiatives. *Business Ethics Quarterly, 22*(3), 527–556.

52. Gond, J. P., Barin Cruz, L., Raufflet, E., & Charron, M. (2015). To frack or not to frack? the interaction of justification and power in a sustainability controversy. *Journal of Management Studies*. doi:10.1111/joms.12166.

53. Korten, D. (2018). *Ecological civilization: The vision*. Retrieved from: https://davidkorten.org/home/ecological-civilization/.

54. For elaboration of this perspective, see Waddock, S. (in press). Generative businesses fostering vitality: Rethinking businesses' relationship to the world. In J. Seitz, C. Hinze, & M. Pirson (Eds.), *Working Alternatives (working title)*. Fordham University Press.
55. Jeurissen, R.J.M. (2000). The social function of business ethics. *Business Ethics Quarterly,10*(4), 821–843; Ulrich, P. (2008). *Integrative economic ethics: Foundations of a civilized market economy*, translated by James Fearns (Cambridge University Press, Cambridge, MA).
56. Moore, S., & Jie Wen, J. (2008). Business ethics? A global comparative study on corporate sustainability approaches. *Social Responsibility Journal, 4*(1–2), 172–184.
57. Porter, M. E., & Kramer, M. R. (2011). The big idea: Creating shared value. *Harvard Business Review, 89*(1), 62–77.
58. Weber, A. (2013). *Enlivenment: Towards a fundamental shift in the concepts of nature, culture and politics*. Berlin: Heinrich-Böll-Stiftung. Retrieved from: www.autor-andreas-weber.de/downloads/Enlivenment_web.pdf.
59. Abram, D. (1996, January 28). Animals and environment deserve more respect. *Daily Gazette*.
60. Purser, R. E., Park, C., & Montuori, A. (1995). Limits to anthropocentrism: Toward an ecocentric organization paradigm? *Academy of Management Review, 20*(4), 1053–1099.
61. Chen, M. J. (2014). Becoming ambicultural. *Academy of Management Review, 39*, 119–137.
62. Chen, X. (2002). Reason and feeling: Confucianism and contractualism. *Journal of Chinese Philosophy, 29*(2), 269–283. doi:10.1111/1540-6253.00081.
63. Shrivastava, P., & Persson, S. (2014). A theory of strategy—Learning from China from walking to sailing. *M@n@gement, 17*, 38–61.
64. Jullien, F. (2015). *The book of beginnings*. New Haven, CT: Yale University Press.
65. Jullien, F. (2007). *Vital nourishment: Departing from happiness*. Brooklyn, NH: Zone Books.
66. Abram, D. (1996, January 28). Animals and environment deserve more respect. *Daily Gazette*, p. 69.
67. Hutchins, G. (2014). *The illusion of separation: Exploring the cause of our current crises*. Edinburgh: Floris Books.
68. Donaldson, T., & Dunfee, T. W. (1999). *Ties that bind: A social contracts approach to business ethics*. Cambridge: Harvard Business School Press.
69. Dunfee, T. W., Smith, N. C., & Ross Jr., W. T. (1999). Social contracts and marketing ethics. *Journal of Marketing, 63*(3), 17.
70. Donaldson, T. (1982). What justice demands. *Review of Social Economy, 40*(3), 301–310.
71. Lewin, P. (2007). Creativity or coercion: Alternative perspectives on rights to intellectual property. *Journal of Business Ethics, 71*(4), 443.
72. Donaldson, T., & Dunfee, T. W. (1999). When ethics travel: The promise and peril of global business ethics. *California Management Review, 41*(4), 45–63.
73. Donaldson, T., & Dunfee, T. W. (1999). *Ties that bind: A social contracts approach to business ethics*. Cambridge: Harvard Business School Press.
74. Donaldson, T. (2009). Compass and dead reckoning: The dynamic implications of ISCT. *Journal of Business Ethics, 88*, 659.
75. Donaldson, T., & Dunfee, T. W. (1994). Toward a unified conception of business ethics: Integrative social contracts theory. *The Academy of Management Review, 19*(2), 265.

76. Haidt, J. (2007). The new synthesis in moral psychology. *Science, 316*(5827), 998–1002.
77. Gauchet, M. (1997). *The disenchantment of the world–A political history of religion*. Princeton, NJ: Princeton University Press.
78. Abram, D. (1996). *The spell of the sensuous: Perception and language in a more-than-human world*. New York: Vintage Books.
79. Purser, R. E., Park, C., & Montuori, A. (1995). Limits to anthropocentrism: Toward an ecocentric organization paradigm? *Academy of Management Review, 20*(4), 1053–1099.
80. Persson, S., & Wasieleski, D. M. (2015). The seasons of the psychological contract: Overcoming the silent transformations of the employer-employee relationship. *Human Resource Management Review, 12*(3), 503–524.
81. Jullien, F. (2011). *The silent transformations*. London: Seagull. Also, Jullien, F. (2007). *Vital nourishment departing from happiness*. New York: Zone Books.
82. Rousseau, D. M. (2006). Is there such a thing as "evidence-based management"? 2005 presidential address. *Academy of Management Review, 31*, 256–269.
83. Zhu, Y., & Bargiela-Chiappini, F. (2013). Balancing emic and etic: Situated learning and ethnography of communication in cross-cultural management education. *Academy of Management Review, 12*(3), 308–395.
84. Jullien, F. (2007). *Vital nourishment: Departing from happiness* (p. 155). New York: Zone Books.

4 Individual-Level Tensions Contributing to Disconnectedness

Modern human beings are of two minds, physically as well as in their thinking about dualisms. This "split" mind builds on the physiological distinction in functioning and apparent purposes between the left and right halves of the brain, which Ian McGilchrist has called the "master and his emissary"[1] and Jaynes called the "bicameral" (two-sided) mind.[2] Here we focus on the idea of split mind, split brain—and the implications that have arisen from that split, which has fractured, in a sense, the human chain that links us to our heritage in nature. This internal split is part of the reason for the dualisms that exist in Western thinking that have created some of the paradoxes of sustainability that we have already observed.

Dual Processes in the Brain

Decision-making is a cognitive operation. The cognitive process can be partitioned into two main families: System 1 and System 2. "System 1 quickly proposes intuitive answers to judgment problems as they arise, and system 2 monitors the quality of these proposals, which it may endorse, correct or override."[3] System 1 is associated with the more immediate and holistic right brain processes, as described by McGilchrist in *The Master and His Emissary*.[4] Moral judgments, in contrast, are affected by controlled cognitive reasoning processes that are more focused on the consequences of an action or potential decision (teleological) as well as intuition, which is highly susceptible to emotions and bias.[5] Dual-process theories all claim that human behavior is a product of the "interplay of these two broad types of decision processes, which . . . capture the difference between reasoned/reflective thinking and impulsive/reactive decisions."[6]

On the basis of Nobel Laureate, Daniel Kahneman's cognitive systems model, we acknowledge the separation of two mental systems at the individual level.[7] System 1 is in charge of automatic processing of information. Individuals have no control over the activation of this system. When faced with a situation, System 1 constructs an immediate interpretation through the activation of heuristics. Heuristics are efficient, quick modes of decision-making. For instance, when faced with a familiar situation, System 1 will innately generate an automatic response such as recalling the previous action taken to address the situation. System 2 deals with concentration, effortful mental activities and active processing, including what is subjectively perceived as agency and choice. It can override the automatic metrics for behavior dictated by System 1 through *cognitive expenditure*.[8] Reasoning through complex dilemmas and the construction of imaginative solutions are System 2 cognitive activities. Both systems are affected by human emotions. Emotions profoundly influence individuals' tendencies to make choices.[9] Emotions affect what heuristics are activated (System 1) and how analytic processes are used (System 2). Responses based on intuition or emotion can have a significant role in how issues are initially framed and perceived.[10] Humans' cognitive tendencies and abilities are naturally formed and are largely universal. Automatic processing of information as elicited through the activation of heuristics served survival goals. But, as we have identified in this section, our cognitive abilities are often flawed and constrained. So it seems to be useful to us to discuss the concept of bounded awareness and how it affects individuals' perception of issues.

Cognition thus involves two separate mental systems.[11] System 1 is in charge of automatic processing of information. Individuals have no control over the activation of this system. When faced with a situation, System 1 constructs an immediate interpretation through the activation of heuristics. Through evolutionary history, heuristics developed as efficient, quick modes of decision-making. For instance, when faced with a familiar situation, System 1 will innately generate an automatic response such as recalling the previous action taken to address the situation. The characteristic process involves automatic, effortless, associative, rapid, experiential responses. Often a mental rule is applied to arrive at a quick decision. Rapid and intuitive assessments of a situation (ethical or not) "are likely to depart from the laws of logic and probability."[12] A system that assesses utility and longer-term consequences is needed to overcome biases associated with System 1.

System 2 deals with effortful mental activities and active processing— what we know as reasoning or logic (the left-brain functions, as described by McGilchrist). "The operations of System 2 are often associated with the subjective experience of agency, choice, and concentration."[13] It can override the automatic metrics for behavior dictated by System 1 through cognitive expenditure.[14] Reasoning through complex dilemmas and the construction of imaginative solutions are System 2 cognitive activities. Both systems are affected by human emotions. Emotions profoundly influence individuals' tendencies to make choices.[15] Emotions affect what heuristics are activated (System 1) and how analytic processes are used (System 2). System 2 thinking should result in more neutral decision-making as quick heuristics are not relied upon to make judgment calls and decisions.

Bounded Awareness

Rooted in the premise that individuals' intended rationality is limited by shortcomings in a person's ability to thoroughly gather and process information,[16] bounded awareness represents a cognitive blocking of perceptions or phenomena.[17] When influenced by bounded awareness, people fail to perceive visible and important information while demonstrating awareness of other, but irrelevant information associated with an event, object, or issue.[18] Essentially, bounded awareness can cause an ethical "blind spot" regarding an issue and is likely to generate decision failures.[19] We believe bounded awareness is partially responsible for causing *sustainability blind spots*, as important information regarding ecological issues is unconsciously ignored by decision-makers.

Given that we see sustainability issues as having an implicit ethical component because of the potential harm to current and future generations, it is relevant to our arguments in this present paper to link this discussion of bounded awareness to bounded *ethicality*. This concept builds on work on bounded awareness and relates to the cognitive processes that cause individuals to engage in unethical acts.[20] People can depart from their ethical values and moral identities when they are not aware of the moral implications of their choices on a particular issue. Chronic failures to act in accordance with one's moral identity are largely affected by the lack of moral awareness of the issue at hand (e.g., sustainability).[21] Even more potentially problematic, bounded awareness can prevent actors from emotionally processing the unethical nature of their behavior, blinding them to the consequences of their actions and encouraging the continuation of unethical actions.[22] To overcome the bounds of ethicality, individuals are encouraged to be more reflective in their decision-making and to take measures to engage System 2 thinking.[23]

Dual-process models of moral judgment typically characterize deontological (rules-based) evaluations of ethical issues as being governed by automatic, emotional responses and utilitarian judgments as being driven by active, controlled cognition.[24] These dual-process theories have received recent support through functional magnetic resonance imaging from cognitive neuroscience research.[25] The negative emotion felt by an individual drives an automatic disapproval of a harmful action, but can be overridden by a utilitarian evaluation of the action that causes the harm. Utilitarian judgments involve increased activity in the dorsolateral prefrontal cortex of the brain, which interacts with the base ganglia region of the brain governing "gut" intuition.[26] These utility judgments are also associated with more cognitive reflection that is associated with

System 2 thinking.[27] This more measured approach to an ethical analysis is slower and requires more cognitive expenditure.

Dual processes of cognition are normally characterized as a dualism of competing networks of thinking. They are positioned as being in opposition between fast and slow processing, and straight cognition versus affect. We contend, however, that these processes, automatic and controlled, are in fact a duality. Psychology researchers propose that dual-process models "co-determine" human behavior with a mix of intuition, affect, and deliberate evaluations of information.[28],[29] This insight is important and relevant to our thesis that a better understanding of these cognitive processes through cognitive neuroscience can help us all to make efficient decisions with fewer ethical lapses. It can lead to a more integrated and holistic approach, and help us all better integrate the paradoxes of sustainability into our thinking so that human societies and institutions can function in the future without the harmful impacts that dualistic thinking has wrought.

Neurocognitive processes of decision-making (including ethical decision-making), then, involve different systems that are networked together and operate interactively, much as we have suggested that dualities operate as wholes that cannot be teased apart. Both systems are necessary for understanding the world, acting responsibility, and making good decisions, and for integrating economistic with ecological values as we argue is needed. Even though ethical decisions tend to be treated distinctly from other types of decisions, that they are "dissociable from other forms of thinking,"[30] creates yet another unnecessary dualism and commits the separation fallacy in yet another form.

Different cognitive systems, located in the amygdala and prefrontal cortex, are responsible for evaluating short-term and long-term issues, respectively.[31] The implication is that there exists a time-oriented analytical conflict between an automatic and reflective cognitive system.[32] The neural competition between these two areas of the brain compromises the information gathering process and the accuracy of the actual decision.[33] This competition can also lead to ethical lapses of judgment towards the natural environment; for example, not paying attention to ecological impacts of human decision making or economistic thinking that fails to take socio-ecological consequences into account, as we discuss later in the book.

Intuitive processes in the brain involve storing and accessing information automatically. The way in which knowledge and information is stored and recalled affects the quality of the intuitive judgment as well as how fast the information is retrieved.[34] Experience with situations indeed affects the speed and quality of the intuitions, but it is not the only factor. How the subconscious mind is programmed by conscious processes is also a critical factor for making more effective decisions. Thus, the two systems of thinking interact and can inform each other to avoid lapses in judgment, and help integrate the dualities existent in paradoxical situations, not to mention helping humans to reintegrate with nature.

The information filed in the subconscious circuits of the brain must not be random, but rather, this information needs to be labeled and logically organized, which is aided by System 2 controlled processing. "Integration of knowledge by essentials not only makes retrieving information faster and more accurate, it also gives decision makers an indispensable tool: guiding principles"[35] or standard operating rules. These rules are useful for condensing information into useful and easily accessible generalizations that can be applied to cause-effect relationships across a variety of situations.[36] For ethical decisions, cognitive processes that organize information from experiences into guiding principles are useful for decreasing the frequency of ethical lapses in judgment, including creating distinctions and oppositional tendencies in situations, like the need for long-term flourishing of and on the planet, where dualisms get human beings into trouble. So initially, the evaluative process associated with decision-making must be "slowed down" to transform the information gathered through experience into more useful intuitive rules of thumb for future decisions. We are not advocating what Kahneman calls slow thinking[37] all the time for managers or other decision makers, but arguing that it can help minimize ethical lapses in judgment caused by cognitive bias from System 1, as well as helping us to form more integrated or holistic perspectives on the paradoxes that we face in our challenged world. In thinking about how to deal with sustainability paradoxes, we argue, reflective System 2 processing can be used to supplement more intuitive System 1 responses and make for more effective intuition that both recognizes and accepts the paradoxes that exist and begins to help us figure out how to deal with them more effectively.

Scientists believe that "automatic and controlled processes interact in a sequential way,"[38] whereas controlled processes associated with System 2 suppress the initial System 1 automatic response to affect the overall decision.[39] Intuitions occur by default and then reflective processes may intervene, if prompted.[40] System 2 can override System 1.[41] Thus, while there is processual competition, the systems can interact and influence one another. Social neuroscience researchers have discovered that automatic processing is associated with the X-system in the brain, while the reflective type is associated with another neurological system, the C-system.[42] Through brain scanning techniques, neuroscientists find that these two systems do indeed interact. The X-system is guided by the base ganglia region and the C-system is associated with the prefrontal cortex.

This dual processing approach, when combined with thinking about the bicameral mind, provides us with an understanding of why, in Western civilization, so many paradoxes are dealt with dualistically rather than as more holistic dualities (although it does not fully explain why this dichotomization did not occur as much in Eastern and Indigenous ways of seeing the world). As we started in the previous chapter, McGilchrist argued,[43] the left-brain functions of analysis, fragmentation, atomization, rationality, and reason, have in Western cultures, have come to dominate over the right brain functions of integrative, holistic, and more intuitive thinking. It is the latter right brain functions, however, that provide the potential for working effectively with the dualities associated with paradox, for seeing the system as a whole, and for integrating seemingly paradoxical ideas, yet in so many ways Western ways of conceptualizing the world completely overlook the need to understand both aspects of paradox. For instance, by only protecting the short-term economic interests of the present global society rather than also and simultaneously thinking about future generations' economic, social, and ecological interests, future generations will suffer.

Tension Between Rationality and Emotion

There is also a duality that exists, sometimes perceived as a dualism, between cognition or rationality and emotion. Once again as with left- and right-brain thinking, Western culture favors cognition and rationality over the more intuitive-seeming emotional responses to situations. Logic, reason, and analysis are valued, along with readily quantifiable information and data, over more instinctual, more "emotional" considerations like beauty, aesthetics, art, and even nature valued for itself. This splitting of emotion and reason aligns with humans' desire to split themselves off from nature in many developed parts of the world. Below we explore the physiological origins of this split with an eye towards seeing how it, like the bicameral mind, might once again be reunited.

The bulk of human behavior involves constant interactions between controlled and automatic processes as well as interactions between cognitive and emotional systems. First, much of the brain implements "automatic" processes, which are faster than conscious deliberations and which occur with little awareness or feeling of effort.[44] Situations have specific and limited action possibilities or which provide unconscious signals to help select an action (e.g., a written word induces reading, an extended hand induces a handshake). Also, learned habits unconsciously suggest what comes next in action sequences. These influences are far from subtle as they are the basis of cognitive efficiency. Habits provide expert execution and coordination for actions in a familiar situation, which makes them generally more efficient than deliberate goal-controlled processes. Habits, however, are less flexible than deliberate processes as they adapt much more slowly to novel parameters or to complex, variable and multidimensional situations.

A sociocultural–evolutionary approach to morality, moral foundations theory,[45] contends that there are foundations of moral intuition that are present cognitively, regardless of a particular culture.[46] This work posits that conceptions of morality go beyond a mere concern for others in terms of justice, and that it also includes concerns about maintaining community and stability in groups.[47] The foundations of moral intuition that are proposed by moral foundations theory are rooted in evolutionary processes to regulate group interactions. Moral foundations theory proposes five moral intuition foundations broken into two main categories: one that emphasizes protection of individuals (harm/care and fairness/reciprocity)[48] and the other that refers to group bonds (ingroup/loyalty, authority/respect, and purity/sanctity).[49],[50] The former is rooted more in concerns for economic factors (external goods), while the latter is more focused on social concerns.[51] Foundations are based in a common "other-regarding" concern that served an adaptive advantage to our ancestors, resulting in an automatic affective response.[52] Thus, emotions and cognition are intimately linked and they shape our responses to the world around us—and to the paradoxes that we see.

Further support for these dualisms and the need to integrate them into dualities comes from work on global values, and on the differences that exist between conservatives and progressives in the U.S. by moral psychologist Jonathan Haidt and his collaborators. Haidt finds in global studies that the five core sets of values—or moral foundations described above—exist in a range of cultures. These values include care or the cherishing and protection of others, i.e., the opposite of harm, fairness or the idea of achieving justice on the basis of shared rules, loyalty or standing with one's "ingroup" (tribe, clan, family, or other social unit), authority or respect or the willingness to cede to tradition and authority, and sanctity or purity, which is the revulsion for disgusting things.[53] In later work, Haidt hypothesizes about a sixth moral foundation, liberty (opposed to oppression).[54]

Relevant to the idea of dualisms, Haidt, along with Lakoff, points to differences in values systems between people of conservative and progressive beliefs. While progressives orient largely towards values of care and fairness, paying little attention to loyalty, authority, and sanctity or purity, conservatives tend to value all five of the moral foundations as being important. He also notes in his book *The Righteous Mind* that libertarians tend to emphasize the sixth foundation of liberty at the expense of all of the others.[55] Understanding these differences, which are similar in many ways to the "nurturing parent" and "good father" distinctions between progressives and conservatives that linguist George Lakoff identified, can help us think through how to develop approaches and as we will argue in Chapter 8, the need for new narratives and stories, that integrate and value everyone's perspectives.

Cognitive neuroscience research has discovered that there is indeed a neural algorithmic link between emotional expressions and functions of the brain.[56],[57] Emotion is activated in the amygdala and reason is found in the prefrontal cortex. Emotions are more likely to become involved with cognitive processes when issues take on an ethical component.[58] The relevance of moral foundations theory to our arguments is partially related to the dual-process model. Humans use two differential processes when analyzing a situation, viewing duality, or resolving a dilemma with (or without) a moral component. A decision-making process incorporates evolutionarily derived moral intuitions in concert with calculated analysis and dialogue. (This same dual-process thinking operates in the aesthetic rationality concept discussed in a subsequent chapter.) This dual-process perspective connects human cognition with emotion. When making categorical inferences about a phenomenon or situation, dual-process models require additional cognitive activity which can lead to more effective reasoning.[59]

These individual characteristics and differences shed insight into why dualisms or tensions of the opposite have arisen and become so problematic, especially in Western/developed cultures. Taken to the system level of analysis, as discussed in the next chapter, they can help us see and potentially integrate other dualities that characterize much of modern society, constituting what we have called the broken human chain.

Notes

1. McGilchrist, I. (2009). *The master and his emissary: The divided brain and the making of the western world.* New Haven: Yale University Press.
2. Jaynes, J. (2000). *The origin of consciousness in the breakdown of the bicameral mind.* New York: Houghton Mifflin Harcourt.
3. Kahneman, D., & Frederick, S. (2005). A model of heuristic judgment. In H. Holoyoak & R. G. Morrison (Eds.), *The Cambridge handbook of thinking and reasoning* (pp. 267–294). Cambridge, UK: Cambridge University Press.
4. McGilchrist, I. (2009). *The master and his emissary: The divided brain and the making of the western world.* New Haven: Yale University Press.
5. Greene, J. D. (2007). The secret joke of Kant's soul: In moral psychology. In W. Sinott-Armstrong (Ed.), *The neuroscience of morality: Emotion, disease, and development* (Vol. 3, pp. 105–118). Cambridge, MA: MIT Press.
6. Alos-Ferrer, C., & Strack, F. (2014). From dual processes to multiple selves: Implications for economic behavior. *Journal of Economic Psychology, 41,* 2.
7. Kahneman, D. (2011). *Thinking fast and slow.* New York: Strauss and Giroux.
8. Street, M. D., Douglas, S. C., Geiger, S. W., & Martinko, M. J. (2001). The impact of cognitive expenditure on the ethical decision-making process: The cognitive elaboration model. *Organizational Behavior and Human Decision Processes, 86,* 256–277.
9. Druckman, J. N., & McDermott, R. (2008). Emotion and the framing of risky choice. *Political Behavior, 30,* 297–321.
10. De Martino, B., Kumaran, D., Seymour, B., & Dolan, R. J. (2006). Frames, biases and rational decision-making in the human brain. *Science, 313,* 684–687.
11. Kahneman, D. (2011). *Thinking, fast and slow.* New York: Straus and Giroux.
12. Hodgkinson, G. P., Sadler-Smith, E., Burke, L. A., Claxton, G., & Sparrow, P. R. (2009). Intuition in organizations: Implications for strategic management. *Long Range Planning, 42,* 277–297.

13. Kahneman, D. (2011). *Thinking fast and slow* (p. 21). New York: Straus and Giroux.
14. Kahneman, D., & Frederick, S. (2002). Representativeness revisited: Attribute substitution in intuitive judgment. In T. Gilovich, D. Griffin & D. Kahneman (Eds.), *Heuristics and biases: The psychology of intuitive judgment* (pp.49–81). New York: Cambridge University Press.
15. Druckman, J. N., & McDermott, R. (2008). Emotion and the framing of risky choice. *Political Behavior*, *30*, 297.
16. Simon, H. (1983). Search and reasoning in problem solving. *Artificial Intelligence*, *21*(1–2), 7–29.
17. Werhane, P. (2006). A place for philosophers in applied ethics and the role of moral reasoning in moral imagination: A response to Richard Rorty. *Business Ethics Quarterly*, *16*(3), 401–408.
18. Bazerman, M., & Chugh, D. (2006). Decisions without blinders. *Harvard Business Review*, January, 88–97.
19. Werhane, P. H., Hartman, L. P., Moberg, D., Englehardt, E., Pritchard, M., & Parmar, B. (2011). Social constructivism, mental models, and problems of obedience. *Journal of Business Ethics*, *100*, 103–118.
20. Chugh, D., & Kern, M. C. (2016). A dynamic and cyclical model of bounded ethicality. *Research in Organizational Behavior*, *36*, 85–100.
21. Bazerman, M. H., & Sezer, O. (2016). Bounded awareness: Implications for ethical decision making. *Organizational Behavior and Human Decision Processes*, *136*, 95–105.
22. Chugh, D., & Kern, M. C. (2016). A dynamic and cyclical model of bounded ethicality. *Research in Organizational Behavior*, *36*, 95.
23. Bazerman, M. H., & Pugh, O. (2016). Bounded awareness: Implications for ethical decision making. *Organizational Behavior and Human Decision Processes*, *136*, 95–105; Greene, J. (2014). *Moral tribes: Emotion, reason and the gap between us and them*. New York: Penguin Press.
24. Greene, J. D. (2007). The secret joke of Kant's soul. In moral psychology. In W. Sinott-Armstrong (Ed.), *The neuroscience of morality: Emotion, disease, and development* (Vol. 3, pp. 105–118), Cambridge, MA: MIT Press.
25. Greene, J. D. (2009). Dual-process morality and the personal/impersonal distinction: A reply to McGuire, Landon, Coltheart, and Mackenzie. *Journal of Experimental Social Psychology*, *45*, 581–584.
26. see Miller, E. K., & Cohen, J. D. (2001). An integrative theory of prefrontal cortex function. *Annual Review of Neuroscience*, *24*, 167–202.
27. Hardman (2008); Strack, F., & Deutsch, R. (2004). Reflective and impulsive determinants of social behavior. *Personality and Social Psychology Review*, *8*, 220–247.
28. Hsee, C. K., & Rottenstreich, Y. (2004). Music, pandas, and muggers: On the affective psychology of value. *Journal of Experimental Psychology: General*, *133*(1), 23–30.
29. Metcalfe, J., & Mischel, W. (1999). A hot/cool-system analysis of delay of gratification: Dynamics of willpower. *Psychological Review*, *106*, 3–19. doi:10.1037/0033-295X.106.1.3.
30. Salvador, R., & Folger, R. G. (2009). Business ethics and the brain: Rommel Salvador and Robert G. Folger. *Business Ethics Quarterly*, *19*(1), 5.
31. Bechara, A. (2005). Decision making, impulse control and loss of willpower to resist drugs: A neurocognitive perspective. *Nature Neuroscience*, *8*(11), 1458.
32. McClure, S. M., Laibson, D. I., Loewenstein, G., & Cohen, J. D. (2004). Separate neural systems value immediate and delayed monetary rewards. *Science*, *306*(5695), 503–507.

33. Brocas, I., & Carrillo, J. D. (2014). Dual-process theories of decision-making: A selective survey. *Journal of Economic Psychology, 41*, 45–54.
34. Woiceshyn, J. (2009). Lessons from "good minds": How CEOs use intuition, analysis and guiding principles to make strategic decisions. *Long Range Planning, 42*(3), 298–319.
35. Woiceshyn, J. (2009). Lessons from "good minds": How CEOs use intuition, analysis and guiding principles to make strategic decisions. *Long Range Planning, 42*(3), 301.
36. Woiceshyn, J. (2009). Lessons from "good minds": How CEOs use intuition, analysis and guiding principles to make strategic decisions. *Long Range Planning, 42*(3), 298–319.
37. Kahneman, D. (2011). *Thinking, fast and slow.* New York: Macmillan.
38. Alós-Ferrer, C., & Strack, F. (2014). From dual processes to multiple selves: Implications for economic behavior. *Journal of Economic Psychology, 41*, 4.
39. Kahneman, D., & Frederick, S. (2005). A model of heuristic judgment. *The Cambridge Handbook of Thinking and Reasoning, 267*, 293.
40. Evans, J. S. B., & Stanovich, K. E. (2013). Dual-process theories of higher cognition: Advancing the debate. *Perspectives on Psychological Science, 8*(3), 223–241.
41. Stanovich, K. E. (2010). *Decision making and rationality in the modern world.* New York: Oxford University Press.
42. Lieberman, M. D., Jarcho, J. M., & Satpute, A. B. (2004). Evidence-based and intuition-based self-knowledge: An fMRI study. *Journal of Personality and Social Psychology, 87*, 421–435.
43. McGilchrist, I. (2009). *The master and his emissary: The divided brain and the making of the western world.* New Haven: Yale University Press.
44. Kahneman, D. (2011). *Thinking, fast and slow.* London: Macmillan.
45. Haidt, J. (2001). The emotional dog and its rational tail: A social intuitionist approach to moral judgment. *Psychological Review, 108*, 814–834.
46. Weber, C. R., & Federico, C. M. (2013). Moral foundations and heterogeneity in ideological preferences. *Political Psychology, 34*(1), 109.
47. Lakoff, G. (2008). *The political mind: Why you can't understand 21st-century politics with an 18th-century brain.* New York: Penguin.
48. Haidt, J., & Graham, J. (2007). When morality opposes justice: Conservatives have moral intuitions that liberals may not recognize. *Social Justice Research, 20*(1), 98–116.
49. Haidt, J., & Graham, J. (2007). When morality opposes justice: Conservatives have moral intuitions that liberals may not recognize. *Social Justice Research, 20*(1), 98–116.
50. Haidt, J., & Joseph, C. (2004). Intuitive ethics: How innately prepared intuitions generate culturally variable virtues. *Daedalus, 133*(4), 55–66.
51. Stenner, K. (2009). Three kinds of "conservatism." *Psychological Inquiry, 20*(2–3), 142–159.
52. Haidt, J. (2013). Moral psychology for the twenty-first century. *Journal of Moral Education, 42*(3), 290.
53. See, e.g., Haidt, J. (2007). The new synthesis in moral psychology. *Science, 316*(5827), 998–1002; Haidt, J. (2008). Morality. *Perspectives on Psychological Science, 3*(1), 65–72.
54. Haidt, J. (2012). *The righteous mind: Why good people are divided by politics and religion.* New York: Vintage.
55. Haidt, J. (2012). *The righteous mind: Why good people are divided by politics and religion.* New York: Vintage; Haidt, J. (2008). Morality. *Perspectives on Psychological Science, 3*(1), 65–72.

56. Salzman, C. D., & Fusi, S. (2010). Emotion, cognition, and mental state representation in amygdala and prefrontal cortex. *Annual Review of Neuroscience, 33*, 173–202.
57. Schulte-Rüther, M., Markowitsch, H. J., Fink, G. R., & Piefke, M. (2007). Mirror neuron and theory of mind mechanisms involved in face-to-face interactions: A functional magnetic resonance imaging approach to empathy. *Journal of Cognitive Neuroscience, 19*(8), 1354–1372.
58. Sonenshein, S. (2009). Emergence of ethical issues during strategic change implementation. *Organization Science, 20*(1), 223–239.
59. Markovits, H., Lortie-Forgues, H., & Brunet, M-L. (2012). More evidence for a dual-process model of conditional reasoning. *Memory & Cognition, 40*, 736–747. doi:10.3758/s13421-012-0186-4.

5   Systemic-Level Tensions

Organizations, businesses, and whole systems like societies—or even the global governance infrastructure, which is different from global government and currently is largely voluntary—also experience dualisms or tensions of the opposite. That is, they too encounter the paradoxes of sustainability on which we focus, further breaking the human chain, that is, our deep connection to nature. As noted earlier, many Eastern, Southern, and Indigenous cultures have retained their more holistic perspectives, and attendant understanding that human beings are of and connected to nature. In the West, however, as we have tried to demonstrate, that link has been broken. In our left-brained efforts to control the world around us, we in "developed" nations have tended to emphasize a positivist and empirical science, strongly built on materialistic foundations, almost to the exclusion of other values, spirituality, or other aspects of a living world that cannot readily be measured. One reason, in this context, that money and wealth have become such important measures of "success" is that such short-term indicators are readily quantifiable, something that appeals to the left brain.

These tendencies have manifested in practice in what Riane Eisler calls Dominator cultures, infused with "masculine" (at least from a Western perspective) values, which we explore in more depth in a following section. Here we are arguing for a more integrated approach that values both masculine *and* feminine values, that recognizes both economizing *and* ecologizing, and individualism and the collective. This type of approach to culture, which we call ecologizing, following Bill Frederick, relates well with what Eisler calls Partnership cultures, as we will discuss presently.

The emphasis that humans in industrialized nations now place on materialism, along with today's dominant market-based ideology of neoliberalism, also focuses many of our institutions, particularly businesses, decidedly on the short term. A short-term orientation virtually ignores the effects of today's decisions on longer-term or slower-moving outcomes, which helps to explain our climate change and sustainability crises. These orientations emphasize domination over collaboration and partnership, materialism/empiricism over values, nature, and spirit. They prioritize, for example, exploitation to gain maximum rewards over approaches that recognize the intrinsic value of people and place. Thus, they represent an important break or split in the human chain.

All of these dualisms, we will argue, have resulted in the dominance of today's largely economic narrative of neoliberalism evidences itself as an orientation towards values of economizing and power aggrandizing. Neoliberalism manifests itself in neoclassical economics. It is a major factor in how many economies and enterprises operate today (at least on the surface) and is a highly problematic approach to the world. Neoliberalism rests in the economizing (economistic), power-aggrandizing, and technological values uncovered and articulated by Frederick[1] as discussed earlier. Somehow, we need to shift that neoliberal and economizing narrative away from economizing values towards values of ecologizing and civilizing, while retaining the best aspects of economizing and power aggrandizing.

Below, we address these dualisms: science and positivism versus more qualitative and less measurable values, short- versus long term orientation, masculine versus feminine values, individualism versus collectivism, and the implications of all of these dualisms. These dualisms hopefully can be united into integrated dualities that recognize and honor their paradoxical nature, as we consider how to move from today's dominant economic narrative—based in the left-brained oriented sides of the dualisms—to move towards a more integrated approach of ecologizing and ecocentrism, which incorporate but are not dominated by anthropocentrism and corporate-centric logics and language.

Temporal Tensions

Time is a fundamental and critical variable for organizational analysis. Recently, it is receiving much research attention in sociology, cultural studies, and organizational studies. Time certainly shapes many organizational processes fundamentally. Evaluation mechanisms, accounting, and delivery schedules are subject to conceptualizations and measurements of time. But time is also a source of tension for individuals and organizations. Organizational scholars have recognized a lack of theorizing about time and organizations.[2] This absence of treatment about time can create many problems. Problems include the following. a) There is a gross mismatch between the quarterly and annual accounting of financial information and the longer time cycles in nature. b) There is a lack of sensitivity to time aging of knowledge assets in organizations, which allows abundant knowledge to be lost with retiring employees. c) The social acceleration of production/operations time has a bimodal impact of performance/productivity—too slow affects productivity, too fast causes burn-out and fatigue—the need is to find optimal speed of operations. d) There is a lack of attention to rhythms (human, biotic, meteorological, seasonal, etc.), which can be a source of harmful disruption in natural cycles, overloading of natural systems, and cause of destruction/catastrophe.

One of the reasons sustainability initiatives are so difficult to enact may be due, in part, to the temporal expectations on which business decisions are made. Business managers are typically evaluated on a short-term basis (annually, quarterly, or even daily), but sustainable development is a long-term issue. In terms of moral intensity, the perceived degree of moral imperative in a particular issue,[3] there is not enough temporal immediacy around sustainability for individuals, organizations, or nations to act.

Think about it. Despite debates around climate change and even climate crisis, most scientists predict global average temperatures will rise by at least 2.5C in the next 50 years or less. The consequences of this warming are quite horrible and well documented.[4] But try telling a manager who is being evaluated on a quarterly basis that she has to engage in sustainable behaviors in her organization because we are reaching our planetary boundary in a couple of generations. Without the temporal immediacy, managers are less motivated to act towards sustainability. Managers are constantly faced with this tension between short-and-long term horizons.

Our understanding of time could discriminate sustainability from other concepts including, responsibility.[5] Management scholars' general neglect in accounting for time in our theories leads to a short-term view of the world, which has huge implications for sustainability. Benefits accruing in the future are, from the Western and disconnected-from-nature perspective, valued less than present benefits.[6] This atomistic view, of course, keeps sustainability debates rooted in the Western mode of thinking, by reducing sustainable development to economic terms and ignoring the moral and ecological consequences of business as usual. Ironically, from this perspective, current Western perspectives, when dealing with the environment, could be viewed as being ethically neutral,[7] rather than providing needed guidance about how humans can live more responsibly on the planet. Such a framing is ethically agnostic or amoral, which is aligned with (we believe wrong-headed) economistic thinking that believes that economic decisions have no moral valence.

In management, there is great value placed on making fast decisions.[8] Across many competitive contexts, shorter business and technology cycles and quicker competitor responses are forcing speedier strategic decisions onto the business firm.[9] As a result, this trend towards more speed and more efficiency has caused firms to value flexibility of operations very highly. If a manager must change the direction and functioning of the company more rapidly than ever before, the ability to quickly alter everything from cost structures, to business processes, to organizational culture is coveted at a premium.[10]

According to sociologist, Harmut Rosa, time has been neglected in social science analyzes of modernity. Rosa introduces a new perspective on time, one rooted in understanding the causes and effects of time acceleration. "Acceleration of time" is defined by him as an objective fact, *not* as a *speeding* up of processes, but as *an exponential increase in the quantity of activities in the same allocated time period.*[11] His definition corresponds more to the notion of rhythm in music, but with the difference that "acceleration" reflects here an objective fact, and not a subjective perception. (We discuss objectivity versus subjectivity more later in this chapter).

This definition represents the basis for his analysis of the process of speeding up of modern society. Acceleration in modernity is manifested in three forms: technological acceleration, the acceleration of social change, and the speeding up of the pace of life, driven by economic, social and cultural factors.

If this is indeed true and society, through technological advancement, is increasing its pace, then we worry about the effects on the social and ecological environment. The accelerated rhythm of life may lead to the compression of space through time.[12] The "ideological value placed on being fast and decisive has led to the avoidance of difficult questions, myopic thinking, repression of doubt, and the stifling of reflexivity . . . leaving no space for inquiry and improvements".[13] The effects of this space–time compression are manifested in the form of anomie and alienation of the individual.[14] Business organizations rely on acceleration and dynamism in the modern social environment, leading to humanistic consequences to the employee as well, as the meaning of work could be severely altered.[15] At a faster work pace, employees could suffer by being forced to fit more and more work into the same amount of time in their day, which could affect their physical and mental well-being.

Research has also attempted to address attentional failures due to temporal and spatial scales of organizational processes.[16] This work argues that both small and large-scale issues escape organizational attention as a result. Related to our split minds (dual-process brain) discussed earlier in this book, humans' cognitive architecture may make decision-making errors as a result of this newfound speed in organizations and society. There "is a bio-socially grounded tendency for humans to infer the future by extending the past, prospective cognitions are susceptible to processing failures".[17] Once again, our awareness becomes bounded by such pressures on our cognition.

Although time is recognized as a central feature of change,[18] scholars have recently claimed that our theories of change are largely a-temporal.[19] Especially in the West, we see, or look for, change, rather than the process of "changing". We don't see the silent transformations that are happening continuously within us and around us.[20] As a metaphor, we notice only the river itself, without paying any attention to its flow and current.

Thus, we notice change only after the state of the object is changed. But we are limited in our ability to see that the transformations are continuous and often subtle, as time lapse photography of natural processes vividly demonstrates. Thus, there is a temporal tension centered around how we recognize time. We tend to witness change only at two independent time periods. In other words, we measure change by pitting the object in question against two moments in time—before and after. Since time is constantly moving at, as Rosa contends, an accelerated pace, we can no longer be blind to the changes that take place all the time. For sustainability, it does not do enough good to compare "progress" on environmental measures in the Year 2040 against what the world looked like in 1980. Ironically, there is not enough time to save the planet if we continue along this trajectory.

Distal Versus Proximal Thinking

Recently, organizational theorists have recognized that it is important to try to understand time when we analyze organizational processes.[21] We need new ways to control the future, which is dependent, in part, on how we conceptualize and relate to time.[22] Change is understood as the adaptation of a subjective movement from past to present. We cannot be limited by this subjective and narrow interpretation of time, if we are going to solve long-term social and environmental problems. The dominant Western tendency is to view time as always forward flowing, leading to a future state from the past or present moment.[23] The only way to address the future is to recognize the dynamic and flowing nature of events and phenomena.

The type of thinking we are describing here is called distal thinking. This type of thinking about time emphasizes outcomes and results. It illustrates our focus on completed end products, things, or even decisions and thoughts.[24] On the other hand, proximal thinking views any type of organization as a flowing, continuous conglomeration of objects or, as Cooper and Law called it, "assemblages of organizing".[25] We believe that organizations should be viewed in terms of proximal thinking in order to overcome the temporal limitations that may be causing some of our decision failures. Organizational theorists and managers need to pay attention to what has been forgotten or even that is invisible. In the face of time acceleration, this perspective becomes even more important.

Distal thinking views time in a linear manner, focusing on teleological or purposeful outcomes.[26] In the West, we see that institutions are treated as independent bodies. The corporation is viewed as a single entity for legal purposes. The past is thought to be completely known, that we possess complete objective information. Our actions are always tied to some measurable, objective goal. This goal is usually tied to short-termism. Organizational identities are expected to be stoic over time and unwavering. This way of thinking leads to the mimicking of past actions for future applications and problems.[27] Thus, we tend to deny that times have changed or that the context has changed. We ignore time. It is not difficult to see the implications for sustainability in this distal notion of time. In contrast, proximal thinking involves trying to understand the contingent nature of processes. Time is reframed as an ever-changing effect in itself; not as something that is fixed and easily manipulated.[28] Laclau referred to this as "dislocated time" where organizations are networks of organizing processes and objects rather than fixed and unchangeable.[29]

In his Theory of Structuration, Giddens defines modernity as the regularized control of social relations across indefinite time–space distances.[30] In modernity, structural principles stress consistency of the time and space dimension and the resulting mechanisms in organizations perpetuate the objectivity of time.[31] As a consequence, time "then becomes a primary 'medium of exchange' which contributes to the process of macro-system integration because it facilitates social homogenization by enabling practices/relations to be disembedded from local contexts and re-articulated across indefinite tracts of time and space".[32]

Our present-day socially constructed organizations operate on the premise that the exact coordination of activities requires that all stakeholders develop and synchronize the same temporal orientation. Thus, scheduling within organizations is ordered to "ensure" predictability of outcomes. Shared time becomes necessary in each system. The "linear character of modern time presents new problems for social systems because the contingency of an open future threatens continuity in the form of 'what comes next'".[33] This perspective has huge implications for sustainability as the needs of future generations are discounted. Related to Rosa's notion of time acceleration, technological developments attempt to compress time and space. The "ideological value placed on being fast and decisive has led to the avoidance of difficult questions, myopic thinking, repression of doubt, and the stifling of reflexivity . . . leaving no space for inquiry and improvements."[34]

There are two primary research traditions on time that really separate an analysis of time across the long- and short-term dimensions. These two traditions are also consistent with the linearity of Western thinking about time versus the circular perspectives on time from Indigenous cultures. And they represent yet another related tension. The first tradition centers research around structuralism and functionalism,[35] which we see driving much organizational research today. The second tradition classically analyzes particular and transitory behavioral elements by applying a cultural perspective in the social sciences.[36] In this tradition, culture is used as a substitute for society, which implies a tension between local and global. For sustainability, this is problematic since efforts to curb climate change need to be configured on a global level.

The definitional distinctions between society and culture helps shed light on the evolutionary views of human behavior. Natural science theories (which we delve more deeply into in Chapter 6) help us understand the permanent elements of behavior and the social science view emphasizes the transitory elements more often. Thus, change is normally explained from a Western cultural lens. This line of thinking leads us to another tension related to objectivity and subjectivity.

Objectivity Versus Subjectivity

A related tension to the temporal one relates to objectivity v. subjectivity. Subjective perspectives are not only possessed by an individual but can be shared by a group of individuals. An inter-subjectivity involves the shared understanding of an issue or phenomenon within a group. Objectivity, in contrast, refers to facts or knowledge that are not necessarily related to human awareness. In other words, what is objective fact in the natural sciences may not be equivalent to objectivity in the social sciences.

This clarification helps to define the central role of a time orientation in the broken chain between humans and the natural environment. Time is subjectively determined by society in social science.[37] The subjective dimension of time involves the observations of decision-makers, whereas the objective form involves the longer-term tendencies of organizations. In the short term, managers try to affect the time horizon with their decisions. As we will see this view of time is related to the economizing value set of self-organizing structures. A concern for the longer term, which is needed for sustainable development, can only be realized if the managers and leaders with the discretion to act are able to perceive that short-term decisions affect future generations. We advocate a long-term time orientation in this book, which is related to ecologizing values. This orientation is often challenged by our current organizational systems, which are designed to deliver results in the short term. The 2007–2008 global financial crisis provides an excellent illustration for the importance of this distinction and potential links. As for the future trends in financial markets, it is not sufficient for scholars to know the duration of economic and political processes. They must also pay attention to the time horizon of the financial decision makers themselves who actually perceive and interpret these processes, and finally decide to act or not to address sustainability.

Masculine Versus Feminine Values

Another important dualism that manifests in today's culture in a variety of ways, and that is possibly also a product of left-brain dominance in Western cultures, is an apparent split between masculine and feminine traits. Although there are clear biological differences between males and females in the human (and many other) species, attributes associated with masculinity and femininity are socially constructed, or made up in societies. Different conceptions of males and females, masculinity and femininity are relevant to different cultures as we will explore below. Thinking of this masculine–feminine dichotomy as a duality, an integrated whole rather than a dualism of opposites, we can begin to see that both masculinity and femininity clearly share some overlapping traits. Further, individuals of either gender (or individuals who fall "between" stereotypical genders), as well as whole cultures, of course, can, and we believe need to, exhibit *both* masculine and feminine traits. That said, since the dominant culture today in Western civilization seems associated with masculine attributes, and emerging ideas about ecologizing seem to somewhat more associated with feminine qualities, it may be important to consider the dualism of masculine–feminine as opposites, before thinking about how to integrate them more completely into a more holistic notion.

Many modern Westernized cultures that exhibit masculine traits view such traits as being more positive than are the opposite-seeming tendencies of femininity. In contrast to the (apparently positive) attributes of strength, energy, and apparent decisiveness associated with masculinity, femininity, for example, is stereotypically portrayed as exhibiting gentleness, caring, compassion, tolerance, nurturance, empathy, and sensitivity. Femininity in Western cultures is even associated with (apparently weak or even negative) traits of fragility, passiveness, and dependency. In contrast, in the Chinese yin/yang symbol discussed earlier, masculinity is depicted as the white side, while femininity is the dark side of the symbol, yet they are actually part of one integrated entity that like other dualities cannot be separated and retain their integrity.

These attributes of Westernized masculinity and femininity exhibit themselves at the individual level, in the expectations and stereotypes of how males and females (men and women) are expected to behave in different culture. Of course, the relative importance of various aspects of these traits differs by culture as well. One important set of insights at the societal level about masculinity and femininity, conceived as a dualism, that is, with the belief that one is either masculine or feminine, versus being able to integrate both aspects, comes from the work of Geert Hofstede and colleagues.[38] These scholars laid out six important dimensions on which national cultures (not individual behaviors) can be assessed. These dimensions are important to our argument because they pick up on important aspects of different cultures. Hofstede's six dimensions are: power distance (the degree to which people with less power expect that power to be distributed unequally); individualism versus collectivism (see the following section, as that is another important dualism needing integration to heal our relationship with nature); masculinity versus femininity; uncertainty avoidance; long-term versus short-term orientation, which was discussed previously; and indulgence versus restraint. Here we focus explicitly on the masculine–feminine differentiation, with a discussion of individualism and collectivism to follow.

Hofstede and his colleagues emphasized differences in masculinity and femininity at the national level as they relate to the division of emotional roles between men and women.[39] Hofstede polarized these dimensions in a continuum ranging from an assertive (masculine) pole to a caring (feminine) pole at the societal level. Similar to the attributes at the individual level, masculine cultures emphasize emotional and social role differentiation between the genders, assertiveness and ambition (for men), with work taking precedence over family, admiration for the strong, fathers dealing with facts and mothers with feelings. In masculine cultures, girls but not boys can cry, boys but not girls should fight back, men are elected to political positions, religions and gods are male, and there is strong moralism about sexuality.

In contrast, more feminine cultures minimize social and emotional role differentiation, both men and women need to be modest and caring, there is balance between work and family, and sympathy for the weak. Further, feminine cultures allow mothers *and* fathers to deal with facts and feelings, and both genders can cry but not fight, women have decision making power over how many children to have and can act in elected positions or political life. Religion in more feminine cultures focuses on fellow human beings, and sexuality is accepted as a fact of life.[40]

Interestingly, Hofstede's research indicates that masculinity tends to be high in developed countries like Japan, Germany, Italy, and Mexico, and moderately high in English-speaking Western nations like the United States and the United Kingdom.[41] Consider Hofstede's work in the context of many years of work by cultural historian Riane Eisler, who in a pathbreaking early book called *The Chalice and the Blade*,[42] studied social systems of antiquity as a way of seeking out the roots of the cultures that we experience today. Eisler found that there a significant tension—paradox of sustainability—between what she terms dominator or masculine cultures and partnership or more feminine societies (to align with Hofstede's terms). Eisler argues, based on extensive anthropological, mythological, and linguistic evidence, that many cultures in prehistoric times were what she calls partnership cultures, where relationships between the genders were relatively egalitarian, activities were peaceful, and there was a matriarchal emphasis on lifegiving, nurturance, and caring. Importantly, there was general equity between the genders rather than dominance of one over the other in partnership cultures.

Consider somewhat simplistically, for example, traits that are generally (and stereotypically) considered to be masculine at the individual level. These traits include power, strength, courage, independence, violence, energy, assertiveness, integrity, equality, and virility (high sex drive). These traits derive from stories of gods and heroes in human civilization's earliest days, and have become part and parcel of what Eisler identifies as "Dominator cultures," which exhibit political values of acceptance of inequality, control, authoritarianism, and coercion.[43] Eisler contrasts Dominator cultures with Partnership cultures, which are (and were) based on values of equality, freedom, democracy, and caring,[44] qualities often associated with femininity.

Partnership-oriented cultures, which today Eisler calls "caring economies,"[45] are directly aligned with the values of ecologizing as we will discuss later. According to Eisler, partnership cultures in ancient times were eventually upended by invading hordes of nomadic warriors, who instituted domination systems that included rigid hierarchies (especially of men over women), power differences, and violence. These Domination systems still exist today, as Eisler noted in a speech to the United Nations in 2017, in commonly found domination practices related to "the kind of system we have been trying to leave behind, be it man over man, man over woman, race over race, religion over religion, and, yes, man over nature."[46] Eisler argues, as we do, that we need to move to a more feminized, partnership culture, one that we call ecologizing or eco-centric as opposed to economizing or economistic, in which balancing human activity with nature, equity among peoples, and collaboration is valued more than domination and superiority over others.

It is important to note here that we are not rejecting the positive aspects of masculine culture in our efforts to move the system towards ecologizing. We *all*—and "all" is the point—need strength, assertiveness, decisiveness, power, strength, courage, independence, energy, integrity, equality—traits associated with masculinity, at least in Western cultures. Similarly, we *all* need to recognize our interconnectedness, gentleness, caring, compassion, tolerance, nurturance, empathy, sensitivity, and other attributes associated with femininity. Thus, it is in the integration of the dualism into the duality of a combined masculine-feminine or ecologizing cultures, values, and attributes for our societies with their economies that we seek. In other words, by integrating the best of masculine and feminine traits together into our broader socio-economic-ecological systems, we will all benefit in the long run, as will the other living beings on the planet that are affected by human activities. Similarly, for the next set of dualisms, individualism and collectivism, the desired end state is a more integral approach, as philosopher Ken Wilber[47] might say.

Individualism Versus Collectivism

Another dualism that affects how we humans view ourselves and our world and needs reconciliation is the one between individualism and collectivism, to use the terms that Hofstede used.[48] Human beings have always lived in collectivities—in nomadic tribes during the preagricultural era and in villages during pre-industrial times. During those eras, the concept of the individual person or personality simply did not exist absent the existence of the tribe. A dualistic perspective on the individual and the collective emerged with the advent of agricultural production and societies in which social hierarchies also began to evolve, where individuals had specific places, roles, and functions.[49] It was not until the 18th century when the 1789 French Declaration of the Rights of Man [sic] and the 1774 American Bill of Rights were adopted that the idea of the individual began to take precedence over the collective.[50] Sometimes the dualism that exists between individuals and collective or communities is perceived as a "threat to the organic unity between individuals and society,"[51] rather than as a way of integrating individuals into the broader whole of the community.

The tension that exists at the individual level about whether an individual defines him- or herself in the context of the group or more explicitly as part of a collective plays out at the societal or cultural level as well in the tension between individualism and collectivism. It can be seen in the work of sociologists like Geert Hofstede. Hofstede usefully defines collectivism as the "degree to which people in a society are integrated into groups," as opposed to individualism, in which "the ties between individuals are loose: everyone is expected to look after him/herself and his/her immediate family."[52] In other words, cultures can also currently be differentiated by the extent to which people view themselves as individual actors versus being part of a collectivity or community that needs to be integrated to function effectively.

In individualistic cultures, according to Hofstede, individuals primarily care for themselves and their immediate families. In other words, there is a clear sense of "I," that is, the individual, both in society and as an indispensable part of the language. From this perspective, individuals have inherent rights to privacy, and speaking one's mind, having strong opinions, and a task orientation, which are all considered good. Individualistic cultures see people largely as individuals—separate from any sense of community, education is viewed as learning how to learn, and there is a decided task orientation that prevails over a relational orientation.

Collectivist societies, in contrast, see people as being integral and necessarily loyal parts of their extended families or clans, stress belonging and harmony. Language focuses in collectivist cultures on "we," and "I" is avoided. Such cultures emphasize what Hofstede calls "we" consciousness. People in collectivist societies perceive others as either being in their "in-group" or in an "out-group," that is, not part of their own collectivity. In contrast to individualist cultures, in which transgression of norms results in guilt, in collectivist cultures, such transgressions result in shame. In such cultures, relationships are considered more important than tasks. Hofstede further claimed that as countries became more industrialized and developed, they became more individualist, while less wealthy and more traditional societies remained collectivist.[53]

Thinking about the differences between individualism and collectivism, Schwartz argued that certain core values, for example, hedonism, achievement, self-direction, social power, and stimulation, favor individualist ends. At the same time, other values, for example, prosocial, restrictive conformity, security, and tradition support collectivism, while maturity or the appreciation, understanding, and acceptance of self and others, supports both.[54] Schwartz then goes on to argue, based on empirical evidence from multiple cultures, that thinking in dichotomous terms (dualisms) overlooks the fact that some values serve *both* individual and collective interests, some are needed to foster broader goals than those any particular ingroup, and it is mistaken to think that individualistic and collectivist values are actually in opposition.

In the end Schwartz argues that collectivist or communal societies exhibit extended primary groups (like clans or other networks of groups), while more individualistic societies have relatively narrow groupings (e.g., families). He points to the need to think carefully about the values that can be linked to both ends of the polarity between individualism and collectivism, with values like maturity, security, achievement, and hedonism, for example, exhibiting at best weak differences.[55]

Interestingly, recent work by Cuddy and her colleagues indicates that the implicit association of individualism with male values and collectivist values as being female is itself culturally and context-dependent. That is, in individualistic cultures like the U.S., men were seen as more individualistic, while in highly collectivist cultures like Korea, men were seen as more communal and as having more networks than women.[56] Cuddy and colleagues also determined that there is a relationship between the degree of individualism or collectivism at the country level and how masculinity was assessed, with collectivist cultures rating collectivist traits as masculine and individualistic countries rating individualistic traits as masculine. In other words, the definition of masculinity varies depending on the country's orientation to individualism or collectivism.[57]

Such hypotheses and research findings get us to our own sense that what is needed is an integration across the range of cultural orientations, with Schwartz's work pointing in the direction of using shared values— values that all believe are important—as one way of approaching the idea of integration of the dualism into a duality. These considerations become important when we consider the impact of and need to shift today's dominant narrative, neoliberalism or economism, towards a more integrated narrative of ecologizing or ecocentrism, as we discuss in the next section.

One way of thinking about how to integrate these dualisms is to reflect on the pan-African concept of *ubuntu*. *Ubuntu*, often translated as "I am because we are," reflects both individual moral qualities as well as a philosophical approach that argues that we are all connected.[58] The word *ubuntu*, from the Nguni language in South Africa, carries multiple meanings and tends to evolve over time and circumstance. Although similar words in different languages may have different meanings as well, the general concept of *ubuntu* implies that the individual exists in the context of community, and that people in the context of community are interconnected.[59]

Building on this notion of *ubuntu* as interconnected people in the context of community, we can relate it to recent findings in quantum physics. Quantum physics indicates that we are all interconnected, at the quantum level—and perhaps beyond it, just as ecologists recognize the interdependencies and interconnections among elements of an ecosystem. Indeed, others argue that there is no mutual exclusivity between individualism and collectivism, and that, as we want to argue, conceived as a duality, individualism (when not carried to extremes) can be an important consideration in the emergence of healthy societies. Allik and Realo, following this line of thinking, for example, claim "the growth of individuality, autonomy, and self-sufficiency may be perceived as necessary conditions for the development of interpersonal cooperation, mutual dependence, and social solidarity,"[60] conditions that are important for building healthy societies in the long term.

Without culturally appropriating the pan-African notion of *ubuntu*, but rather using the idea as a way of thinking, that approach might help us gain perspective through the both/and logic inherent to resolving both the masculine/feminine and individual/collective dualisms into dualities that recognize both the individual and the whole. Both/and thinking can help us see all people as individuals, with moral worth and purposes, as ends in themselves, while at the same time recognizing that as the English poet John Donne writes, "No man [sic] is an island." Given our biological heritage and the fact that we humans are born helpless, if for no other reason, we all necessarily live and thrive in the context of community.

Neoliberalism/Economizing Versus Ecocentrism/Ecologizing

In the developed world today, much of our economic activity—and indeed, as we will elaborate in Chapter 8, the metanarrative that tells the equivalent of the modern "origin story"—revolves around economic concepts related to neoliberalism, particularly in developed Western cultures. Neoliberalism, which we counterpose to an ecologizing narrative that is still emergent, is a highly dominant "story" that we tell ourselves about how today's world, particularly our economic systems (and by inference our societies) work. Yet it is a story that has been deliberately developed and promulgated to promote a certain perspective, one that Eisler might call a Dominator culture.

Neoliberalism, as it has emerged in today's rather extreme form, was developed and strategized at a meeting in 1947 after World War II by a group of economists, historians, and others. They met in Mont Pelerin in Switzerland to deal with what they perceived to be a threat to liberty and free markets. In the framing that eventually became neoclassical economics, now deeply embedded in economics and finance textbooks, and guiding much thinking about how businesses need to operate, the neoliberal narrative emphasizes individualism, free markets, free (global) trade, continual material and economic growth, and limited government regulation and a strong military.[61]

This economic philosophy manifested itself in politics in developed nations, particularly in the United States and the United Kingdom in the early 1980s under the leadership of U.S. President Ronald Reagan. Reagan famously advocated for "keeping government off our backs," while the UK's Prime Minister Margaret Thatcher claimed both that "there is no alternative" (with the acronym TINA) to neoliberalism and that "there is no such thing as society."[62] In a very real way, these claims obliterated the dualism by privileging only one side and suggesting that any different perspectives were simply wrong.

In considering the dualisms of individualism and collectivism, conservative and progressive, and masculine and feminine, it seems clear that the neoliberal narrative tends to orient to the individualist, conservative, and masculine pole of these dualisms. That is, neoliberalism orients towards what Eisler, whose work was discussed earlier, calls Dominator cultures.[63] The important question becomes how to develop a new narrative that bridges these dualisms into dualities. Such a new narrative would help in constructing a more holistic approach that encompasses not just human beings but also the rest of Nature's manifestations and living beings.

Riane Eisler argues as we do that there may in fact be alternatives to the cutthroat form of economic activity embedded in today's neoliberalism and modern understanding of capitalism that operates without regard to social or ecological consequences. She points out clearly that, in contrast to what she terms "caring economies," what exist today are Dominator economics. She made this point explicitly in her UN speech, arguing that "neoliberalism represents a regression to Dominator economics: a top-down economic system with those on top in control of resources." A core problem is that neoliberalism fails to take into account any of the social or ecological consequences of its model of continual growth, exploitation of natural resources, and exploitation of human beings (human beings are not "resources" in our view).[64] From Eisler's perspective, which is very much aligned with our own, we need to move beyond—or, in Ken Wilber's terms, transcend and include[65]—these old dominator systems in favor of "economic systems that give visibility and real value to the most important human work—the work of caring for people . . . and caring for our Mother Earth."[66]

Speaking of economic dimensions of the dominator and partnership cultures identified by Eisler, Loye further argues that Domination is based in an economy of scarcity that permits or even encourages exploitation of nature and even other humans, benefitting the few at the expense of the many.[67] Partnership economies, in contrast, are grounded in beliefs of abundance that should be widely shared, as are Nature's healthy ecosystems,[68] thereby spreading the wealth around. In addition, partnership societies recognize interdependence and mutuality of purpose by companies and their employees, rather than the exploitation of workers common in Dominator cultures.[69]

Notably, to our minds at least, the dimensions of masculinity and femininity align rather neatly with work by American linguist George Lakoff, who finds that conservatives tend to value what he terms the "good father" (a very masculine) model of behavior at an individual level, while progressives favor the "nurturing parent" (more feminine) model.[70] Although Lakoff's work has a different orientation, it is very relevant to the idea of dualisms because it suggests a reason why conservatives, who tend to adhere to neoliberalism, and progressives, who are in favor of economic opportunity for all, diverse perspectives, equity and equality, social justice, tolerance, and care for others, find it hard to talk to each other. Eisler also argues that dominator cultures emphasize "technologies of destruction" over more creative endeavors that are included in what she calls "technologies of conservation."[71] These technologies of conservation, however, things like recycling, waste management, wilderness preservation, and a general orientation towards nature that emphasizes harmony and balance between humans and nature, are very much what is needed in tomorrow's world to cope with the issues of ecological sustainability we have been alluding to. Ecologizing, as opposed to economizing, values draw on the creative resources of all people—including some whose work is traditionally left out of or ignored in the "productive" economic (Dominator) system (e.g., mainly women's work of care, in Eisler's view).

Notes

1. Frederick, W. C. (1995). *Values, nature, and culture in the American corporation*. Oxford: Oxford University Press. See also Frederick, W. C. (2012). *Natural corporate management: From the big bang to wall street*. Sheffield, UK: Greenleaf.
2. Bansal, P., & Des Jardine, M. R. (2014). Business sustainability: It is about time. *Strategic Organization*, 12(1), 70–78.
3. Jones, T. J. (1991). Ethical decision-making by individuals in organizations: An issue-contingent model. *Academy of Management Review*, 16(2), 366–395.
4. IPCC (Intergovernmental Panel on Climate Change), 2018. Global Warming of 1.5 °C: All Chapters, www.ipcc.ch/report/sr15/.
5. Bansal, P., & Desjardine, M. R. (2014). Business sustainability: It's about time. *Strategic Organization*, 12(1), 70–78.
6. Cowen, T., & Parfit, D. (1992). Against the social discount rate. In P. Laslett & J. S. Fishkin (Eds.), *Justice between age groups and generations* (pp. 144–161). New Haven: Yale University Press.

7. Jonas, H. (1984). *The imperative of responsibility: In search of an ethics for the technological age.* Chicago: University of Chicago Press.

8. Bourgeois, I. J., & Eisenhardt, K. M. (1988). Strategic decision processes in high velocity environments: Four cases in the microcomputer industry. *Management Science, 34,* 816–835.

9. D'Aveni, R. A. (1994). *Hypercompetition: Managing the dynamics of strategic maneuvering.* New York: Free Press.

10. Galunic and Anderson: From Security to Mobility: An Examination of Employee Commitment and an Emerging PC.

11. Rosa, H. (2009). Social acceleration: Ethical and political consequences of a desynchronized high-speed society. In H. Rosa & W. Scheuerman (Eds.), *High Speed Society.* State College, PA: The Pennsylvania State University Press.

12. Harvey, D. (1991). Flexibility: Threat or opportunity. *Socialist Review, 21,* 65–78.

13. Alvesson, M., & Spicer, A. (2012). A stupidity-based theory of organizations. *Journal of Management Studies, 49*(7), 1194–1209.

14. Rosa, H. (2010). *Alienation and acceleration, toward a critical theory of late-modern temporality.* Oslo: Nordic Summer University Press; Rosa, H. (2013). *Social acceleration: A new theory of modernity.* New York: Columbia University Press.

15. Pirson, M. (2017). *Humanistic management.* Cambridge, UK: Cambridge University Press.

16. Bansal, P., Kim, A., & Wood, M. O. (2018). Hidden in plain sight: The importance of scale in organizations' attention to issues. *Academy of Management Review, 43*(2), 217–234.

17. Lord, R. G., Dinh, J. E., & Hoffman, E. L. (2015). A quantum approach to time and organizational change. *Academy of Management Review, 40*(2), 263–290.

18. Giddens, A. (1984). *The constitution of society.* Berkeley, CA: University of California University Press.

19. Tsoukas, H., & Chia, R. (2003). On organizational becoming: Rethinking organizational change. *Organization Science, 13*(5), 567–582.

20. Jullien, F. (2015). *Silent transformations.* New Haven, CT: Yale University Press.

21. Ancona, D. G., Okhuysen, G. A., & Perlow, L. A. (2001). Taking time to integrate temporal research. *Academy of Management Review, 26*(4), 512–529.

22. Lord, R. G., Dinh, J. E., & Hoffman, E. L. (2015). A quantum approach to time and organizational change. *Academy of Management Review, 40*(2), 263–290.

23. Lord, R. G., Dinh, J. E., & Hoffman, E. L. (2015). A quantum approach to time and organizational change. *Academy of Management Review, 40*(2), 263–290.

24. Holmer-Nadesan, M. (1997). Dislocating (Instrumental) organizational time. *Organization Studies, 18*(3), 481–510.

25. Cooper, R., & Law, J. (1995). Organization: Distal and proximate views. *Research in the Sociology of Organizations, 13,* 239.

26. Lord, R. G., Dinh, J. E., & Hoffman, E. L. (2015). A quantum approach to time and organizational change. *Academy of Management Review, 40*(2), 263–290.

27. Holmer-Nadesan, M. (1997). Dislocating (Instrumental) organizational time. *Organization Studies, 18*(3), 481–510.

28. Cooper, R., & Law, J. (1995). Organization: Distal and proximate views. *Research in the Sociology of Organizations, 13,* 242.

29. Laclau, E. (1990). *New reflections on the revolution of our time*. London: Verso.
30. Giddens, A. (1991). *Modernity and self-identity: Self and society in the late modern age*. Stanford, CN: Stanford University Press.
31. Jonas, H. (1984). *The imperative of responsibility: In search of an ethics for the technological age*. Chicago: University of Chicago Press.
32. Giddens, A. (1991). *Modernity and self-identity: Self and society in the late modern age* (p. 18). Stanford, CN: Stanford University Press.
33. Luhman, N. (1996). *Social systems*. Stanford, CA: Stanford University Press.
34. Alvesson, M., & Spicer, A. (2012). A stupidity-based theory of organizations. *Journal of Management Studies, 49*(7), 1194.
35. Durkheim, E. (1967). *De la division du travail social (1893)*. Paris: Presses Universitaires de France (PUF); Pareto, V. (1902 [1982]). Di un nuovo errore nello interpretare le teorie dell'economia matematica. *Giornale degli Economisti, 12*(15), 401–433, reprinted in *Ouvres Complètes 26: Écrites d'économie politique*, edited by Giovanni Busino, Genéve: Librairie Droz, 1982, 488–520.
36. see Kant, I. (1784). *Idee zu einer allgemeinen Geschichte in weltbürgerlicher Absicht*. In Kant, Immanuel, Werke, Akademie Textausgabe: Akademie-Textausgabe. Bd.8, Abhandlungen nach 1781, Gruyter September 1, 1971, Berlin, New York.
37. Mumford, L. (1952). *Art and technics*. New York: Columbia University Press.
38. Hofstede, G., & Hofstede, G. J. (2005). *Cultures and organizations: Software of the mind* (Rev. and expanded 2nd ed.). New York: McGraw Hill.
39. Hofstede, G. (2011). Dimensionalizing cultures: The Hofstede model in context. *Online Readings in Psychology and Culture, 2*(1), 8. Retrieved from: https://scholarworks.gvsu.edu/cgi/viewcontent.cgi?article=1014&context=orpc.
40. These details are taken from Table 4 in: Hofstede, G. (2011). Dimensionalizing cultures: The Hofstede model in context. *Online Readings in Psychology and Culture, 2*(1), 8. Retrieved from: https://scholarworks.gvsu.edu/cgi/viewcontent.cgi?article=1014&context=orpc.
41. Hofstede, G. (2011). Dimensionalizing cultures: The Hofstede model in context. *Online Readings in Psychology and Culture, 2*(1), 8, 13. Retrieved from: https://scholarworks.gvsu.edu/cgi/viewcontent.cgi?article=1014&context=orpc.
42. Eisler, R. T. (1988). *The chalice and the blade: Our history, our future*. San Francisco, CA: Harper & Row.
43. Loye, D. (2015). Untangling partnership and domination morality. *Interdisciplinary Journal of Partnership, 1*(1), 1–17. Retrieved from: https://pubs.lib.umn.edu/index.php/ijps/article/view/91/85.
44. See Loye, D. (2015). Untangling partnership and domination morality. *Interdisciplinary Journal of Partnership, 1*(1), 1–17. Retrieved from: https://pubs.lib.umn.edu/index.php/ijps/article/view/91/85.
45. Eisler, R. (2008). *The real wealth of nations: Creating a caring economics*. San Francisco, CA: Berrett-Koehler Publishers.
46. Eisler, R. (2017). The real wealth of nations: From global warming to global partnership. *Interdisciplinary Journal of Partnership, 4*(3). Retrieved from: http://pubs.lib.umn.edu/ijps/vol4/iss3/13.
47. Wilber, K. (1998). *The eye of spirit: An integral vision for a world gone slightly mad*. Boston: Shambhala Publications. Also, Wilber, K. (2002). *A theory of everything: An integral vision for business, politics, science, and spirituality*. Boston: Shambhala, among other works by Wilber.

48. Hofstede, G. (2011). Dimensionalizing cultures: The Hofstede model in context. *Online Readings in Psychology and Culture*, 2(1), 8. Retrieved from: https://scholarworks.gvsu.edu/cgi/viewcontent.cgi?article=1014& context=orpc.
49. Allik, J., & Realo, A. (2004). Individualism-collectivism and social capital. *Journal of Cross-Cultural Psychology*, 35(1), 29–49.
50. Allik, J., & Realo, A. (2004). Individualism-collectivism and social capital. *Journal of Cross-Cultural Psychology*, 35(1), 29–49, 30.
51. Allik, J., & Realo, A. (2004). Individualism-collectivism and social capital. *Journal of Cross-Cultural Psychology*, 35(1), 29–49, 31.
52. Hofstede, G. (2011). Dimensionalizing cultures: The Hofstede model in context. *Online Readings in Psychology and Culture*, 2(1), 8, 11. Retrieved from: https://scholarworks.gvsu.edu/cgi/viewcontent.cgi?article= 1014&context=orpc. Characteristics discussed in this and the next paragraph are from Table 3.
53. Hofstede, G., Hofstede, G. J., & Minkov, M. (2010). *Cultures and organizations: Software of the mind: Intercultural cooperation and its importance for survival*. New York: McGraw-Hill.
54. Schwartz, S. H. (1990). Individualism-collectivism: Critique and proposed refinements. *Journal of Cross-Cultural Psychology*, 21(2), 139–157.
55. Schwartz, S. H. (1990). Individualism-collectivism: Critique and proposed refinements. *Journal of Cross-Cultural Psychology*, 21(2), 139–157.
56. Cuddy, A. J., Wolf, E. B., Glick, P., Crotty, S., Chong, J., & Norton, M. I. (2015). Men as cultural ideals: Cultural values moderate gender stereotype content. *Journal of Personality and Social Psychology*, 109(4), 622–635.
57. Cuddy, A. J., Wolf, E. B., Glick, P., Crotty, S., Chong, J., & Norton, M. I. (2015). Men as cultural ideals: Cultural values moderate gender stereotype content. *Journal of Personality and Social Psychology*, 109(4), 622–635, 631.
58. Gade, C. B. N. (2012). What is ubuntu? Different interpretations among South Africans of African descent. *South African Journal of Philosophy*, 31(3), 484–503.
59. Gade, C. B. N. (2012). What is ubuntu? Different interpretations among South Africans of African descent. *South African Journal of Philosophy*, 31(3), 484–503, 487.
60. Allik, J., & Realo, A. (2004). Individualism-collectivism and social capital. *Journal of Cross-Cultural Psychology*, 35(1), 29–49, 32.
61. For more background see Waddock, S. (2016). Foundational Memes for a new narrative about the role of business in society. *Humanistic Management Journal*, online. doi:10.1007/s41463-016-0012-4l; Monbiot, G. (2016, April 15). Neoliberalism—the ideology at the root of all of our problems. *The Guardian*. Retrieved from: www.theguardian.com/books/2016/apr/15/ neoliberalism-ideology-problem-george-monbiot; Mont Pelerin Society. (undated). *Statement of aims*. Retrieved from: www.montpelerin.org/ statement-of-aims/.
62. See, e.g., Monbiot, G. (2016, April 15). Neoliberalism—the ideology at the root of all of our problems. *The Guardian*. Retrieved from: www.theguardian. com/books/2016/apr/15/neoliberalism-ideology-problem-george-monbiot.
63. Eisler, R. T. (1988). *The chalice and the blade: Our history, our future*. San Francisco, CA: Harper & Row.
64. E.g., Lovins, L. H., Wallis, S., Wijkman, A., & Fullerton, J. (2018). *A finer future: Creating an economy in service to life, A report to the club of Rome*. Gabriola Island, BC, Canada: New Society Publishers; Waddock, S. (2016).

Foundational memes for a new narrative about the role of business in society. *Humanistic Management Journal, 1*, 91–105.

65. Wilber, K. (2017). Trump and a post-truth world: An evolutionary self-correction. *Integral Life.com.* Retrieved from: https://integrallife.com/trump-post-truth-world/.

66. Eisler, R. (2017). The real wealth of nations: From global warming to global partnership. *Interdisciplinary Journal of Partnership*, 4(3), 8. Retrieved from: http://pubs.lib.umn.edu/ijps/vol4/iss3/13.

67. Loye, D. (2015). Untangling partnership and domination morality. *Interdisciplinary Journal of Partnership*, 1(1), 1–17. Retrieved from: https://pubs.lib.umn.edu/index.php/ijps/article/view/91/85.

68. Weber, A. (2013). *Enlivenment. Towards a fundamental shift in the concepts of nature, culture and politics.* Berlin: Heinrich-Böll-Stiftung. Retrieved from: www.autor-andreas-weber.de/downloads/Enlivenment_web.pdf.

69. Loye, D. (2015). Untangling partnership and domination morality. *Interdisciplinary Journal of Partnership*, 1(1), 1–17, 10. Retrieved from: https://pubs.lib.umn.edu/index.php/ijps/article/view/91/85, Figure 4.

70. Lakoff, G. (2014). *The all new don't think of an elephant! Know your values and frame the debate.* White River Junction, VT: Chelsea Green Publishing.

71. Eisler, R., Donnelly, G., & Montuori, A. (2016). Creativity, society, and gender: Contextualizing and redefining creativity. *Interdisciplinary Journal of Partnership*, 3(2), 23. Retrieved from: https://pubs.lib.umn.edu/index.php/ijps/article/view/130/124.

6 Natural Values Tensions

From Economizing to Ecologizing

Scholar William C. Frederick developed a theory of business values rooted in nature, as introduced earlier. Frederick argued that there are three predominant sets of values of humankind that are at the core of tensions that exist between businesses and society, in part because the values that dominate in business are quite different from societal values.[1] Business, he argued, is dominated by values of economizing and power aggrandizement, while societies lean more towards the third value set of ecologizing and even civilizing, as Waddock elaborated.[2] We argue here that the values of economizing and power aggrandizing, particularly as they have manifested in businesses, though also in many governments and other large institutions, have resulted in an unbalanced and ultimately destructive human mindset. This "split mind" has resulted in a "split worldview" that has, as we saw with Sergio in the prologue, divorced humanity from our inextricable and absolutely fundamental connections to each other and, just as importantly, to nature.

We elaborate in the following section by starting with a discussion on energy and how it relates to the natural values sets. Energy serves as the basis for the values sets, all of which is rooted in natural science.

Thermodynamic Laws of Nature

Natural systems transform continuously as time moves forward. Evolutionary processes move towards ever greater complexity when living systems are healthy. Among all life forms, change is driven by the transformation of energy. The laws of thermodynamics provide insight into how useful energy is converted into a wasteful product that generates little utility for the organism. The premise is that all energy in the universe "devolves" from a form that fuels and sustains life to a state that provides no value. This end state is referred to as thermodynamic equilibrium. There is no escape from this end result. Eventually, our solar system's sun will die, which means all of its useful energy will burn off and cease to sustain life.

Within these laws of thermodynamics are definitions of open systems, the rules of energy flows, and the boundaries within which they operate and exist.[3] Over time, no organism nor its environment can ever return to its original state of high-density energy.[4] The progression from high-density energy, which is necessary for all life forms, to low-density energy cannot be reversed.[5] Thermodynamic equilibrium results when all useful energy is transduced into a zero value. What drives this degradation of energy is entropy. At this point, a system has exhausted all of its potential for change. Entropy is "a quantity that relentlessly grows with dissipation and attains its maximum value when all the potential for further work is spent."[6] At thermodynamic equilibrium, entropy has reached its maximum value within a particular system. As time moves forward, entropy increases, as dictated by the Second Law of Thermodynamics. According to this physics principle, physical systems continuously drift from organized states to maximum disorder.[7]

These organized states are described by the First Law of Thermodynamics. This law outlines the principle of energy conservation within a physical system. Energy is conserved within a physical process, even though it changes into different forms over time.[8] Living systems survive, even developing over time to ever-greater complexity, connectedness, and diversity when they are flourishing. (See the discussion of living systems in Chapter 8.) Flourishing living systems thrive despite processes dictated by the second law, which implies that in the short-term, energy can be harnessed to sustain life in a (relatively) closed system. We need to think about business within the context of these natural laws. We normally think of the business organization as being a socially constructed reality. Although it is true that the idea of business is indeed a culturally determined institution, its formation is a naturally driven way of self-organizing to aid in our survival. As we will see when we discuss technologizing values later on, the business organization is a natural human invention helping us flourish in society. The natural laws that govern physical systems are present within business organizations as well.[9] These thermodynamic laws are unavoidable. Institutions like business are a natural manifestation of anti-entropic tendencies from the First Law.

In the short term, life counters the second law by staving off entropy. In business, we see this take the form of innovation. As a form of technologizing values, innovation allows businesses to self-organize and renew themselves, just as living systems do. But in the long term, entropy wins in the end. Functional order is generated out of these self-organizing (economizing) structures.[10]

Evolutionary theorists acknowledge that life forms are constantly influenced by natural forces, which ultimately cause them to degrade and transform. Even Darwin wrote about self-contained organizing in terms of helping a species adapt and preserve its existence. Natural selection "inevitably leads to the gradual advancement of the organization of the greater number of living beings throughout the world."[11] This process driving evolution is an example of the First Law at work.[12] All life forms are organized so as to maintain themselves, propagate, and survive. The efficiency of the transformation of energy is affected by the influence of economic and ecological systems, according to the Second Law.

Economizing in Depth

Frederick, an astute observer of business as it exists, posited that *business* values are mainly supported by two value clusters, economizing and power aggrandizing, which we briefly introduced earlier. Economizing (or Value Cluster I) contains a set of values that emphasize efficiency and prudence in resource use and that are particularly applicable to business enterprises—and to the masculine and individualized societies discussed in the last chapter. This efficiency orientation—or economizing—establishes core values for businesses as they currently exist and with their dominant imperative today of maximizing profitability (at virtually all costs).[13] Economizing values represent a "short-term" self-organizing process that drives organisms to stave off entropy as long as possible. But, as we explained above, the avoidance of entropy is unavoidable in the long-term.

As today's businesses have evolved, economizing values account for the orientation towards mass production, scale, and consequent need for mass markets and associated advertising/marketing campaigns that have characterized many businesses since the dawn of the Industrial Era. Even today, when many production-oriented businesses are switching production on demand or mass customization rather than simply scale, there are still massive companies that dominate their various industries. As University of Michigan's Gerald Davis points out, though, today's big businesses tend not to be the industrial, product-oriented, mass-production companies of the 20th century, but rather are digitally driven, platform-based, or service-oriented businesses. Davis even argues that giant corporations are on the decline overall. Yet giants still exist. Today's giants, instead of being manufacturers like General Motors, which in 2018 was once again downsizing, are retail companies like Wal-Mart and digitally driven companies with (relatively) few employees, at least compared to the old industrial giants. These new behemoths include the likes of Facebook, Amazon, and Google. Even companies like Uber, Airbnb, and Lyft, which are big players in what is known as the sharing economy and tend to use the resources of others—for example, for room rentals or ride services—thereby employ even fewer employees than companies like Facebook and Google.[14] Despite their relatively fewer employees, however, all of these companies still exist under the same imperative of profitability at all costs without regard for the systemic consequences of their business models.

Indeed, along these lines, Frederick claimed that "Economizing is . . . the central, indispensable, defining characteristic of business. It emerges as the main normative value of business activity."[15] Economizing has four parts in Frederick's framing of it. First, of course, is the idea of economizing itself, the efficiency orientation. That value is supported by three other parts, though, what Frederick terms sustained input–output balance (or steady-state economizing), growth (or productivity increase), and systemic integrity (organizational bonding). Businesses' apparent need for endless growth, market dominance, and hierarchy can be explained when these economizing values are combined with the power aggrandizing values of Frederick's Value Cluster II, power aggrandizing. Power aggrandizing values orient human institutions of all sorts towards acquiring, accumulating, and holding onto coercive power, both internally in a given organization as well as externally in societies, markets, and the world.[16] The particular values that support power aggrandizing are status hierarchy, status-based decision power, power–system dynamic equilibrium, and power aggrandizement itself. All of these values when combined lead to ever-greater accumulation and deployment of power in the context of organizations, providing what Frederick calls the "motivational power" of business firms.[17]

There is a third set of values that Frederick says are also important but that, in his view, do not play much of a role in business as it has evolved today. Value Cluster III values are oriented towards what Frederick termed ecologizing, values that are both derived from nature as well as learned by human beings. It is these ecologizing values that we believe are an imperative for a thriving future of humanity, not to mention other living beings on the planet. Ecologizing values are rooted in natural relationships and processes. They encompass not just humanity and its interests but also Nature and all of her manifestations. As Frederick puts it, Value Cluster III emphasizes flora and fauna, ecosystems, and the activities that, in a sense, "give life"[18] to communities, groups, and natural ecosystems.[19] Ecologizing, in contrast to economizing and power aggrandizing, provides a context where what Capra calls the web of life, that is the inherent connectedness of all beings within their contexts, and what Frederick called the "interweav[ing of] life activities in ways conducive to the perpetuation of an entire community"[20] can occur.

In moderation and oriented towards efficient use of resources and the stabilization of organizations and communities, of course, both economizing and power aggrandizing have provided many benefits for humanity. The problem is that, as McGilchrist argues, in Western modern cultures in particular, the "emissary" (left brain, which analyzes and breaks things down into their component parts) now dominates in many ways over the "master" (right brain, which views things more holistically and creatively). Economizing and power-aggrandizing values, that is, now dominate over the third set of values, those of ecologizing even as it is becoming increasingly clear from the panoply of emerging crises facing humanity that a more ecologizing framework of values is needed.

Indeed, many people are so embedded in left-brain values that they find it hard to see themselves as a part of nature or as a natural being. From that perspective, nature is only here to meet humanity's needs, with resources subject to exploitation, and when the linear material through-put of our current economic system is no longer useful, as a place to dump what is no longer wanted. In a global context of climate change, potentially collapsing ecosystems, political divisiveness, and growing inequality, to mention only a few problems that threaten the very future of humankind, we argue that there is a growing imperative to bring ecologizing values to the fore.

Somehow, in the splitting into dualisms that we have been discussing over the past several chapters, we humans have forgotten our origins— the human chain that connects us not only to the past (and future), but also to each other and, inextricably, to nature. We have largely, at least in Western and highly industrialized nations, become less aware that we are beings in and of nature, whose very existence and certainly ability to thrive depends on the integrated whole of nature with us humans embedded in it. Indigenous people, and particularly their shamans (as healers, connectors, and storytellers/sensemakers),[21] know about these integral connections. Yet particularly in the "developed" world, where that development seems to emphasize endless growth in material acquisitions and population, we seem to have forgotten our origins in and links to nature. Hence the broken human chain around which this book revolves.

Fundamentally, everything we do, have, eat, and are, is part of nature, as is our behavior, thinking, and culture. To recognize that reality we need a mindset shift from economizing as a dominant way of thinking towards ecologizing. This shift most likely needs to include yet transcend economizing and power aggrandizing to provide a more holistic perspective on the way we humans live and need to live to thrive in the world. Below, we will explain what that shift means in more detail, as we move from economizing to ecologizing.

From Economizing to Ecologizing

Underlying our natural senses are evolutionarily formed value clusters derived from natural processes in physics and evolutionary biology.[22] The first dominant values that drive human behavior, especially in business today, are *economizing values*. These values are representative "of natural processes that undergird the struggle for life in general and the particular way in which humans have organized themselves for this struggle."[23] Both thermodynamic laws and (Darwinian) evolution (discussed previously) are a consequence of the same process: an influx of external free energy flowing into both chemical and biological systems.[24]

They relate to the tendency for any living being to acquire energy from its environment and utilize it to generate direct value for itself, leading to growth and survival in the short term. As we stated, businesses create self-organized structures that adapt to the changing environment in an open system. We will explore these common structures and how their design often mutes sustainability-related values.

A sustainability or ecologizing orientation underlies the human condition as well. *Ecologizing values* are part of the human condition through their cognition and emotions. They involve and address humans' relationship with the ecological environment.[25] They guide, control, and motivate. An individual's behavior towards his/her own survival and with nature is guided, controlled, and motivated, in part, by this value set. Anthropological evidence and sociological research on human societies through evolutionary history, however, show an inconsistent treatment of the natural environment across cultures and time. The realization of the ethic keeps evolving, although (we argue) the underlying guiding principles may be consistent. The tendency is there, but the drive is muted. Thus, the evolution of these ethical values is discontinuous and not consistent across cultures.

Ecologizing values, which are aligned with values found in Eisler's partnership societies, as discussed in the previous chapter, as well as (from the Western perspective) more feminine values, are quite different from the economizing values that dominate business and even whole nations today. Ecologizing, according to Frederick, emphasizes values of linkage, diversity, homeostatic succession, and community.[26] Although Frederick claims that ecologizing values are not present in the context of businesses, it is our contention that for humanity to thrive—and possibly even survive—in the future, an ecologizing mindset and value structure needs to be deeply embedded into businesses and into every human institution and society. Values of equality, freedom, democracy and caring are the ones that dominate in Eisler's descriptions of partnership societies as opposed to the inequality, control, authoritarianism, and coercion of dominator cultures.[27]

Ecologizing or partnership cultures emphasize our connectedness and need to be in harmony with nature as opposed to exploitation and instrumental use of Nature's bounty.[28] Values of care, connectedness, community, and civility are what Waddock called civilizing or relationship values. These civilizing values supplement technological and ecologizing values fostered by our human (and sometimes animal) natures.[29] In particular civil society (as opposed to business or government) is currently dominated by civilizing values, and it is these very values of care, connectedness, community, and civility that offer the potential to reintegrate; quite literally, to reconnect humans with themselves, with other humans, with other living beings, and, more generally, with Nature. That is, civilizing values can help to fix the broken chain. These civilizing values, we believe, have the potential to make us fully human in what we now know is a connected and interdependent world.

Think about it. Among the major ecological issues facing humankind are the climate crisis, the potential for collapsing ecosystems, increasing desertification, topsoil erosion, the pollution of lakes, rivers, and streams, deforestation, melting ice caps, massive species loss, increasingly dangerous weather events, and many other significant problems. All of these signs indicate that geophysical planetary conditions are changing and doing so at the hands of humans. Scientists from the Stockholm Resilience Center argue that at least four of nine physical planetary boundaries—beyond which humanity's incursions cannot go and maintain an environment that supports civilization as we know it—have already been breached (we will say more about these ideas in Chapter 11).[30]

Human population has more than quadrupled since 1900. Today's economizing mindset and the neoliberal framework it has spawned foster reckless use and even abuse of natural resources by far too many companies and even governments in the interests of constant financial, economic, and GDP growth.[31] The IPCC, or Intergovernmental Panel on Climate Change, has issued several reports that place the responsibility for climate change squarely at the feet of humanity,[32] as did Pope Francis in his important encyclical *Laudato Si'*.[33]

The 2018 IPCC report, even more scarily, argues that the prior goal of limiting global warming to 2°C is too generous, and that the planet had, at that writing, less than twelve years to limit warming to 1.5°C or less before facing dire consequences. Predicted consequences of not achieving that goal range from even more extreme weather events than are already being experienced, including heatwaves, droughts, fires, and desertification, plus the collapse of tropical fisheries, declines in staple food production and decreased nutritional value, and further melting of Arctic ice, creating more rise in sea levels, among others. Both the science-based approach of the IPCC and the more spiritually oriented approach to the problem by Pope Francis also strongly note the important link between climate change and particularly negative impacts on the poor and on developing nations. In light of these findings, an ecologizing mindset, which takes living in harmony with nature into account, becomes more and more of an imperative to avoid what the IPCC calls "climate catastrophe."

To elaborate on the physical science, research by the Stockholm Resilience Center has determined that there are nine systemic processes on the planet that cannot be transgressed without significant risk to the health and wellbeing of humanity. Unfortunately, that work also suggests that four of those boundaries, which constrain what these scientists call a "safe operating space for humanity," have already been exceeded.[34] At the same time, there is also growing concern about inequality, which has significant potential for "wrecking the world"[35] and has been found to be one of the causative factors in civilizational collapse, along—ahem!—with overuse of ecological resources.[36] That linkage is more problematic because of increasing evidence that increased inequality is associated with poorer ecological outcomes and conditions, as well as less healthy people.[37]

Equally frighteningly, the Intergovernmental Science-Policy Platform on Biodiversity and Ecosystem Services (IPBES) issued a report in 2019 indicating that species extinction, already known as the Sixth Great Extinction, is accelerating. In what is the most comprehensive study of the topic yet, the IPBES found that as many as a million species are now threatened with extinction.[38] Because of the break in the human chain, many people might ask, "So what? It is not humans who are threatened." But the reality is that there actually is an unbroken chain between humans and the rest of Nature, and we cannot readily dismiss the disappearance of species in the food chain and our ecosystems, because we humans are integrally linked to all of them.

Problematically, today humanity faces these issues for the first time on a global scale, rather than within the constraints of a single society or region. We will discuss these issues in more depth in Chapter 11.

In this very difficult context, both ecologizing and civilizing values become increasingly essential to the long-term wellbeing of Earth, human beings, and all other living beings that inextricably arise from Nature and on which we humans depend. Hence, there is growing clarity that humans need to operate within Nature's operating rules rather than ignoring or thwarting them. In other words, the human project on Earth could be relatively short-lived in the overall context of living things on Earth—breaking the chain of existence that the idea of the web of life implies, not to mention the human chain with its fractured links as discussed earlier.

Ecologizing values, broadened to encompass the values and characteristics that "give life" to complex living systems, can help human beings live within Nature's operating principles. Thus, we believe that unless and until ecologizing values become the core operating principle for all of humanity's enterprises—whether businesses, governmental institutions, civil society organizations, schools, hospitals, or other types of human-organized entities—we humans are likely to continue down today's destructive path, pursuing short-term material interests over longer term ecological realities.

Since all that we humans (and every other living being) are, do, and believe derives from nature, ecologizing and civilizing values come from Nature just as much as economizing and power aggrandizing values do.[39] Perhaps the connection of ecologizing to natural dynamics is even more evident than economizing values, since ecologizing fundamentally recognizes the foundational role of Nature in all of human existence. Unlike the more destructive qualities embedded in economizing and power aggrandizement, however, ecologizing values lend themselves not to entropy but to an expansion of the web of interconnectedness, diversity, and complexity, that is, the abundance, that constitutes healthy living systems.[40]

The ecologizing value cluster, in Frederick's framing, contains four values.[41] The first is linkage. Linkage means interconnectedness among living and nonliving entities, which physicist Fritjof Capra called the web of life. Interconnectedness recognizes the integral interdependency, interrelationships, and connectedness among living beings and with the Earth itself and will be discussed later as part of "what gives life" to living systems.[42] The second value of ecologizing that Frederick identifies is diversity, another important factor in what gives life. Nature works not from the principle of scarcity, but from that of abundance, meaning that healthy living systems are "alive" in part because of their diversity.[43]

Diversity is closely connected to processes of collaboration, mutual life support, and symbiosis that link living entities to other (sometimes nonliving) entities and to each other and that biologists claim are one of the hallmarks of life.[44] In fact, counter to the second law of thermodynamics, which argues for entropy and decline in systems, living systems grow to greater diversity and abundance of different types of entities when they are healthy and thriving. We will also come back to this important idea of diversity briefly below when we discuss what gives life to natural and human systems. Indeed, biologists now tell us that linkage or symbiosis, including cooperation, and collaboration, is a hallmark of life, perhaps even more so than competition.[45] This insight has important implications for how we shape human societies, enterprises, and even whole nations in a future world more constrained by (human) population growth and ecological limits than the past has been.

What Frederick calls homeostatic succession has been described by physicist Fritjof Capra as the web of life.[46] Homeostatic succession is the dynamic, ever-changing set of interactions and bonds that exist among different entities and organisms in the context of living systems. Just as quantum physicists like Capra now tell us that everything is related at the quantum level, so ecologists find that ecological and human systems have similar relatedness, connectedness, and dynamics at a more macros scale. In systems, that is, things need to be considered holistically because what happens in one part of the system has ripple effects to other parts.[47] Frederick indicates that succession—what is generally called the cycle of life—is homeostatic in the sense that it displays regularity, patterns, and dynamics that tend towards stability to systems that may be striving for but never actually achieve equilibrium. It is a continuous change and, in living systems, an evolving and emergent process, in a constant process of evolution—or decline.[48]

The fourth value that Frederick associates with ecologizing is that of community, by which he means the interweaving of the other three values of linkage, diversity, and homeostatic succession.[49] In other words, communities—whether ecological, biological, or human—survive and thrive because of their interdependencies, similarities and differences (diversity), and relationships. In a sense, as discussed earlier, this value of community reflects the pan-African notion of *Ubuntu*, which means simply "I am, because we are." In other words, one person, community, or species cannot exist without the "web" of others that constitute its broader community and the whole environment or context in which it exists. That notion of connected community applies to all living beings— single-cell organisms, viruses, plants, and animals.

Although some of us might like to believe in our extreme individuality and independence, the reality is that we all actually do exist in a context, in a connected web of life, interdependent with each other and with nature. That web of interconnectedness—community—makes us what we are and make other entities what they are. Without that web of connectivity, we cannot survive, never mind thrive. Hence *Ubuntu*—I am because we are.

Coping more effectively with today's pressing issues, we in the so-called developed world in particular need to reconfigure our mindset in important ways. Ecologizing values better reflect scientific (and human) understanding of our connectedness with nature and with each other than do today's dominant values or economizing, which tend to put economic growth, financial wealth, and materialism ahead of other values. Ecologizing values enable us to reintegrate ourselves as human beings with nature, once again recognizing the need to live, operate our businesses and other institutions, and connect with other humans in harmony with Nature's ways. This shift of mind means accounting for ecological values and the operating principles on which successful ecosystems rely. Only then can we work through some of the dualities, tensions, and paradoxes posed by the split mind and split worldviews that are fracturing the human chain out of which we evolved. To do so we need to better understand and begin to resolve several tensions that have emerged out of the split-mind dynamics discussed in the last chapter.

Ecologizing and *economizing* values need to be integrated. Where economizing predominates, organisms achieve a temporary respite from entropic trends, thus surviving in the short term. The tendency for individuals to economize often takes precedence over our less-pronounced drives to ecologize. Humans economize through technological and other types of innovation to survive. It is natural and unavoidable to human nature to strive to develop and utilize new technologies in order to survive. It became a moral imperative for our ancestors to innovate new solutions to social and ecological challenges to be able to feed growing populations and survive other threats, particularly once humans settled in agriculturally based villages. Thus, in order to survive, humans had (and still have) to navigate the social and environmental world. Technological developments were (and are) necessary to overcome the threats posed by the ecosystem (including those other individuals living in the ecosystem).

Certainly, technological innovation has been a key to development. The problem is that in the recent past it has come to over-dominate all forms of innovation, which has led to one of the major problems of "progress:" it is viewed largely in technological terms.

In Chapter 8, we propose a justification of techno-symbolic values based on the following logic: Economizing values connect self to others through economic relations. Ecologizing values connect self to nature through sustainable practices. But the formation of the self is increasingly moderated by technological and symbolic processes within culture. While this need to create a balance between the value sets is documented, it has not been operationalized in the literature or in practice. Potentially, technological innovation can be utilized to integrate *economizing and ecologizing* values, thus alleviating issues related to sustainability through "mutualistic economizing."[50]

Thus, in the next chapter, we explore how ecologizing and civilizing values and perspectives can help us move from today's atomization, fragmentation, and mechanistic perspectives to a living systems approach to a world in which all the manifestations of Nature are valued and treated as if they had inherent worth, that is, dignity. As we consider this shift, several additional tensions—even paradoxes—arise.

Notes

1. Frederick, W. C. (1995). *Values, nature, and culture in the American corporation*. Oxford: Oxford University Press.
2. Waddock, S. (2002). *Leading corporate citizens: Vision, values, value-added*. New York: McGraw-Hill.
3. Ruth, M. (1993). *Integrating economics, ecology and thermodynamics* (p. 51). Dordrecht, The Netherlands: Kluwer Academic Publishers.
4. Zemansky, M. W. (1937). *Heat and thermodynamics*. New York: McGraw-Hill Book Company.
5. Frederick, W. C. (2012). *Natural corporate management: From the big bang to wall street*. Sheffield, UK: Greenleaf.
6. Coveney, P., & Highfield, C. (1990). *The arrow of time* (p. 51). New York: Fawcett.
7. Feynman, R. P., Leighton, R., & Sands, M. (1963). *The Feynman lectures on physics* (Chap. 42, Sect. 42.3). Reading, MA: The Addison-Wesly Publishing.
8. Coveney, P., & Highfield, C. (1990). *The arrow of time*. New York: Fawcett.
9. Frederick, W. C. (2012). *Natural corporate management: From the big bang to wall street*. Sheffield, UK: Greenleaf.
10. Petzinger, T. (1999). *The new pioneers*. New York: Simon and Schuster.
11. Darwin, C. (1859). *The origin of species* (p. 122, 1958 edition). New York: New American Library.
12. Tooby, J., Cosmides, L., & Barrett, H. C. (2003). The second law of thermodynamics is the first law of psychology: Evolutionary developmental psychology and the theory of tandem, coordi- nated inheritances: Comment on Lickliter and Honeycutt. *Psychological Bulletin, 129*(6), 858–865.
13. Frederick, W. C. (1995). *Values, nature, and culture in the American corporation*. Oxford: Oxford University Press; see also Frederick, W. C. (1992).

Anchoring values in nature: Toward a theory of business values. *Business Ethics Quarterly*, 2(3), 283–303.
14. Davis, G. F. (2016). *The vanishing American corporation: Navigating the hazards of new economy.* San Francisco, CA: Berrett-Koehler.
15. Frederick, W. C. (1992). Anchoring values in nature: Toward a theory of business values. *Business Ethics Quarterly*, 2(3), 290.
16. Frederick, W. C. (1992). Anchoring values in nature: Toward a theory of business values. *Business Ethics Quarterly*, 2(3), 283–303; Frederick, W. C. (1995). *Values, nature, and culture in the American corporation.* Oxford: Oxford University Press.
17. Frederick, W. C. (1992). Anchoring values in nature: Toward a theory of business values. *Business Ethics Quarterly*, 2(3), 287.
18. Waddock, S., & Kuenkel, P. (2018). *What gives life to large system change?* Boston College Working Paper.
19. Frederick, W. C. (1995). *Values, nature, and culture in the American corporation* (p. 9). Oxford: Oxford University Press.
20. Frederick, W. C. (1995). *Values, nature, and culture in the American corporation* (p. 9). Oxford: Oxford University Press.
21. See Waddock, S. (2017). *Healing the world: Today's shamans as difference makers.* Salt Mills, UK: Greenleaf and Routledge.
22. Frederick, W. C. (1995). *Values, nature, and culture in the American corporation* (p. 9). Oxford: Oxford University Press; Frederick, W. C. (2012). *Natural corporate management: From the big bang to wall street.* Sheffield, UK: Greenleaf.
23. Frederick, W. C. (1999). *Values, nature, and culture in the American corporation* (p. 207). Oxford: Oxford University Press.
24. Kaila, Ville R. I., & Annila, Arto. (2008). Natural selection for least action. *Proceedings of The Royal Society A.* doi:10.1098/rspa.2008.0178.
25. Frederick, W. C. (1999). *Values, nature, and culture in the American corporation.* Oxford: Oxford University Press.
26. Frederick, W. C. (1992). Anchoring values in nature: Toward a theory of business values. *Business Ethics Quarterly*, 2(3), 283–303; Frederick, W. C. (1995). *Values, nature, and culture in the American corporation.* Oxford: Oxford University Press; Frederick, W. C. (2012). *Natural corporate management: From the big bang to wall street.* Sheffield, UK: Greenleaf. Note that the first set of values Frederic described in his 1992 article described the values slightly differently from the version published in the 1995 book. The 1992 ecologizing values were described as: symbiosis, collaboration and mutual life support, group defense and integrity, and equilibrium that sustains the community. Here we use the four values identified in the 1995 book: linkage, diversity, homeostatic succession, and community.
27. Loye, D. (2015). Untangling partnership and domination morality. *Interdisciplinary Journal of Partnership*, 1(1), 1–17. Retrieved from: https://pubs.lib.umn.edu/index.php/ijps/article/view/91/85.
28. Loye, D. (2015). Untangling partnership and domination morality. *Interdisciplinary Journal of Partnership*, 1(1), 1–17. Retrieved from: https://pubs.lib.umn.edu/index.php/ijps/article/view/91/85; Loye, D. (2015). Untangling partnership and domination morality. *Interdisciplinary Journal of Partnership*, 1(1), 1–17. Retrieved from: https://pubs.lib.umn.edu/index.php/ijps/article/view/91/85. Also Lovins, L. H., Wallis, S., Wijkman, A., & Fullerton, J. (2018). *A finer future: Creating an economy in service to life, A report to the club of Rome.* Gabriola Island, BC, Canada: New Society Publishers.
29. Waddock, S. A. (2002). *Leading corporate citizens: Vision, values, value-added.* New York: McGraw-Hill.

30. Steffen, W., Richardson, K., Rockström, J., Cornell, S. E., Fetzer, I., Bennett, E. M., . . . Folke, C. (2015). Planetary boundaries: Guiding human development on a changing planet. *Science, 347*(6223), 1259855; Biermann, F. (2012). Planetary boundaries and earth system governance: Exploring the links. *Ecological Economics, 81,* 4–9.
31. IPCC. (2014). Summary for policymakers. In C. B. Field, V. R. Barros, D. J. Dokken, K. J. Mach, M. D. Mastrandrea, T. E. Bilir, M. Chatterjee, K. L. Ebi, Y. O. Estrada, R. C. Genova, B. Girma, E. S. Kissel, A. N. Levy, S. MacCracken, P. R. Mastrandrea, & L. L. White (Eds.), *Climate change 2014: Impacts, adaptation, and vulnerability. Part A: Global and sectoral aspects. Contribution of working group II to the fifth assessment report of the intergovernmental panel on climate change* (pp. 1–32). Cambridge and New York: Cambridge University Press.
32. IPCC. (2014). Summary for policymakers. In C. B. Field, V. R. Barros, D. J. Dokken, K. J. Mach, M. D. Mastrandrea, T. E. Bilir, M. Chatterjee, K. L. Ebi, Y. O. Estrada, R. C. Genova, B. Girma, E. S. Kissel, A. N. Levy, S. MacCracken, P. R. Mastrandrea, & L. L. White (Eds.), *Climate change 2014: Impacts, adaptation, and vulnerability. Part A: Global and sectoral aspects. Contribution of working group II to the fifth assessment report of the intergovernmental panel on climate change* (pp. 1–32). Cambridge and New York: Cambridge University Press.
33. Francis, H. F. (2015). *Encyclical letter Laudato Si': On care for our common home.* Rome and The Vatican: The Holy See. Retrieved from: http://w2.vatican.va/content/dam/francesco/pdf/encyclicals/documents/papa-francesco_20150524_enciclica-laudato-si_en.pdf.
34. The original work is found in Rockström, J., Steffen, W. L., Noone, K., Persson, Å., Chapin III, F. S., Lambin, E. et al. (2009). Planetary boundaries: Exploring the safe operating space for humanity. *Ecology & Society, 14*(2), 32. Retrieved from: www.ecologyandsociety.org/vol14/iss2/art32/. The Stockholm Resilience Centre updated its findings in Steffen, W., Richardson, K., Rockström, J., Cornell, S. E., Fetzer, I., Bennett, E. M., . . . Folke, C. (2015). Planetary boundaries: Guiding human development on a changing planet. *Science, 347*(6223), 1259855.
35. Collins, C., & Ehrenreich, B. (2012). *99 to 1: How wealth inequality is wrecking the world and what we can do about it.* San Francisco, CA: Berrett-Koehler. See also, Stiglitz, J. E. (2012). *The price of inequality: How today's divided society endangers our future.* New York: WW Norton & Company.
36. Diamond, J. (2005). *Collapse: How societies choose to fail or succeed.* New York: Penguin.
37. Cushing, L., Morello-Frosch, R., Wander, M., & Pastor, M. (2015). The haves, the have-nots, and the health of everyone: The relationship between social inequality and environmental quality. *Annual Review of Public Health, 36,* 193–209.
38. Diaz, S., Settele, J., & Brondizio, E. (2019). *Summary for policymakers of the global assessment report on biodiversity and ecosystem services of the intergovernmental science-policy platform on biodiversity and ecosystem services.* Retrieved from: www.ipbes.net/system/tdf/spm_global_unedited_advance.pdf?file=1&type=node&id=35245.
39. Frederick, W. C. (1995). *Values, nature, and culture in the American corporation.* Oxford: Oxford University Press; Frederick, W. C. (2012). *Natural corporate management: From the big bang to Wall Street.* Sheffield, UK: Greenleaf.
40. Capra, F. (1995). *The web of life.* New York: Anchor Doubleday.
41. Frederick, W. C. (1992). Anchoring values in nature: Toward a theory of business values. *Business Ethics Quarterly, 2*(3), 283–303; Frederick, W. C.

(1995). *Values, nature, and culture in the American corporation*. Oxford: Oxford University Press.

42. Capra, F. (1995). *The web of life*. New York: Anchor Doubleday; Capra, F. (2005). Complexity and life. *Theory, Culture & Society, 22*(5), 33–44; Capra, F., & Luisi, P. L. (2014). *The systems view of life: A unifying vision*. Cambridge, UK: Cambridge University Press.
43. Weber, A. (2013). *Enlivenment. Towards a fundamental shift in the concepts of nature, culture and politics*. Berlin: Heinrich-Böll-Stiftung. Retrieved from: www.autor-andreas-weber.de/downloads/Enlivenment_web.pdf.
44. Frederick had outlined these characteristics of ecologizing in his 1992 paper, cited above.
45. E.g., De Waal, F. B. (1996). *Good natured* (No. 87). Harvard University Press.
46. Capra, F. (1995). *The web of life*. New York: Anchor Doubleday.
47. See, e.g., Capra, F. (1995). *The web of life*. New York: Anchor Doubleday; Capra, F., & Luisi, P. L. (2014). *The systems view of life: A unifying vision*. Cambridge, UK: Cambridge University Press.
48. Frederick, W. C. (1995). *Values, nature, and culture in the American corporation* (p. 143). Oxford: Oxford University Press.
49. Frederick, W. C. (1995). *Values, nature, and culture in the American corporation* (pp. 145–146). Oxford: Oxford University Press.
50. Frederick, W. C. (2012). *Natural corporate management: From the big bang to wall street*. Sheffield, UK: Greenleaf.

Section II

New Narratives, Stories, and Memes

To this point in the book, we have presented a series of tensions—dualisms—that have paradoxical relationships that can be resolved when integrated into dualities, that is, integrated wholes that provide for the both/and of opposites existing simultaneously. Moving from linear, "masculine" ways of thinking that emphasize individualism, scientific positivism, and material wealth and growth towards a more ecological perspective demands that we consider important aspects of systemic change. An ecologizing culture and perspective is likely to be more based on collectivism (community) and what in the West are viewed as feminine values, principles that give life rather than material or financial wealth, and a whole range of other integrated dualisms. Part of what needs to happen, we argue below, is a change of story.

Reminiscent of the origin stories with which we started this book, we believe that part of what is needed to begin to move towards values of ecologizing and enlivenment is to create new stories, or what are called metanarratives, to replace today's dominant stories in ways that foster new types of interactions, initiatives, and engagement. Powerful new narratives can, we believe, help frame and reframe our important relationships—to each other, to our communities and societies, and to the natural environment.

7 Our Muted Sustainability Values

Shifting to Ecologizing and Civilizing

What Ecologizing and Civilizing Looks Like

Ecologizing means moving away from almost purely economistic and materialistic values to the type of ecologizing values that Frederick outlined. It also includes developing more civilizing or humanistic values in our institutions and organizations, including businesses, and a recognition that things other than financial wealth can be inherently valuable. Such a massive mindset change also means integration of perspectives that move away from linearity to understanding of cycles, circularity, and living systems, that is, principles that give life (as opposed to simply financial wealth outcomes).

In the next chapter, we will explore the important roles that metanarrative and memes play in that change process. In turn, this shift means that ways of thinking will likely transition from Western/Occidental-dominated atomistic and positivistic scientific frameworks to include Eastern/Oriental, Indigenous, Southern, and other perspectives that are more organic and holistic, moving towards what has been called the sustainability mindset.[1] This latter shift means a move away from predominantly non-systems science and thinking towards more systems-oriented ways of interacting with the world and conceptualization. It might even mean re-incorporation of spiritual values (whether based in religion or more secular beliefs) into how we view the world, along the lines suggested by David Abram in his book *The Spell of the Sensuous*, in which we humans once again allow ourselves to be awed by the power of the natural Earth.[2]

Civilizing/Humanistic/Ecologizing Values

Among the shifts implied by incorporation of ecologizing are a movement away from economies dominated solely economistic values towards economies that encompass a more realistic and nature-based set of humanistic values. As mentioned in Chapter 2, the economizing mindset that dominates today has resulted in economism as reflected in the neoliberal narrative outlined there and discussed in the next chapter. In addition, it emphasizes a set of values that privilege empiricism, tangibility, and various forms of atomization or fragmentation, viewing the world through a scientific, masculine-oriented (in the Western sense) lens with its (left-brained) tendency to look at the parts rather than more integrated wholes. In that context, the human drives of defending and acquisition have dominated over drives of bonding and comprehension, with their implications of community, connectedness, and cohesion, as well as continued development cognitively, morally, and in other important ways, that is, "head" over "heart," left brain over right brain dominance as discussed in Chapter 4.

One consequence of the split mind is that we view our economic system as well as our businesses—never mind ourselves—as largely separate (divorced from) societies and nature. Even the academic language frequently used of "business *and* society" (versus business *in* society, which is itself *in* Nature) suggests that somehow businesses are separate from society, distinct entities that do not all draw from the resources and bounty of Nature. Importantly, this language overlooks the reality that too many businesses put their too often toxic wastes back into nature on the other side of consumption, rather than reusing, recycling, or regenerating them in some way. Further, too much production and consumption are incredibly short-term in orientation, creating mounds (and, indeed, oceans full) of plastic and other detritus from items used once and thrown "away" or otherwise used for a very short time.

The very real and integral links of businesses to nature are seldom seriously considered in the neoliberal context, in part because neoliberalism fails to acknowledge anything outside the economy—including Nature and societies. Today's emphasis on sustainability does, however, bring some of these issues to the fore. One consequence of the split mind that McGilchrist discusses and we outlined earlier,[3] is that it has created a tension, even a paradox, between today's dominant economic perspective, of neoliberalism or neoclassical economics, and important societal and ecological considerations. Ecologizing values and thinking can help create bridges to better integrate these dualities or paradoxes.

Take some of the assumptions of neoliberalism, also known as neoclassical economics. In that belief system, human beings are considered to be self-interested maximizers, usually of financial wealth, when biological research demonstrates built in altruism among humans (and, indeed, some animals) exists alongside self-interest.[4] Another problematic assumption is that purportedly free markets and free trade are always superior to other forms of organizing, with constant growth and even consequent inequality not problematic in any way because they create incentives for innovation in the process of what Schumpeter called creative destruction.[5] The fundamental belief is that such growth deriving from free markets will invariably result in the benefit of all or the 'common good.' That thought derives from Adam Smiths original treatise, though neoliberals do not really believe in the common good or even in society. That belief was asserted in a famous statement by former British Prime Minister Margaret Thatcher, in a 1987 interview in *Women's Own*, "there is no such thing as society. There are individual men and women and there are families. And no government can do anything except through people, and people must look after themselves first. It is our duty to look after ourselves and then, also, to look after our neighbors."[6]

Ecological and social consequences of managerial actions, then, typically are not incorporated into business costs. They are considered externalities, that is, side effects or consequences of commercial activities that are not accounted for in products' and services' costs. From a systems perspective, however, there is no "outside" or "away" place where these so-called externalities can go. Understood holistically, everything is part of the system, including waste products, excessive consumption, and overproduction. The real costs remain in the system, in things like pollution, lack of social cohesion, and failing ecosystems, to be paid for in a variety of ways, including species extinction, rising health care costs and sickness, shifting weather patterns, and many more impacts.

The ethical and ecological implications of some practices thus do not really count in the neoliberal economic model. That model, for example, valorizes "efficient" practices like crop monocultures, not to mention the over-fertilization and pesticide use that literally kills the life in agricultural soils. It promotes clear-cutting of forests, industrial farming practices in animal husbandry, exploitation and burning of rainforests, because these are quick and dirty ways to get results that, on the surface, look "efficient" despite their short- and long-term ecological costs. It encourages production of high-fat, -sugar, and -salt "food products" with little nutritional value, because they are considered cost-effective and provide a lot of calories. It supports placing cities into deserts, as well as the constant human "development" of land, eroding habitats for many creatures and contributing to the human-caused sixth great extinction of living beings on the planet.[7]

These practices ought to be a good thing, in the sense of being thrifty and frugal with resources. Instead, our have emerged with very different meanings in today's economizing mindset. Such practices, unfortunately, have significant negative social and ecological consequences that are not contained or even measured within the current economic calculus, which ignores ecological costs—or even perversely counts them as beneficial when they generate economic activity.

The imperatives of economizing and the economizing mindset are deeply embedded in the mainstream theory of the firm, which argues that there are two primary governance mechanisms: markets and hierarchies. That dominance still exists, despite recognition by scholars of several other types of governance mechanisms: clans or communities, associations,[8] government hierarchies, and the increasingly prevalent network form.[9] The narrowness of the economizing perspective exists in part because of the way that corporate purpose is typically described per the neoliberal model, that is, as the maximization of profits or, sometimes, the maximization of shareholder wealth. This definition stands in stark contrast to a proposal that businesses exist to create "collective value" absent dignity violations, offered by scholars Thomas Donaldson and James P. Walsh.[10] It stands in contrast to definitions of wealth that recognize that there are many forms of capital that go beyond financial capital, including social, political, intellectual, and others.

More holistic socio-ecological values are largely ignored in our Northern/Western "modern" or "developed" context. They are, however, more prominent in Indigenous, Eastern, and Southern cultures, thereby creating even more of the dualities, tensions, and even paradoxes in our thinking discussed in earlier chapters. Attaining more integrated perspectives means first understanding these tensions or dualities, then attempting to integrate the apparent paradoxes that they generate into new, more holistic frameworks that speak to today's systemic realities, integrating dualisms into coherent, integrated dualities.

Below we continue that exploration, starting with the need to move from mechanistic to living systems, in the process exploring ideas about what gives life to systems. Then we briefly explore the ways in which humans have separated themselves from nature, and the need to now understand ourselves as integrally connected to nature, along with the numerous cycles present in that natural context. The final part of the chapter explores the movement from non-systems sciences towards systems science, and from linear ways of thinking to more organic and holistic thinking.

From Mechanistic to Living Systems

Ecologizing values made a decided shift away from the more positivist and mechanistic values of economizing. Despite the greater complexity inherent in a systems perspective, particularly a living systems perspective, on human organizing and socializing, the more realistic assumptions of systems thinking provide a better basis for considerations about the wellbeing of the whole than do the more limited and narrow assumptions of economizing.

To cope with many of the issues facing the world, it is increasingly clear that today's scientific orientation of fragmentation, positivism, and atomization as ways of understanding living (and other) entities needs to give way towards a living systems perspective. Building in systemic features that give life to systems, it may be possible to avoid continuing to reproduce today's problems tomorrow. A living systems perspective can provide an integration of scientific (and mechanistic) perspectives with a recognition of the holism, connectedness, and, indeed, awe and the sacred integral to living systems. A general systems approach provides key insights that can be enhanced by understanding of the characteristics of systems that give life or what architect Christopher Alexander called the "quality without a name" to living systems.[11]

Mechanistic approaches to complex systems rely on a Newtonian view of physics, now made quite dated by emerging concepts in quantum physics[12] and more integral approaches to organizing that encompass, as philosopher Ken Wilber might note,[13] subjective and objective, as well as individual and collective levels of analysis.[14] Even as general systems theory began to inform social sciences about the nature of human systems, there was an aversion to understanding them, as Frederick did, as natural systems.[15] Yet humans are living aspects of nature, just as any other creature would be, and their social constructions, be they communities, organizations, or societies are equally submitted to natural constraints, limits, and possibilities.

General systems theory tells us that there are core components to anything that can be called a system. Systems are comprised of subsystems or components, typically arranged in some sort of hierarchy (or sometimes a network), with energetic inputs, transformations, and outputs because they are viewed as open, at least to some extent, with boundaries that are somewhat permeable to those inputs and outputs. These energetic inputs and transformations create internal and external feedback loops that give rise to what is known as negative entropy in living systems. When they are healthy and successful, energetic inputs allow the system to thrive rather than deteriorating from entropic forces. Healthy (living) systems, that is, move towards greater complexity, connectedness, and interrelatedness among their parts through processes of internal elaboration, that help create the dynamic equilibrium and homeostasis needed for system components to achieve their variety of "goals" or purposes.[16]

In an important paper, Bansal and Song articulated the key differences between non-systems science and systems science along similar lines, arguing that "a system defies reductivism."[17] We would note here that living organisms, and all human-created constructions like families, communities, enterprises, institutions of all sorts, and societies are systems. Further, they are typically complex adaptive systems, typically fraught with problems best described as wicked.[18]

The movement from more positivist, economizing orientations to understanding shifts from a reductivist (atomization, fragmentation into component parts) perspective towards more holistic perspectives. As noted, systems need to be viewed as wholes to maintain their systemic integrity. Further, non-systems approaches tend to be linear and simplistic versus living systems' inherent nonlinearity and complexity, deriving their scientific orientation from quantum physics and complexity theory rather than Newtonian physics and a more Darwinian perspective. Bansal and

Song[19] recognize further that systems are non-deterministic with multiple points of (temporary) equilibrium, because they are dynamic and unstable, with multiple interdependent, inherently connected components that cannot be teased apart if the system is to maintain its integrity. Further, living systems in particular have a characteristic that Chilean biologists Humberto Maturana and Francisco Varela called autopoiesis, that is, self-organization or the capacity to reproduce and maintain themselves.[20]

Living Systems: What Gives Life?

Living systems deeply embed specific characteristics. Living systems theory, along with ecologizing principles, is inherently systemic, not reductionist or atomistic (left-brained thinking). Living systems have properties that emerge as they become more complex, components that are integrally connected with each other to comprise the system, and, as they become more complex, greater adaptive capacity,[21] as a way of coping with entropy as seen in the second law of thermodynamics, discussed earlier. In other words, living systems, including human systems like organizations and economies, cannot be reduced to their parts; in many ways, they must be considered as whole entities.

Work by Sandra Waddock and Petra Kuenkel synthesizing a number of different literatures, from architecture, urban design, biology, consciousness, physics, and ecology, among others, developed six core principles that "give life" to systems.[22] These principles include intentional generative, permeable containment, emerging novelty, contextual interconnectedness and requisite diversity, mutually enhancing wholeness, and proprioceptive consciousness. As we begin to unpack these ideas a bit, it is important to note that these principles are aimed at understanding *living* systems of the sort that we believe will be better supported by ecologizing rather than economizing values. Economizing values are built on the more mechanistic or non-systems assumptions rather than principles that enhance life. Ecologizing values build on life-giving features of systems.

One of those features is intentionality, or intentional generativity, which combines elements of purposiveness (even the "purpose" of survival)[23] and the capacity that healthy systems have for generativity, or the ability to renew, replenish, and restore themselves through creating something new, a process that can result in resilience and the potential for future elaboration, as we will see shortly. It is this principle of intentional generativity that is implied in Maturana and Varela's idea of autopoiesis or self-creation,[24] which basically means a drive to continue to exist that Weber calls enlivenment in a book by that name.[25] The idea of generativity is reflected in Weber's notion that "the biosphere does not grow," at least not in the sense implied by economizing values of constant material, profitability, or economic growth. Rather, what is generative is, as he puts it, "the diversity of experiences: ways of feeling, modes of expression, variations of appearance, novelties of patterns and forms," a generative pattern he describes as depth.[26]

Another principle of what gives life to systems is that of wholeness (mutually consistent wholeness), which we have already seen to be important to systemic perspectives like ecologizing, in noting that systems cannot be fully understood by breaking them down into their parts because the system itself is something more than the parts. Systems are comprised of parts, which Koestler called "holons."[27] Holons are nested wholes that are integrally connected to each other, which constitute a whole that has its own integrity in what Weber calls a relationship of interbeing, or inherent connections.[28] Economizing values fail to recognize this interconnectedness among different aspects of a system, among communities, and between people and nature, in its quest to separate human activities solely into economic realms. Ecologizing in contrast places humans firmly into the context of the whole of nature, the fabric of their communities and societies (and families), and with each other, recognizing that essence of wholeness.

Systems can be thought of as open or closed. Living systems are inevitably open systems, because they require energetic inputs (i.e., human systems need food and liquids to survive), transformation, and outputs to survive, for example, that waste matter be released when necessary. Inputs typically undergo some sort of transformation process to convert those inputs into useful form and ultimately into output of wastes into the broader system, where they can, as the authors of *Cradle to Cradle* note, become food for other systems.[29] What that means, as the principle of permeable containment suggests, is that systems, even social and ecological systems, need to have some sort of boundary that helps define them, give them identity, and in some sense contain them, and also some sort of openness that allows for these energetic exchanges.[30]

Healthy living systems, founded on ecologizing principles, also exhibit novelty (emergent novelty), or a capacity to change as is appropriate to their circumstances. Living systems are constantly dynamic, evolving, and emerging new aspects of themselves, or being, as Weber argues, fundamentally creative and emergently self-constructing.[31] It is this process of emerging novelty that allows healthy systems to avoid the dissolution implied by entropy, creating a form of what the physicist Schrödinger called negative entropy (negentropy).[32] But, as noted, healthy ecologizing systems do not necessarily grow in the material sense; rather, they grow in diversity and abundance. In a sense, they thwart efficiency, for as Weber tartly points out, "The biosphere is not efficient."[33] Instead, the biosphere trades in abundance, and as the principle of interconnectedness and requisite diversity suggests, diversity.

Interconnectedness and diversity combine two system features that generate the "quality without a name" or what we are calling life. We have already noted numerous times that ecologizing recognizes life, as does quantum physics, even applied at the more macro level of ecology.[34] In a breakthrough book on human social systems and "quantum mind,"[35] Wendt recognizes and documents the inherent interconnectedness of everything in our world. Human systems like organizations, communities, and societies, that is, are comprised of complexly connected, dynamic, and interrelated parts[36] that, most likely, cannot be fully understood, but must at least to some extent be considered holistically as entities in and of themselves. With organisms, social, and natural systems, fragmenting them into their component parts takes the "life" right out of them.

Diversity or, drawing on the idea of requisite variety,[37] requisite diversity, is also fundamental to healthy living systems. The abundance that healthy living systems creates depends on diversity, not monocultures, huge megalithic companies that control markets and financial systems, or scaled-up production systems that produce vast quantities of unneeded products in the name of efficiency. Indeed, urban ecologist Jane Jacobs in her seminal book *The Death and Life of American Cities*, claimed that sufficient or requisite diversity was the core principle to *life* in cities.[38] Requisite diversity provides the capacity for resilience because the system does not overly rely on any one element. Should one part fail in some way, other parts can replace the failing elements.

There is another important element to health *human* systems, and that is human consciousness and awareness,[39] which allows for humans to design systems, organizations, and whole societies (deliberately or not). It is human awareness/consciousness that has allowed humans to create or "contrive"[40] social and organizational systems, and to do so deliberately, in some ways setting them apart from other types of living systems.

Regenerativity

Consistently with ecologizing values and the principles that give life to systems, former Wall Street executive John Fullerton has articulated eight core principles for what he terms regenerative capitalism and a regenerative economy.[41] According to Fullerton, a regenerative economy is underpinned by an assumption that "economic vigor is a product of human and societal vitality, rooted in ecological health and the inclusive development of human capabilities and potential."[42] Such an economy would be one in which the idea of interdependence and connectivity is understood in ways so that economic actions work towards long-term overall health of the society, integrates financial, human, societal, and ecological health, values richness and diversity, integrity and fairness working through what Fullerton terms "constructive competition," and responds to all human needs.[43]

To support the idea of regenerativity, Fullerton outlines eight principles of regenerative economy vitality. The first principle is "in right relationship," an idea that draws on the interconnectivity and interdependence between humans and nature, discussed above. The second principle "views wealth holistically" expands the use of the term capital to encompass multiple forms of capital better aligned with human (ecologizing) values. Fullerton claims there are eight types of capital that create what he terms holistic wealth: intellectual, spiritual, social, material, financial, living, cultural, and experiential, pointing out that these capitals go well beyond financial wealth. The principle, "innovative, adaptive, responsive," speaks to the reality that living systems are dynamic, need to be adaptable and responsive to events external to themselves, and, as the life principle of novelty discussed above suggests, create new things as needed.[44]

Another key principle, according to Fullerton is empowered participation, which means that sub-elements of the system need to be able to meet their own needs and add their unique contributions to the wellbeing of the whole. Along these lines, the fifth principle "honors community and place" recognizes the importance of resilience and distinctive local identifies and cultures, while the sixth, "edge effect abundance" recognizes the importance of boundaries—and the fertility that is associated with the edges or boundaries of systems. Fullerton's seventh principle, "robust circulatory flow," emphasizes that just as living entities need good circulation to thrive, so do human systems of all sorts. Finally, the eighth principle, "seeks balance," recognizes the need for harmony among the elements of the system into a unified whole.[45]

From Dominance Over Nature to Stewardship "Of and With" Nature

Shifting from economizing to ecologizing as the basis of society and economy, as we have argued, entails redefining—or more accurately—rediscovering the original meaning of economy. The English word "economy" is derived from two Greek words, *oikos*, meaning house, and *nemein*, meaning manage, a word in use around 1530. Thus, the original meaning of the Greek word *oikonomia* was to manage the household, or, more colorfully, to manage hearth and home. Far from the constant growth, endless material resource use, and maximization of wealth implied by today's economic system and neoliberalism, the original meaning of economics had implications of frugality, thrift, and stewardship of resources, thereby creating a balance between what is needed and what is spent.

Combined with the belief that Nature would provide in abundance if resources were carefully stewarded and used to advance the good life, the general idea of *oikos* was that wealth generation in "man's [*sic*] needs needed to be limited or the good life might be lost in the perceived abundance of Nature."[46] (Of course, early Greek life was fraught with misogyny, slavery, and hierarchies in which only a few male heads of householder were able to achieve the good life by participating in politics and philosophy,[47] realities that also need to be taken into account.) Ethics enters the economic picture in Greek life because of the need to limit Nature's potential excesses.

For the sake of the future of humanity, we humans now need to consider the whole Earth to be our home. Hence, we need to undertake careful stewardship of that home and its many resources, not just for humanity, but in the interest of flourishing life more generally, something that today's growth-oriented yet 'economizing' approach fails to do. Indeed, Milton Friedman, who was perhaps the most noted proponent of today's economistic thinking, argued the economic theory is "in principle independent of any particular ethical position."[48] Yet economizing as we have seen does incorporate clear values: financial wealth, constant growth in material and monetary goods, and freedom from the restraints that might be felt if the common good were taken into account. Economizing is hardly value-free.

Ecologizing aims to replace economizing with a different set of values, grounded also in nature, and yet going beyond the tenets of economizing. Since these values draw from emergent knowledge in physics, biology, and psychology to name only a few disciplines, we believe that ecologizing values better reflect the realities of the world, enabling us to rethink the fundamentals of human beings' relationship to Nature, though, of course, we still need economizing values to promote frugality and measured use of resources. From "man's" dominance or dominion over nature as expressed in the Bible, we need to move towards the caretaking or stewardship idea for all of use that may well be inherent in the original Biblical phrasing. Indeed, in many ways ecologizing values reflect what today might be perceived as more feminine values, at least in Western cultures, as noted earlier, than today's dominant masculine-oriented values, because of their emphasis on circularity, dynamism, and connectivity, among other factors.

What the various ways of approaching ecologizing values discussed in this chapter suggest is that *healthy* living and natural systems are supported by a set of principles and, in a sense, operating standards quite different from the neoliberal norms currently dominating economies and, not incidentally, societies, in much of the world. The principles that give life, are regenerative, allowing for ecologizing to recognize that what gives life to systems is inherent to developing a thriving (not just sustaining, which implies stasis or more of the same) world in which dignity and wellbeing can be achieved for all. Note that "all" here goes beyond human communities, to encompass all of the living beings, plant, animal, and other, on the planet, and the ecosystems they collectively create. The clear message from these various approaches to ecologizing tell us that humans cannot thrive long term without the rest of the world's living beings, natural resources, and ecologies also thriving. That is because we humans are in and of nature, not separate from it, and our constructions—our families, communities, cities, nations, societies, for example—cannot thrive if the world around is us failing.

Notes

1. Kassel, K., & Rimanoczy, I. (2018). *Developing a sustainability mindset in management education*. London: Routledge; Rimanoczy, I., & Laszlo, E. (2013). *Big bang being: Developing the sustainability mindset*. Sheffield, UK: Greenleaf Publishing.
2. Abram, D. (2012). *The spell of the sensuous: Perception and language in a more-than-human world*. New York: Vintage.
3. McGilchrist, I. (2009). *The master and his emissary: The divided brain and the making of the western world*. New Haven: Yale University Press.
4. Flack, J. C., & De Waal, F. (2004). Monkey business and business ethics: Evolution origins of human morality. *The Ruffin Series of the Society for Business Ethics*, 4, 7–41; De Waal, F. B. (1996). *Good natured* (No. 87). Cambridge, MA: Harvard University Press; Waal, F. B. (2013). *The bonobo and the atheist: In search of humanism among the primates*. New York: WW Norton & Company.
5. Schumpeter, J. A. (1962). *Capitalism, socialism and democracy*. New York: Harper & Row.
6. Cited from *Women's Own*, October 3, 1987, in Margaret Thatcher: A life in quotes, *The Guardian*, April 8, 2018. Retrieved from: www.theguardian.com/politics/2013/apr/08/margaret-thatcher-quotes.
7. E.g., Barnosky, A. D., Matzke, N., Tomiya, S., Wogan, G. O., Swartz, B., Quental, T. B., Marshall, C., McGuire, J. L., Linsey, E. L., Maguire, K. C., Mersey, B., & Ferrer, E. A. (2011). Has the Earth's sixth mass extinction already arrived? *Nature*, 471(7336), 51–57.
8. Turnbull, S. (2017). Grounding a theory of firms in the natural sciences. *Humanistic Management Journal*, 159–186, citing Ouchi, W. G. (1980). Markets, bureaucracies, and clans. *Administrative Science Quarterly*, 25, 125–141; North, D. C. (1985). Transaction costs in history. *Journal of European Economic History*, 4, 557–572.
9. Hollingsworth, J. R. (2000). Doing institutional analysis for the study of innovations. *Review of International Political Economy*, 7(4), 4595–644.
10. Donaldson, T., & Walsh, J. P. (2015). Toward a theory of business. *Research in Organizational Behavior*, 35, 181–207.
11. Alexander, C. (1979). *The timeless way of building*. New York: Oxford University Press; also, Alexander, C. (1999). The origins of pattern theory: The future of the theory, and the generation of a living world. *IEEE Software*, 16(5), 71–82.
12. Capra, F., & Luisi, P. L. (2014). *The systems view of life: A unifying vision*. Cambridge, UK: Cambridge University Press.
13. E.g., Wilber, K. (2002). *A theory of everything: An integral vision for business, politics, science, and spirituality*. Boston: Shambhala.
14. E.g., Laloux, F. (2014). *Reinventing organizations: A guide to creating organizations inspired by the next stage in human consciousness*. Millis, MA: Parker Nelson.
15. David, S. (1971). *The theory of organizations*. New York: Basic Books, quoted in Kast, F. E., & Rosenzweig, J. E. (1972). General systems theory: Applications for organization and management. *Academy of Management Journal*, 15(4), 447–465.

16. These characteristics of general systems, which we apply to living systems, are described in Kast, F. E., & Rosenzweig, J. E. (1972). General systems theory: Applications for organization and management. *Academy of Management Journal, 15*(4), 447–465, 450.
17. Bansal, P., & Song, H-C. (2017). Similar but not the same: Differentiating corporate sustainability from corporate responsibility. *Academy of Management Annals, 11*(1), 105–149.
18. Waddock, S., Dentoni, D., Meszoely, G., & Waddell, S. (2015). The complexity of wicked problems in large system change. *Journal of Organizational Change Management, 28*(6), 993–1012.
19. Bansal, P., & Song, H.-C. (2017). Similar but not the same: Differentiating corporate sustainability from corporate responsibility. *Academy of Management Annals, 11*(1), 105–149.
20. Maturana, H. R., & Varela, F. J. (1991). *Autopoiesis and cognition: The realization of the living* (Vol. 42). New York: Springer Science & Business Media, see also Bansal and Song, cited above.
21. Miller, J. G. (1972). I: The nature of living systems. *Biosystems, 4*(2), 55–77.
22. Ideas in the next several paragraphs are drawn from this work, Waddock, S., & Kuenkel, P. (2019, May). What gives life to large system change? *Organization & Environment.* published online first. Retrieved from: https://journals.sagepub.com/doi/10.1177/1086026619842482, and Kuenkel, P., & Waddock, S. (2019). Stewarding aliveness in a troubled earth system. *Cadmus, 4*(1), 14–38.
23. See Swanson, G. A., & Miller, J. G. (2009). Living systems theory. *Systems Science and Cybernetics: Synergetics, 1* (System Theories), 136–148.
24. Maturana, H. R., & Varela, F. J. (1991). *Autopoiesis and cognition: The realization of the living* (Vol. 42). New York: Springer Science & Business Media.
25. Weber, A. (2013). *Enlivenment. Towards a fundamental shift in the concepts of nature, culture and politics.* Berlin: Heinrich-Böll-Stiftung. Retrieved from: www.autor-andreas-weber.de/downloads/Enlivenment_web.pdf.
26. Weber, A. (2013). *Enlivenment. Towards a fundamental shift in the concepts of nature, culture and politics* (p. 27). Berlin: Heinrich-Böll-Stiftung. Retrieved from: www.autor-andreas-weber.de/downloads/Enlivenment_web.pdf.
27. Koestler, A. (1968). *The ghost in the machine.* New York: Random House.
28. Weber, A. (2013). *Enlivenment. Towards a fundamental shift in the concepts of nature, culture and politics.* Berlin: Heinrich-Böll-Stiftung. Retrieved from: www.autor-andreas-weber.de/downloads/Enlivenment_web.pdf.
29. McDonough, W., & Braungart, M. (2010). *Cradle to cradle: Remaking the way we make things.* New York: Macmillan.
30. Both Jane Jacobs work on successful urban centers and Christopher Alexander's pattern language theory argue for such permeable containment, e.g., Jacobs, J. (1961). *The death and life of great American cities.* New York: Vintage; Alexander, C. (1979). *The timeless way of building.* New York: Oxford University Press.
31. Weber, A. (2013). *Enlivenment. Towards a fundamental shift in the concepts of nature, culture and politics.* Berlin: Heinrich-Böll-Stiftung. Retrieved from: www.autor-andreas-weber.de/downloads/Enlivenment_web.pdf.
32. Schrödinger, E. (1992). *What is life? With mind and matter and autobiographical sketches.* Cambridge, UK: Cambridge University Press.
33. Weber, A. (2013). *Enlivenment. Towards a fundamental shift in the concepts of nature, culture and politics* (p. 27). Berlin: Heinrich-Böll-Stiftung.

Retrieved from: www.autor-andreas-weber.de/downloads/Enlivenment_web.pdf.
34. Capra, F., & Luisi, P. L. (2014). *The systems view of life: A unifying vision.* Cambridge, UK: Cambridge University Press.
35. Wendt, A. (2015). *Quantum mind and social science: Unifying physical and social ontology.* Cambridge, UK: Cambridge University Press.
36. E.g., Alexander, C. (1979). *The timeless way of building.* New York: Oxford University Press; Weber, A. (2013). *Enlivenment. Towards a fundamental shift in the concepts of nature, culture and politics* (p. 27). Berlin: Heinrich-Böll-Stiftung. Retrieved from: www.autor-andreas-weber.de/downloads/Enlivenment_web.pdf; Swanson, G. A., & Miller, J. G. (2009). Living systems theory. *Systems Science and Cybernetics: Synergetics, 1* (System Theories), 136–148.
37. Ashby, W. R. (2011). Variety, constraint, and the law of requisite variety. *Emergence: Complexity and Organization, 13*(1–2), 190–207.
38. Jacobs, J. (1961). *The death and life of great American cities.* New York: Vintage.
39. In the Waddock and Kuenkel paper, this trait is called proprioceptive consciousness. See Waddock, S., & Kuenkel, P. (2018). *What gives life to large system change.* Working paper.
40. Kast, F. E., & Rosenzweig, J. E. (1972). General systems theory: Applications for organization and management. *Academy of Management Journal, 15*(4), 447–465.
41. Fullerton, J. (2015). *Regenerative capitalism: How universal principles and patterns will shape our new economy.* Greenwich, CT: Capital Institute. Retrieved from: http://capitalinstitute.org/wp-content/uploads/2015/04/2015-Regenerative-Capitalism-4-20-15-final.pdf.
42. Fullerton, J. (2015). *Regenerative capitalism: How universal principles and patterns will shape our new economy* (p. 40). Greenwich, CT: Capital Institute. Retrieved from: http://capitalinstitute.org/wp-content/uploads/2015/04/2015-Regenerative-Capitalism-4-20-15-final.pdf.
43. Fullerton, J. (2015). *Regenerative capitalism: How universal principles and patterns will shape our new economy* (p. 40). Greenwich, CT: Capital Institute. Retrieved from: http://capitalinstitute.org/wp-content/uploads/2015/04/2015-Regenerative-Capitalism-4-20-15-final.pdf.
44. Fullerton, J. (2015). *Regenerative capitalism: How universal principles and patterns will shape our new economy.* Greenwich, CT: Capital Institute. Retrieved from: http://capitalinstitute.org/wp-content/uploads/2015/04/2015-Regenerative-Capitalism-4-20-15-final.pdf.
45. Fullerton, J. (2015). *Regenerative capitalism: How universal principles and patterns will shape our new economy.* Greenwich, CT: Capital Institute. Retrieved from: http://capitalinstitute.org/wp-content/uploads/2015/04/2015-Regenerative-Capitalism-4-20-15-final.pdf.
46. Leshem, D. (2016). Retrospectives: What did the ancient Greeks mean by *Oikonomia? Journal of Economic Perspectives,* Winter, *30*(1), 225–231, 226.
47. Lesham, D. (2016, Winter). Retrospectives: What did the ancient Greeks mean by *Oikonomia? Journal of Economic Perspectives, 30*(1), 225–231, 226.
48. Friedman, M. (1953). *The methodology of positive economics. Essays in positive economics* (pp. 3–34, 4). Chicago: Chicago University Press, cited in Leshem, D. (2016, Winter). Retrospectives: What did the Ancient Greeks mean by *Oikonomia? Journal of Economic Perspectives, 30*(1), 225–231, 226.

8 Enlightenment to Enlivenment

The last couple of chapters emphasized that there is a huge disconnect between the implicit—or, in our view, explicit—goal of creating a flourishing world for all and today's dominant system. We need to move the system from Enlightenment values towards values of ecologizing, or what Weber calls Enlivenment (a term he uses to align with the wording of the idea of Enlightenment), that is, bringing life to systems. To do that, we need to consider how to integrate other important dualisms: power and techno-symbolic values, the status quo and innovation, into what are known as institutional logics. Moving forward to an ecologizing mindset also means thinking in terms of developing a wisdom that has too often been missing, a wisdom that draws on the rich resources of ancient wisdom traditions, while understanding that their more holistic orientation of systems understanding, moral imagination, and aesthetic sensibility or rationality needs to be applied in the current context. Bringing these ideas together can help pave the way towards an ecologizing mindset.

Institutional Logics

Institutional logics, or the broader belief systems that shape how people think and act,[1] are formed and influenced *within* and *across* individuals in an organization. The current managerial and economic paradigm assumes that individuals are rationally self-interested human beings with a short-term focus.[2] A rational human being will strive to satisfy his/her specific short-term needs and desires. These desires are instrumental in nature and decisions are based on objective reality.

Choices, from this perspective, are guided by utilitarian calculations by individuals attempting to maximize their net benefit. For example, rational choice theory can provide justification for the role of social justice in environmental decision-making and governance. If this reasoning were applied, environmental decisions would not need any scientific support or cost–benefit analyses; instead, what enhances utility would be seen as most beneficial.[3] This reasoning would appeal to the current institutional logics, the practices, beliefs, and ideals, that dominate the business field,[4] what we have described as the neoliberal or economizing mindset that dominates in society today. The current institutional logic that perceives sustainability as based on rational choices determines the distribution of resources among individuals, the distribution of opportunities for various lines of behavior, and the distribution and nature of norms and obligations in a situation.[5]

At the macro level, institutional theory presumes that organizational change occurs when the institutional logics are re-framed to reflect new organizing principles representing the values of the organization.[6] These organizing principles, which determine how organizations structure their workforce and gather, spread, and process information, offer guiding principles for both organizations and individuals as they interpret and share information.[7] It is first at the individual level of analysis, however, where support for these organizing principles is perceived and fostered. Individuals understand organization principles in relation to institutional logics, interpreting institutional expectations and values and choosing to accept or reject the principles implicit within in institutional logics.[8] Thus, institutional logics operate at multiple levels of analysis.[9]

To overcome the disconnect between humans and nature, it is necessary to create new individual perceptions of reality that include a sense for sustainable development or what we have called an ecologizing logic. These logics are the basis for individual and organizational decisions, steering interpretations of environmental ambiguities to re-enact and strengthen institutional logics.[10] It should be noted that we see the importance of an unbound moral awareness and broadened moral perception (i.e., what has been called moral imagination, which we discuss below) by individuals to enabling institutional logics change. Indeed, as we discuss below, moral imagination, and aesthetic rationality or sensibility, along with systems understanding, are important aspects of wisdom[11]— and it is wisdom that is inherent, in our view, in moving towards ecologizing. For institutional logics to be revised at the organizational level, the individuals involved with the issue must individually alter their own cognition, somehow reintegrating their left and right brains' understandings of the world. Then, as we have noted, the broader stories that we tell ourselves about how the world works need to shift accordingly.

Moral understanding and imagination require ethical perception or deliberation. Ethical deliberation involves understanding concepts whose adaptive structures represent types of situations and modes of affective responses. Moral imagination allows individuals to consider possibilities/ solutions that extend beyond conventional assumptions, accepted moral norms, and existing circumstances in the short term. Using moral imagination, we can extend our knowledge to include a concern for multiple stakeholder groups (including the natural environment and other living beings) on a long-term time dimension through a revised set of institutional logics that move us towards an ecologizing mindset.[12]

Institutional logics are also relevant for micro-level behaviors and the factors that lead to action.[13] Individual level research in institutional logics is concerned with individual perception of the self. Thus, how logics are linked with individual identities is paramount to how revised logics are institutionalized. It involves how individuals interpret the logics and align them with their own self-perceptions.[14] This point is important, as our ultimate goal is to show how individuals can incorporate seemingly paradoxical sustainability values into their thinking and inherent values.

Studies in institutional logics address the competence of individuals in terms of their ability to revise existing, dominant logics.[15] In fact, individuals reflexively draw not only on the specific logics of their corporation or social group but on a wide range of cultural resources.[16] The idea of reflexibility is an important insight with managerial implications in that we see that organizational actors are capable of revising their thinking. Individuals can switch between distinct logics, although they are often restricted by pragmatic norms associated with the existing conventional structures.[17]

The links we suggest with dual-process theories of cognition and moral imagination potentially add to our understanding of how logics can be changed to reflect new moral values about issues.

Power Versus Techno-Symbolic Values

Another natural value set that affects human behavior in relation to other people, other beings, and the environment involves our human drive to innovate, which involves both the use of power and what are known as techno-symbolic values, and is also one of the principles that give life to systems. Humans' ability to survive as a species in the long term, as well as their efforts to exist and thrive in the short term, depend greatly on our propensity to innovate in order to adapt to new conditions. Both ecologizing and economizing require technological and social innovations and creativity.

Technology does not only encompass robotic or computer-generated innovations, but also any advancement that positively enhances humans' survival. Channeling Bill Frederick, we instead consider technology as "the entire array of technical manifestations," including "behavioral features, organizational patterns . . . that can trace their functions and operations to a symbolic process in genetic systems and expressed in socio-cultural forms."[18] Symbolic elements of technology refer to elements that are culturally generated to enable a particular social group to thrive and economize through some adaptive challenge.

Frederick argued that in open systems, certain value sets direct and guide individuals, as well as organizations, to self-organize in the short term to survive certain environments. Both culture and nature are responsible for generating these value sets. The "natural" values are not completely pre-determined by nature but nurtured by culture. But here we also see the intersection of the short and long term that needs to be reconnected for the human chain. In this book we have discussed the evolutionary and thermodynamic forces that help organisms survive in the short and long term. These same processes interact with the logics and values associated with techno-symbolic tendencies. Humans' ability to adapt is through their technological value set, which leads to innovative solutions to navigating the social and ecological world. As with the other value sets, techno-symbolic values are pragmatic in nature by allowing individuals the ability over time to organize techniques and solutions to adaptive problems. For instance, our ability to communicate through the written and spoken word is an innovation that aided our species through evolutionary time. Technology's development and emergence is cumulative over time and progresses in face of new challenges.

Techno-symbolic values help us as human beings do things that are distinctly human, like thinking, creating philosophies and symbols, and figuring out how to develop our societies, which help us integrate the natural values that Frederick identified.[19] These values are embedded in human nature as a means for reasoning symbolically and innovatively to transform elements of the environment, as well as our societies. Our ability to think in an abstract way is related to our "ability to create culture and moral norms."[20] Thus, persons have an innate tendency to innovate through the manifestation of techno-symbolic values. This notion is consistent with the technological systems perspective,[21] which has its roots in the social sciences. In this perspective, technological systems involve a network of actors interacting within a particular social and environmental context and corresponding institutional structures. As such "techno-economic selection takes place in a socio-cultural environment" and affects the mindsets and narratives that inform how we live our lives.[22]

Wisdom: Integrating Systems Understanding, Moral Imagination, and Aesthetic Sensibility

An ecologizing mindset draws on the deep wisdom of ancient traditions, which tend to speak holistically about our human relationship to the Earth[23],[24]—and which represent, in a sense, a still-unbroken human chain. Wisdom has been said by systems theorist Russell Ackoff to be the ability to think through the long-term consequences of decisions and actions.[25] In other words, a wise person will understand the systemic implications of actions, beliefs, and practices, including those consequences on other people and on the natural environment. Wisdom, in effect, helps heal the broken human chain.

Wisdom can do this because it involves, integrates, and balances three important ways of thinking: systems understanding, moral imagination, and aesthetic sensibility. Waddock synthesized a definition of wisdom in the modern context by arguing that it combines three crucial attributes used in the service of a better world: systems understanding, moral imagination, and aesthetic sensibility[26] (or rationality). When we think about repairing the broken human chain, we arguably need to incorporate all three of these elements into the ecologizing mindset. We discuss these aspects of wisdom that we believe can enhance movement towards ecologizing below.

Systems Understanding

Gaining systems understanding—the ability to see the big picture reasonably accurately, to at least reasonably accurately understand or "see" at least to some extent a system's dynamics, interactions and broad patterns— is an important aspect of wisdom and needed when shifting to an ecologizing mindset.[27] We argued earlier that the dominance of left-brain thinking, especially in Western and Northern cultures, has resulted in a linear and atomistic approach to the world about us for many people. An ecologizing mindset demands a more holistic—systemic—understanding, that is, more use of the right brain's capacity for holistic thinking and for balancing the tensions inherent in paradoxes that inevitably exist in systems. The ability to think systemically relates to what Aristotle called practical wisdom—the ability to make good decisions that make sense in a context. Much of the rest of this book is focused on such systemic thinking as a core aspect of the ecologizing mindset needed to repair the human chain, a task to which we now add the need to develop wisdom, which requires two other attributes of mind: moral imagination and aesthetic sensibility/rationality, to which we now turn.

Amoral to Moral Imagination

Moral imagination is one's cognitive capacity to utilize ideas, images, and metaphors to understand moral dilemmas, ethical principles, and to generate moral responses. In this sense, moral imagination becomes an important way for humans to begin to repair the broken chain because it helps create an ethically grounded way of imagining a different way of being in the world. Thus, it relates to humans' ability to retrieve experience, see the ethical implications of a decision or situation, and make wiser choices. Moral imagination is necessary for making acceptable moral judgments.

Using one's moral imagination is a cognitive and emotional process that enables individuals to "discover and evaluate possibilities not merely determined by that circumstance, or limited by its operative mental models, or merely framed by a set of rules."[28] Moral imagination is part of the ethical decision-making process that involves the perception of norms, roles, and social contracts in a given situation and an emotional commitment to acting on moral compulsions. It allows individuals to think beyond narrow conceptions of consequences of actions and expands thinking to include the consideration of ancillary stakeholders who may be affected by a particular action or decision.

An entrepreneurial mindset, including aspects of creativity and innovation is indeed influenced by emotions.[29] "Rational and emotional elements join together in moral deliberation, and moral imagination illuminates them to create a more complete, critical, and personal scenario."[30] Moral discourse involves both rational and emotional elements. Knowledge is thought to be integrated and pragmatic solutions are achieved through the integration of values and emotions.[31]

Symbols, or representational rules, are created by people in societies based on common belief systems, values, and norms.[32] Furthermore, symbols are memes that are powerful tools for evoking behavioral change. They are a manifestation of techno-symbolic values. Particular patterns in organizational structure and process become similar across industries because of widespread use of these symbols. To move towards ecologizing means creating new symbols of "sustainability" that spread widely and relate to logics that counter embedded social norms that are more narrowly conceived than a sustainability or ecologizing mindset calls for. This process involves imagination; in particular, moral imagination. The deinstitutionalization of endemic disregard for sustainability "requires changes in both the symbolism and substance of institutional orders— through the creation of alternative identities that cognitively and morally frame action differently, and through the development of sustainable habits and practices rooted in such newly constructed frameworks of meaning."[33]

Symbols provide the basis for the formation of new organizational realities. They are usually represented by different physical or abstract forms that stand for the symbol's underlying meaning. Communication of information is often done through symbol use through narratives, which we have already argued are vitally important in shifting mindsets. Symbols are "usually represented by a variety of physical or abstract forms that stand for or represent the symbol's underlying meaning."[34] This techno-symbolic innovation is important for survival. We advocate for new symbols to be used through new narratives to convey the need for a greater connection with nature.

Moral imagination plays a critical role in manufacturing social and moral ideas, which are part of our human nature, stir emotions, and connect sentiment with understanding (Burke, 1790). Universal unity around a standard behavior cannot be achieved without moral imagination, which is why developing moral imagination is needed when we consider issues of sustainability and moving towards an ecologizing mindset. Managers must appeal to individual's conceptual imagination to be able to understand standards that can provide guidance into how to resolve moral issues and how to adapt to change.[35] To find shared values that reconnect the human chain with nature, individuals must use all human ways of knowing, feeling, and understanding. It is "primarily through imagination and intuition that we can deepen the understanding we require to make decisions on ethical matters."[36] Of course, this process involves a grounded understanding of the action being evaluated in terms of the general natural-organic issues associated with the decision.

Related back to the dual-process theories of the mind (from Chapter 4), cognitive ease and positive emotions are linked to System 1 thinking by evolutionary processes. Negative emotions often require more cognitive effort than do positive ones. Consequently, information generating a negative emotion is processed more thoroughly and completely.[37] Eliciting those negative emotions may make individuals more cognitively aware of what is happening around them. Perhaps, in discussions about sustainability, the evocation of these negative emotions related to the degradation of the natural environment is necessary to promote change and to reconnect the human chain. Art often is a useful vehicle by which these negative emotions can be elicited among individuals. Changes in emotional response are expected byproducts of the manipulation of symbols through a moral imagination process. Moral imagination involves System 2 processes which override automatic cognition of System 1.[38]

Aesthetic Sensibility/Rationality

An aesthetic sensibility is the ability to see the design and aesthetic (beauty) aspects or implications of a context, situation, or decision.[39] To illustrate, John Dewey's popular notion of aesthetics from his philosophy on art and the human experience. Dewey considers aesthetics as a way of knowing or understanding the developmental nature of experience. Aesthetics allows meaning to be shared across individuals for the consummating their experience by using it to create shared ideals.[40] Dewey argues that aesthetic experiences are rooted in common human experiences that occur throughout peoples' lives. Aesthetic experiences produce knowledge by giving individuals a more intense experience of reality, offering new possibilities, and creating deeper and more insightful interactions between individuals.[41] They can serve as new narratives for communicating ecologizing values through the symbols they evoke. Aesthetics encourages the examination of how form is connected to both appearance and understanding, demonstrating how the same common form can elicit different interpretations across different people.[42] Thus, we think art and aesthetics can help lead to shared meaning about a particular phenomenon, like sustainability.

Aesthetics is a process that involves (on the individual level) a person's subjective experience with an object, symbol or form of creative expression followed by that person's communication of that particular experience to a group, which conveys the felt meaning to others.[43] This step occurs through dialogue, but also through the perception of other peoples' changed behaviors. The subjective experience involves an emotional component which is generated by the perceived beauty exhibited by the focal object.

The second step involves rational discourse as individuals intersubjectively communicate their experience to others in an effort to achieve a shared meaning.[44] Thus, implicit within our conception of aesthetics is a reasoned effort to rationally communicate a particular interpretation of an aesthetic experience. The way individuals perceive conventions of society and the world is manifested in the reasoned dialogue between organizational members. Although we believe that humans universally experience aesthetic responses, we acknowledge that one's particular experience is subject to cultural influences.[45] Aesthetic rationality, characterizing the second stage, shows that art, or any artifact, however subjectively it may be perceived, often leads to the expression of emotions intersubjectively or in an objectivized manner.

Aesthetic judgment is universally valid despite its large subjectivity component.[46] Interpretations of what is aesthetically pleasing involve an individual in searching for what is considered as good and enduring over time. This position assumes that humans are not only self-interested but are also emotional and social beings trying to navigate a complex environment. Therefore, we do not reject rational, economic assumptions of human behavior that emphasize personal instrumentality and extrinsic motivational tools (i.e., money, rewards). Rather, we expand on them by including assumptions from cognitive and social psychology that posit that humans are intrinsically motivated by other factors as well. Artistic expression in any form allows individuals to experience and share their interpretation of the meaning of art reflecting common belief systems. Works of art invite us to experience culturally shared meanings and values that are rooted in a commonly held constellation of beliefs and emotions. Experiences in nature can do much the same for human beings. This aesthetic experience varies from culture to culture but is often widely shared within a particular culture.[47]

Aesthetics is used here as more than a metaphor for appealing designs within organizations and in societies. Rather, aesthetics is deeply ingrained in every individual's cognition and thus can be used to achieve a broader shared understanding of critical issues facing organizations and human societies. In other words, given a near universal propensity of individuals to appreciate aesthetics (for which art of various forms is a common medium), we direct the conversation towards understanding a process by which aesthetics can be used as a tool for altering the perception of current shared understandings.

To purposely create a sustainable system requires an examination of the ways in which institutions affect cognitive frameworks and behavioral drives.[48] New institutional logics generated by both instrumental and aesthetic rationality must be coupled with new guidelines, practices, and actions led by institutional entrepreneurs who create change. Otherwise, the status quo is unlikely to be altered in the long term. The micro-level features of institutional logics influence how individuals understand their own identities.[49] Sustainability needs to be perceived as a core part of the organization's functioning through a change of the logics.

In other words, aesthetic sensibility or rationality is an important aspect of beginning to understand the need for system change towards ecologizing rather than economizing. When we can appreciate the beauty of a business, system, product, or work of art, we begin to see and experience new possibilities that were previously unavailable to us.

Notes

1. Thornton, P. H., & Ocasio, W. (2008). Institutional logics. In R. Greenwood, C. Oliver, K. Sahlin, & R. Suddaby (Eds.), *Handbook of organizational institutionalism*. Washington, DC: Sage.
2. Misangyi, V. F., Weaver, G. R., & Elms, H. (2008). Ending corruption: The interplay among institutional logics, resources, and institutional entrepreneurs. *Academy of Management Review*, 33(3), 750–770.
3. Paavola, J. (2008). Science and social justice in the governance of adaptation to climate change. *Environmental Politics*, 17(4), 644–659.
4. Scott, W. R. (2001). *Institutions and organizations* (2nd ed., p. 139). Thousand Oaks, CA: Sage Publications.
5. Bicchieri, C. (2003). Trust in society (Book). *Journal of Economic Literature*, 41(2), 630; Turner, R. (1991). *Truth and modality for knowledge representation*. Cambridge, MA: MIT Press.
6. Friedland, R., & Alford, R. R. (1991). Bringing society back in: Symbols, practices, and institutional contradictions. In W. W. Powell & P. J. Dimaggio (Eds.), *The new institutionalism in organizational analysis* Chicago: University of Chicago Press (pp. 232–263). Chicago and London; Thornton, P. H., & Ocasio, W. (1999). Institutional logics and the historical contingency of power in organizations: Executive succession in the higher education publishing industry, 1958–1990. *American Journal of Sociology*, 105(3), 801.
7. Perrone, V., Zaheer, A., & McEvily, B. (2003). Free to be trusted? Organizational constraints on trust in boundary spanners. *Organization Science*, 12(4), 92.
8. Sonpar, K., Handelman, J. M., & Dastmalchian, A. (2009). Implementing new institutional logics in pioneering organizations: The burden of justifying ethical appropriateness and trustworthiness. *Journal of Business Ethics*, 90(3), 348.
9. Hinings, B. (2012). Connections between institutional logics and organizational culture. *Journal of Management Inquiry*, 21(1), 98–101.
10. Tan, J., & Wang, L. (2011). MNC strategic responses to ethical pressure: An institutional logic perspective. *Journal of Business Ethics*, 98(3), 375.
11. Waddock, S. (2014). Wisdom and responsible leadership: Aesthetic sensibility, moral imagination, and systems thinking. In D. Koehn & D. Elm (Eds.), *Aesthetics and business ethics, issues in business ethics* (Vol. 41, pp. 129–147). Dordrecht, Netherlands: Springer.

12. Werhane, P. H. (1999). *Moral imagination and management decision-making*. New York: Oxford University Press.
13. Bullinger, B. (2014). Family affairs: Drawing on family logic and familiar regime of engagement to contract "close-up" views of individuals in conventalist and institutionalist reasoning. *Journal of Management Inquiry, 23*(3), 328–332.
14. Feinstein, D. Y., & Thornton, M. A. (2012). Reversible logic synthesis bashed on decision diagram variable ordering. *Journal of Multiple-Valued Logic and Soft Computing, 19*(4), 325.
15. Pernkopf-Konhausner, K. (2014). The competent actor: Bridging institutional logics and French pragmatist sociology. *Journal of Management Inquiry, 23*(3), 333–337.
16. Cloutier, C., & Langley, A. (2013). The logic of institutional logics: Insights from French pragmatist sociology. *Journal of Management Inquiry, 22*(4), 360–380.
17. Bullinger, B. (2014). Family affairs: Drawing on family logic and familiar regime of engagement to contract "close-up" views of individuals in conventalist and institutionalist reasoning. *Journal of Management Inquiry, 23*(3), 328–332; Dodier, N. (1993). Review article: Action as a combination of 'common worlds. *Sociological Review, 41*(3), 556–571.
18. Frederick, W. C. (1995). *Values, nature, and culture in the American corporation* (p. 172). New York: Oxford University Press.
19. Fort, T. L. (2007). *Business integrity, and peace: Beyond geopolitical and disciplinary boundaries*. Cambridge, UK: Cambridge University Press.
20. Fort, T. L. (2007). *Business integrity, and peace: Beyond geopolitical and disciplinary boundaries* (p. 654). Cambridge, UK: Cambridge University Press.
21. Carlsson, B., & Stankiewicz, R. (1995). On the nature, function, and composition of technological systems. In B. Carlsson (Ed.), *Technological systems and economic performance: The case of factory automation* (Vol. 5, pp. 21–56). Dordrecht: Springer. Economics of science, technology and innovation series.
22. Midttun, A. (2010). Montesquieu for the twenty-first century: Factoring civil society and business into global governance. *Corporate Governance, 10*(1), 97–109.
23. Narvaez, D., Arrows, F., Halton, E., Collier, B., & Enderle, G. (2019). *People and planet in need of sustainable wisdom. In indigenous sustainable wisdom: First-nation know-how for global flourishing* (pp. 1–24). New York: Peter Lang.
24. Arrows, F. (aka Donald Trent Jacobs) (2016). *Point of departure: Returning to our more authentic worldview for education and survival*. Charlotte, NC: IAP.
25. Ackoff, R. L. (1999). On learning and the systems that facilitate it. *Reflections, 1*(1), 14–24, 14.
26. Waddock, S. (2010). Finding wisdom within—The role of seeing and reflective practice in developing moral imagination, aesthetic sensibility, and systems understanding. *Journal of Business Ethics Education, 7*, 177–196; Waddock, S. (2014). Wisdom and responsible leadership: Aesthetic sensibility, moral imagination, and systems thinking. In D. Koehn & D. Elm (Eds.), *Aesthetics and business ethics, issues in business ethics* (Vol. 41, pp. 129–147). Dordrecht, Netherlands: Springer.
27. Waddock, S. (2014). Wisdom and responsible leadership: Aesthetic sensibility, moral imagination, and systems thinking. In D. Koehn & D. Elm (Eds.), *Aesthetics and business ethics, issues in business ethics* (Vol. 41, pp. 129–147). Dordrecht, Netherlands: Springer.

28. Werhane, P. H. (1999). *Moral imagination and management decision-making* (p. 93). New York: Oxford University Press.
29. Burch, G. F., Humphrey, R. H., & Batchelor, J. H. (2013). How great leaders use emotional labor: Insights from seven corporate executives. *Organizational Dynamic, 42*(2), 119–125.
30. Roca, E. (2010). The exercise of moral imagination in stigmatized work groups. *Journal of Business Ethics, 96*(1), 138.
31. Rooney, D., & McKenna, B. (2007). Wisdom in organizations: Whence and whither. *Social Epistemology, 21*(2), 113–138.
32. Edelman, M. J. (1985). *The symbolic uses of politics*. Urbana: University of Illinois Press.
33. Misangyi, V. F., Weaver, G. R., & Elms, H. (2008). Ending corruption: The interplay among institutional logics, resources, and institutional entrepreneurs. *The Academy of Management Review, 33*(3), 751.
34. Frederick, W. C. (2012). *Natural corporate management: From the big bang to wall street* (p. 141). Sheffield, UK: Greenleaf Publishing.
35. Babbit, 1919.
36. Somerville, M. A. (2006). *The ethical imagination: Journeys of the human spirit* (p. 71). Montreal: McGill-Queens University Press.
37. Nass, C., & Yen, C. (2010). *The man who lied to his laptop: What machines teach us about human relationships*. New York: Penguin Group.
38. Kool, W., McGuire, J. T., Rosen, Z. B., & Botvinick, M. M. (2010). Decision making and the avoidance of cognitive demand. *Journal of Experimental Psychology: General, 139*(4), 665–682.
39. Waddock, S. (2014). Wisdom and responsible leadership: Aesthetic sensibility, moral imagination, and systems thinking. In D. Koehn & D. Elm (Eds.), *Aesthetics and business ethics, issues in business ethics* (Vol. 41, pp. 129–147, 135). Dordrecht, Netherlands: Springer.
40. Dewey, J. (1931). *Philosophy and civilization*. New York: Minton, Balch & Company.
41. Harter, L. M., Leeman, M., Norander, S., Young, S. L., & Rawlins, W. K. (2008). The intermingling of aesthetic sensibilities and instrumental rationalities in collaborative arts studio. *Management Communication Quarterly, 21*(4), 426.
42. Linstead, S. (2006). Exploring culture with The Radio Ballads: Using aesthetics to facilitate change. *Management Decision, 44*(4), 474–485.
43. Shrivastava, P., Schumacher, G., Wasieleski, D. M., & Tasic, M. (2017). Aesthetic rationality in organizations: Toward developing a sensitivity for sustainability. *Journal of Applied Behavioral Science, 53*(3), 369–411.
44. Habermas, J. (1988). *Theory and practice*. London: Beacon.
45. Dutton, D. (2009). *Aesthetics and evolutionary psychology*. Oxford University Press.
46. Kant, I. (1790). *Critique of Judgment*. Prussia.
47. Schama, S. (1996). *Landscape and memory*. London: Vintage.
48. Misangi, V. F., Weaver, G. R., & Elms, H. (2008). Ending corruption: The interplay among institutional logics, resources, and institutional entrepreneurs. *The Academy of Management Review, 33*(3), 754.
49. Thornton, P. H., Ocasio, W., & Lounsbury, M. (2012). *The Institutional logics perspective: A new approach to culture, structure and process*. Oxford: Oxford University Press.

9 Narratives, Stories, and Memes

Balancing Economizing and Ecologizing

How do we even begin to think about moving societies and systems from economizing to ecologizing values? In this chapter, we argue that one vital starting point for considering the type of value change inherent in moving from economizing to ecologizing is to consider what stories we are telling ourselves about the world around us. It involves, as the previous chapter suggested, using moral imagination. Stories or narratives are important guides to behaviors, attitudes, and practices, whether at the individual, group, organizational, or societal/cultural level, as we have seen in earlier discussions of some of the dualities of individualism and collectivism, masculinity and femininity, and economizing and ecologizing.

Prominent stories and narratives are important because they help people understand their socio-ecological contexts and what is and is not appropriate in a given setting. They are cultural or public mythologies that shape our lives and frame the world for us.[1] Myths and stories—narratives—shape the values that people live by, as well their attitudes about each other, our localities, and about the natural environment. They shape how we develop our institutions, whether governmental, business, or in civil society. If we are influenced by stories, for example, that tell us that domination (dominion) over Nature is humankind's birthright, or that men should dominate over women, or that the rich should have power over the poor, then our behaviors and attitudes are likely to reflect those stories. These types of ideas are reflected in the values of economizing and power aggrandizement that we discussed earlier.

Narratives, stories, and the underlying memes—or core units of culture[2]—that support such narratives—are particularly important when we think about the major cultural and mindset shifts that are needed to bring about a flourishing world for all. Indeed, it is mindset shift that, according to systems theorist Donella Meadows, is the most important lever of systemic change—and the ability to transcend mindsets is even more important, as she articulated in a revised version of her article.[3] That is because human socio-economic systems are set in the context of ecological systems, which inherently have ecologizing built into them, unlike too many of today's human systems. Human institutions of all sorts, societies, economic systems, and natural ecological systems are all complex adaptive systems fraught with wicked problems, which we will explore in more depth below. These characteristics and the importance of narrative and memes have significant implications for efforts to bring about systemic change, that is, a shift towards ecologizing (or partnership) mindsets and cultures.

Narratives

Today's dominant logic, story, or narrative, as we have discussed earlier, is an economic one: that of neoliberalism. After being developed explicitly in the years after World War II and implemented explicitly and deliberately into economic, finance, business, and societal thinking for many years, neoliberalism's tenets have become so ingrained that we hardly realize they are part of a story we tell ourselves about how the world works.[4] Neoliberalism is in fact today's (economic) metanarrative.

A meta-narrative is an overarching narrative or story that interprets the world, circumstances, and events for people, much as the origin stories that we started this book with do for their particular cultures. The overarching nature of a metanarrative or, for that matter, other powerful narratives, provides a powerful guiding framework that helps structure what people believe and why they believe it, not to mention how institutions like businesses and other organizations operate. Sometimes called a grand narrative, a metanarrative is, like the origin stories explored in Chapter 1, an important device for framing our relationships to each other and to the world around us. That is why origin stories are so important: they can help us define who we are and what we need to do in the world around us. They provide guidance for how we think about the world, and how we develop the institutions and practices that ultimately shape cultures and the world.

The most classic form of narrative is what the great mythologist Joseph Campbell called the monomyth—the story of the hero's journey or quest in his classic book *The Hero with a Thousand Faces*. Campbell found versions of that myth in virtually all cultures around the planet, in part because of its universal appeal. Campbell's own words describe the hero's journey: "A hero ventures forth from the world of common day into a region of supernatural wonder: fabulous forces are there encountered and a decisive victory is won: the hero comes back from this mysterious adventure with the power to bestow boons on his fellow man."[5] This story has almost universal appeal—or resonance—which is why it is so common.

Such narratives can be particularly important when people from a diverse array of backgrounds, disciplines, or domains need to agree or unite on something,[6] as will be necessary in any shift towards ecologizing. Good stories and narratives, as Campbell implicitly notes, have

beginnings, middles, and ends, and frequently also antagonists and protagonists, with something important happening in the middle, while
narratives are often more general non-fiction that attempts to shape discourse around something important to its audience.[7] Narratives can, of
course, embed elements of stories in them, especially if they hope to gain
the power of persuasion needed to change mindsets. The hero's journey,
given its ubiquity, provides a useful exemplar for thinking about developing powerful new narratives like the one we posit about ecologizing.
Today's story, however, needs to be one of community or collective action
to reflect the reality that we all need to work together to bring about
needed system changes and that no single hero can accomplish that task
alone.

The original neoliberal narrative was promulgated after World War II
by a group of economists, historians, philosophers, and politicians who
met in Mont Pelerin Switzerland in 1947, though of course it built on
much prior work by a variety of economists. The Mont Pelerin group
met to discuss their fears about the world's economies, and became the
Mont Pelerin Society, which exists to this day. Their ideas contain key
characteristics of good narrative.

In what the Mont Pelerin group called its manifesto (and which became
neoliberalism, then translated into neoclassical economics), the Manifesto identified what the group saw to be a grave threat: "The central
values of civilization are in danger. . . . Dignity and freedom have already
disappeared." They posit an antagonist, that is, liberals, who spread the
threat of "creeds which, claiming the privilege of tolerance . . . seek only
to establish a position of power in which they can suppress and oblit-
erate all views but their own." The group implicitly identifies itself as the
hero or protagonist, that is, this "group of economists, historians, philosophers, and other students of public affairs . . . being desirous of . . .
promoting further intercourse and inviting the collaboration of other
like-minded persons." The Mont Pelerin group then sets forth a doctrine
of (neo)liberal thought to provide a counterpoint (i.e., a battle against)
the perceived threats, especially the "decline of belief in private property
and the competitive market," setting forth the fundamental tenets of neoliberalism to be discussed in the next section.[8] Notably, despite their ideological currency and alignment with conservative and libertarian values
today, the original Mont Pelerin manifesto claimed that "the group does
not aspire to conduct propaganda. It seeks to establish no meticulous and
hampering orthodoxy,"[9] though these ideas are now firmly embedded in
conservative ideological thinking, at least as expressed by conservative
think tanks.[10]

What is important to notice here is the ways in which the Mont Pelerin group used the core elements of narrative and story to make their
ideas compelling. That use of narrative and, importantly, as we will see
in the next section, of the memes that underpin and construct the various

tellings of the story, provide a lesson for considering how to move from today's neoliberal and economizing values towards ecologizing values and a new story that supports them. Key to this shift is understanding the power of memes in the construction and telling of narratives.

Memes

Memes, according to Susan Blackmore who has studied them intensively, are the core units of culture. They can be words, phrases, ideas, symbols, images, pieces of art, or any other cultural artifact that replicates from person to person, or, more accurately, from mind to mind.[11] Memes are important because they provide the foundational elements for narratives. Stories and narratives are constituted from memes, which can be put together in a variety of ways by different actors for their own uses. Because of the replicability of the memes and their underlying meanings, even when the actual stories or narratives differ somewhat from each other, much the same inferences and meanings can be drawn from them. Memes, Blackmore notes, are what shape attitudes, behaviors, beliefs, mindsets, and, in the end, what people think and how they behave.[12] Not only are memes the basic units of culture, they are also the foundational elements in stories and narratives that work well when they resonate broadly and are repeated often.

When the same memes are used over and over again to promote the same message, and when they resonate broadly with a variety of people, then that narrative begins to shape the culture, values, and practices in a context.[13] Resonance happens in part when the memes seem relevant to what people already believe.[14] They become as natural-seeming as the very air that we breathe—until, as former UK Prime Minister Margaret Thatcher famously stated—it seems like there are no alternatives to whatever story they are telling. That is what has happened with neoliberalism, whose memes have been endlessly and quite deliberately repeated by economists and others in sources as diverse as economics and finance textbooks; business education; business and economics conferences; public policy contexts, including through legislators and judges; and in the popular press and all sorts of other media. This deliberateness followed a strategy articulated in 1970 by then future U.S. Supreme Court Justice Lewis F. Powell in what has come to be called the Powell Memorandum.[15] It has been successful in part because neoliberalism is based on a few core tenets or memes that are often repeated by conservative thinkers, while the messaging and memes from more progressive thinkers are much more diffuse and seem to lack similar resonance.[16]

Neoliberalism as Narrative and Memes

The tenets of neoliberalism, briefly alluded to earlier, are based on a set of core memes that apparently have wide resonance and can be shaped into a variety of related narratives depending on the relevant context and purposes. Neoliberalism's memes include dominant economic goals of continual growth and maximization of wealth by companies for one set of stakeholders—the shareholders. These ideas are accompanied by a clear though less explicit emphasis on the accumulation of financial and material wealth through consumption and materialism. Only one form of capital is readily recognized under neoliberalism: financial wealth.

Certain core values (also memes) are stated clearly and often, many of which were articulated at the Mont Pelerin meeting held in Switzerland in 1947.[17] Those memes include individual freedom or liberty (which sometimes gets translated into more extreme forms of individualism, and which is supported by self-interested, rational, and responsible individuals, and even libertarianism. Other values (memes) include free markets, free trade across national boundaries and consequent attendant emphasis on globalization. Under neoliberalism's tenets—and a widespread belief today as a result of it—is the belief that the best government is the least or most limited government, in other words, government should take a laissez-faire approach to businesses and societies (and, actually, societies are not even believed to be real).[18]

This set of ideas or memes represents a set of assumptions that can be built into a range of stories and narratives that humans tell each other about how the world works. One problem, from the perspective of things like climate and sustainability crises, growing inequality, and political divides between conservatives and liberals, is that the narrative has some wrong assumptions. Another is that this set of ideas ignores the impacts of economic activities on people and their communities and societies, not to mention Nature. The economic policies and business practices promoted by this narrative are thus precisely the factors that are resulting in increasing civilizational threats for humanity around climate change and inequality,[19] to name only two significant issues.

Let us explore some of these assumptions a bit. For one thing, there is significant evidence from biology, not to mention spiritual practices and human communities in general, that human beings (and even other creatures) are not entirely and only self-interested maximizers,[20] as neoliberalism would have it. Further, the lack of inclusion of and attention to societal and ecological impacts of continual economic and material growth are having devastating effects on the natural environment and, in particular, on the climate that supports human civilization.[21] Neoliberalism fosters what some ecologists call a take-make-waste attitude in a very linear progression. That progression moves from resource extraction (or exploitation) from nature, to production processes that sometimes produce toxic byproducts (and even products). These products and some of the toxins generated are then released into the world, that is, to a throwaway consumerist culture in which many people in the so-called developed world think nothing of simply discarding items after a few uses.[22] The growth-at-all-costs mentality deeply embedded in neoliberalism and its child, neoclassical economics, causes companies and the financial markets that support them to foster ever greater growth without regard to any social or ecological consequences. All of these processes take place, however, in a context of both complexity and wickedness, as we discuss in the next section, which makes figuring out how to deal with somewhat problematic if we ignore the effects of the dominant narrative on this system.

Bringing About Culture Change Towards Ecologizing Values

If culture is to shift from the economizing values of neoliberalism towards the nature-based values of ecologizing, it is important to understand the nature and complexity of the socio-economic–ecological systems that human societies are. To do so we need to think about three important aspects of systemic change: the power and role of narrative and memes, as discussed in the previous chapter, in providing guidance for human systems; the nature of complex adaptive systems; and the nature of what are known as wicked problems.

Complexity and Wickedness

The reason narratives are important to thinking about shifting towards ecologizing and away from economizing is that the type of systemic change that is needed to contend with the consequences of today's system takes place in a context of both complexity and wickedness. In such contexts, where there is great dynamism and where different elements can interact in unexpected ways, there is little that actually operates in the type of linear, cause–effect pattern that would make planning appropriate changes relatively easy. In such contexts, because of the nature of both complexity and wickedness, little changes can have big impacts, while supposedly large changes might not have the desired effect at all. To understand that reality and hence why narrative and memes are so important, we need to think about the nature of complex adaptive systems and wicked problems briefly.[23]

Complex adaptive systems (for short, complex systems or complexity), a category to which human and ecological systems certainly belong, have certain characteristics. They are made of numerous interacting, interdependent, and interconnected aspects or elements. Interactions tend operate in nonlinear and constantly changing patterns of interaction in processes that are emergent and not entirely predictable. Human social systems, too, are diverse and nonlinear in their operations. Successful or healthy complex systems—like the natural or ecological systems that feel alive as discussed earlier—tend towards ever-greater complexity, often operating at what complexity scientists call the "edge of chaos," in other words, at the edge of some sort of fundamental state change.

Such systems are self-organizing in that there is no central power or source guiding their emerging processes, yet they can exist for substantial periods of time in a state of dynamic equilibrium. For social systems that are healthy, as discussed in thinking about what gives life to systems, that means that change and, to some extent, innovation is constantly taking place.[24] In complex systems, however, there is no clear beginning or end to events, processes, or interactions. Instead, they are tangled up together, so that when something happens in one area, there can be unintended effects or consequences in other areas, making the system inherently dynamic and unpredictable. As with all living systems, the system itself needs to be considered holistically, not broken into its component parts—or it is no longer a system.

Wicked Problems

Compare complex systems with systems embedded wicked problems, with which human social economic and socio-ecological interactions are fraught, and we begin to see many similarities. Wicked problems are human and ecological issues that are inherently complex, whose boundaries span across other issues making it unclear where one begins and making it difficult, if not impossible to determine when they are resolved or solved. Such problems are ill-formulated because of their complexity and poorly structured. They also have numerous different stakeholders, who are likely to have different points of view on everything from the nature, causes, and definitions of the problem(s), to the best means of dealing with it, to what a good solution looks like. Because of these characteristics, there tends to be no obvious "stopping rule" to tell people when the issue is finished or solved—and, in addition, once a change is set in motion, it is virtually impossible to reverse course because of the dynamism, interconnectedness, and interactivity of the various aspects and processes involved.[25]

Narrative, Stories, Memes, and Systemic/Cultural Change

Pulling together all of the ideas raised in this chapter, we begin to see a rationale for focusing so heavily on narrative and memes in the contexts of complexity and wickedness. Since these contexts provide little linearity and a lot of uncertainty and unpredictability, creating major systemic change is very difficult and unpredictable itself. We know from the experience of the former Soviet countries that central planning does not seem to work in such contexts, not to mention how frequently planned change efforts fail. Human systems have multiple component parts, cultural values and norms, and different levels of practice, technologies, and institutions, all of which are subject to change.

As Meadows pointed out, however, there is a hierarchy of what she called levers available to change agents who would change the system.[26] Thinking holistically about a given system, at whatever level is appropriate, means beginning to understand that system in its interconnectivity with other systems, both at its own level and with respect to smaller and larger connected systems. It also means seeing the interrelationships that exist among the problems or issues of interest with other problems and issues, thereby placing the whole system into its broader context. Doing that helps ground the insight that Meadows had in thinking about systemic change that the most powerful change levers are not the technical ones of constants and parameters (like standards or taxes), buffers, structures, delays, negative feedback loops or ways around them, or how information flows, although all of these places are potential intervention points. Nor, she argued, are the most powerful levers changing structures; shifting the rules or goals; or evolving the system by adding, changing, or subtracting system elements, although all of these more structural or infrastructural elements are in fact levers of change and need to be addressed at some point.[27]

What Meadows pointed to in her initial version of her powerful paper, "Leverage Points: Places to Intervene in a System," was the importance of changing the "mindsets or paradigm out of which the system—its goals, structures, rules, delays, parameters—arises."[28] In a revised version of the paper Meadows went even further, arguing that the "power to transcend paradigms" is actually the most effective change lever.[29] What these insights mean in the context of the cultural shift from economizing (neoliberal) values towards ecologizing values is that the guiding or metanarrative embedded with resonant memes may be the most powerful tool in bringing about change. That is because a guiding narrative which as we discussed above is the story provides a framework for developing attitudes, insights, values, and ultimately practices and behaviors that then shape the system. That is, the guiding narrative with its hopefully resonant memes is what infuses minds—and mindsets—with ideas, values, norms, and ways of behaving (much as neoliberalism has done for businesses and, ultimately, whole economies).

Today's mindsets have been infused with neoliberalism—like the very air we breathe. Shifting away from neoliberalism, because it has become so dominant an understanding, at least in Western (and Western-izing) cultures, means finding an equally compelling and resonant set of memes and creating narratives and stories embedded with the core characteristics of good stories, just as the Mont Pelerin and its subsequent adherents have done. Good stories, remember, have heroes or protagonists, antagonists or anti-heroes, and major threats or obstacles that need to be overcome. The move from economizing to ecologizing may well contain the seeds of such a good story and provide viable bases for new types of actions and interactions as we briefly describe next and explore more deeply in the next several chapters.

Restorying Economies to Ecologies

Given neoliberalism's aversion to believing that societies even exist and their neglect of the natural environment, combined with the dominance of its messaging, shifting today's paradigm and mindsets towards ecologizing and civilizing is no easy task. Yet, as reports from the IPCC—which in 2018 stated that there were only twelve years to do so before runaway climate change would happen[30]— and others[31] suggest, there is a clear imperative to move towards something like that—and to do so sooner rather than later.

As we noted earlier, good stories start with identifying a threat or conflict, have both protagonists and antagonists, and, as in the hero's journey, some actions or journeys that the hero takes to find the "boon" to bring back to the regular world. Certainly, issues of climate change, collapsing ecosystems, growing inequality, new diseases, and political divisiveness pose considerable threats to the long-term well-being of humanity. As antagonist, we might posit neoliberalism and all of the ideologues who seem unable to see beyond its tenets—when it is the idea of continual unending material and wealth growth, and, for example, the lack of emphasis on societal and ecological considerations, that fundamentally create the problematic trajectory humanity is currently on. As protagonist, we could posit new storytellers and narrators, who help to frame what a world of ecologizing might look like, while recognizing that the journey to change might be difficult, even extremely difficult, given recent understanding of climate scientists.

Moving towards ecologizing means creating new framings around developing a flourishing world, where dignity and wellbeing for all—values articulated, for example, by the Humanistic Management movement[32]— are paramount rather than financial and material wealth. Very briefly, new memes around wellbeing and dignity for all, including all of the world's living beings and ecosystems, and planetary stewardship, a concept that draws from many of the world's great spiritual traditions, might be resonant. The idea of dignity for all is resonant with ancient and many Indigenous traditions where people believe that there is spirit in all things and that, therefore, they need to be valued in and of themselves.[33] Values oriented towards healthy and flourishing communities at many different levels, and recognition of the "alive" nature of human systems could build in aspects of what gives life to systems as discussed earlier.

In creating narratives that support ecologizing, we will need to reconsider and redefine what is meant by wealth. Perhaps moving towards concepts of wellbeing for all; perhaps towards more relational ways of being in the world, for example, communities in which people take care of each other; perhaps towards according dignity towards all human beings, not to mention all other living beings. Considered much more holistically than in neoliberalism, wealth can take multiple forms— human wealth in social and other relationships; wealth in intellectual capabilities, creativity, and innovativeness; or natural and ecological wealth.[34] From this emergent perspective, the bounty of the planet needs to be replenished, restored, and regenerated in ways that can support the thriving of all living beings, and, of course, spiritual wealth that comes from connectedness—to self, others, nature, and higher purposes and powers. This new mindset of ecologizing needs to recognize and reward understandings of cyclicality, interconnectedness, and the intrinsic value of Nature and all of her creatures—for their own sakes— not just for what material benefit they can bring to human beings.

In any restorying, freedom and democracy build on the five sets of core values that Haidt uncovered, which, as discussed earlier, need to be encompassed to appeal to many people. Those values, as discussed, include care/harm, fairness reciprocity, and liberty. In addition, they encompass loyalty to one's own group—and, we would argue, to the bigger whole, authority and respect for institutions that support the common good, and the integrity (purity and sanctity) of the system as a whole. In such an approach, we would argue not for free but rather for fair markets, not just for globalism but for a federalist system that respects that the best work gets done at the most local possible level, while still respecting the global whole in a both/and logic. Both public and private goods would be respected and bringing in more feminine and collectivist values would foster not just competition but also, and very importantly, collaboration and cooperation at all levels.

The rule of law becomes important to sustaining an ecologizing culture, which means re-energizing and re-integrating the importance of good government (and good governance at the global scale) at relevant levels. Governments can help avoid market failures and cope with any "externalities," that is, negative byproducts in the system, with the recognition that they too are part of the whole that needs to be made healthy and supportive for all of life. In this context, business purposes would shift away from maximization of shareholder wealth towards what Donaldson and Walsh called collective value,[35] value that serves the community without incurring dignity violations.[36] Collective value absent dignity violations, as these authors put it, is an important step towards recognizing that we humans live on and rely on one planet, each other, and a flourishing ecosystem with all of its manifestations for our own well-being. Effectively, the "restorying" is an effort to move towards an understanding of our world as integrated ecologies, linked ecosystems—both human and natural—that deserve to be treated holistically and honored for what they are.

The ideas above obviously only guide us in the direction of a new ecologizing mindset. But they may provide sufficient guidance for us to begin to think, as we do in the next sections, more explicitly about what a flourishing mindset would be. They can indicate how consideration of planetary and human boundaries can be baked into economic and societal thinking in a more ecologizing framework. And they can help us understand how, in the end, we can reconnect the now-broken human chain—the link between humans and our natural environment.

Notes

1. McNeill, W. H. (1982). The care and repair of public myth. *Foreign Affairs*, *61*(1), 1–13.
2. Blackmore, S. (2000). The meme machine (Vol. 25). Oxford: Oxford Paperbacks.
3. Meadows, D. (2007). *Leverage points: Places to intervene in a system*. DonellaMeadows.org. Retrieved from: http://leadership-for-change.souther nafricatrust.org/downloads/session_2_module_2/Leverage-Points-Places-to-Intervene-in-a-System.pdf.
4. Waddock, S. (2016). Foundational memes for a new narrative about the role of business in society. *Humanistic Management Journal*, *1*, 91–105.
5. Campbell, J. (2008). *The hero with a thousand faces* (Vol. 17, p. 23). Novato, CA: New World Library.
6. Moezzi, M., Janda, K. B., & Rotmann, S. (2017). Using stories, narratives, and storytelling in energy and climate change research. *Energy Research & Social Science*, *31*, 1–10.
7. Moezzi, M., Janda, K. B., & Rotmann, S. (2017). Using stories, narratives, and storytelling in energy and climate change research. *Energy Research & Social Science*, *31*, 1–10.
8. Quotes in this paragraph are from: Mont Pelerin Society. (undated). *Statement of aims*. Retrieved from: www.montpelerin.org/statement-of-aims/.
9. Mont Pelerin Society. (undated). *Statement of aims*. Retrieved from: www. montpelerin.org/statement-of-aims/.
10. For an analysis at demonstrates the power of neoliberal ideas, see: Waddock, S. (2018). Narrative, memes and the prospect of large system change. *Humanistic Management Journal*, *3*, 17–45. Retrieved from: http://link-springer-com-443.webvpn.jxutcm.edu.cn/article/10.1007/s41463-018-0039-9.
11. Blackmore, S. (2000). *The meme machine* (Vol. 25). Oxford: Oxford Paperbacks. Also, Blackmore, S. (1998). Imitation and the definition of a meme. *Journal of Metrics*, *2*(2), 1–13; Blackmore, S. (2000). The power of memes. *Scientific American*, *383*(4), 64–73.
12. Blackmore, S. (2000). The power of memes. *Scientific American*, *383*(4), 64–73.
13. Atran, S. (2001). The trouble with memes. *Human Nature*, *12*(4), 351–381.
14. Blackmore, S. (2000). *The meme machine* (Vol. 25). Oxford: Oxford Paperbacks.
15. Powell, L. F. (1971). *Confidential memorandum: Attack of American free enterprise system*. Retrieved from: http://reclaimdemocracy.org/powell_memo_lewis/.
16. Waddock, S. (2018). Narrative, memes and the prospect of large system change. *Humanistic Management Journal*, *3*, 17–45. Retrieved from:

http://link-springer-com-443.webvpn.jxutcm.edu.cn/article/10.1007/s41463-018-0039-9.

17. Mont Pelerin Society. (undated). *Statement of aims*. Retrieved from: www.montpelerin.org/statement-of-aims/. For more history, see, e.g., Butler, E. (undated). *A short history of the Mont Pelerin Society* (Based on a History of the Mont Pelerin Society by Max Hartwell). Retrieved from: www.montpelerin.org/wp-content/uploads/2015/12/Short-History-of-MPS-2014.pdf.

18. These ideas are fully developed in Waddock, S. (2016). Foundational memes for a new narrative about the role of business in society. *Humanistic Management Journal*, 1, 91–105. See also, Waddock, S. (2018). Narrative, memes and the prospect of large system change. *Humanistic Management Journal*, 3, 17–45.

19. E.g., Diamond, J. (2005). *Collapse: How societies choose to fail or succeed.* New York: Penguin. See also Lovins, H., Wijkman, A., Fullerton, J., Wallis, S., & Maxton, G. (2016). *A finer future is possible: How humanity can avoid system collapse and craft a better economic system.* Club of Rome. Retrieved from: www.clubofrome.org/wp-content/uploads/2016/08/A-finer-future.pdf.

20. See, for example, De Waal, F. B. (1996). *Good natured* (No. 87). Cambridge, MA: Harvard University Press; De Waal, F. B. (2008). Putting the altruism back into altruism: The evolution of empathy. *Annual Review of Psychology*, 59, 279–300. Also, Pirson, M. (2017). *Humanistic management: Protecting dignity and promoting well-being.* Cambridge, UK: Cambridge University Press.

21. Lovins, L. H., Wallis, S., Wijkman, A., & Fullerton, J. (2018). *A finer future: Creating an economy in service to life, A Report to the Club of Rome.* Gabriola Island, BC, Canada: New Society Publishers.

22. Hawken, P. (2010). *The ecology of commerce: A declaration of sustainability.* New York: Harper Business.

23. The ideas in this section are drawn from Waddock, S., Dentoni, D., Meszoely, G., & Waddell, S. (2015). The complexity of wicked problems in large system change. *Journal of Organizational Change Management*, 28(6), 993–1012, where they were drawn from a wide range of different sources in complexity science and wicked problems theorizing.

24. Just a sampling of sources about complexity theory along with chaos theory includes Capra, F. (2005). Complexity and life. *Theory, Culture & Society*, 22(5), 33–44; Gleick, J. (1988). *Chaos: Making a new science.* New York: Viking; Kauffman, S. (1995). *At home in the Universe: The search for the laws of self-organization and complexity.* New York: Oxford University Press; Lissack, M. R., & Letiche, H. (2002). Complexity, emergence, resilience, and coherence: Gaining perspective on organizations and their study. *Emergence*, 4(3), 72–94; Nicolis, G., & Prigogine, I. (1989). *Exploring complexity: An introduction.* New York: W. H. Freeman and Company.

25. These ideas were first articulated by Rittel, H. W., & Webber, M. M. (1973). Dilemmas in a general theory of planning. *Policy Sciences*, 4(2), 155–169, though Churchman published his own insights about them earlier in Churchman, C. W. (1967). Guest editorial: Wicked problems. *Management Science*, 14(4), B141–B142.

26. Meadows, D. (2007). *Leverage points: Places to intervene in a system.* DonellaMeadows.org. Retrieved from: http://leadership-for-change.southernafricatrust.org/downloads/session_2_module_2/Leverage-Points-Places-to-Intervene-in-a-System.pdf.

27. Meadows, D. (2007). *Leverage points: Places to intervene in a system.* DonellaMeadows.org. Retrieved from: http://leadership-for-change.souther

nafricatrust.org/downloads/session_2_module_2/Leverage-Points-Places-to-Intervene-in-a-System.pdf.

28. Meadows, D. (2007). *Leverage points: Places to intervene in a system.* DonellaMeadows.org. Retrieved from: http://leadership-for-change.souther nafricatrust.org/downloads/session_2_module_2/Leverage-Points-Places-to-Intervene-in-a-System.pdf.

29. Meadows, D. (2007). *Leverage points: Places to intervene in a system.* DonellaMeadows.org. Retrieved from: http://leadership-for-change.souther-nafricatrust.org/downloads/session_2_module_2/Leverage-Points-Places-to-Intervene-in-a-System.pdf.

30. IPCC (Intergovernmental Panel on Climate Change) (2018). Global warming of 1.5°C, Summary for Policymakers. Retrieved from: http://report.ipcc.ch/ sr15/pdf/sr15_spm_final.pdf.

31. E.g., Bendell, J. (2018). Deep adaptation: A map for navigating climate tragedy. IFLAS Occasional Paper 2 (www.iflas.info). Retrieved from: www.life worth.com/deepadaptation.pdf.

32. E.g., International Humanistic Management Association. Retrieved from: http://humanisticmanagement.international/what-is-humanistic-manage ment/, and the Humanistic Management Network, www.humanetwork. org/. For an academic perspective, see, e.g., Melé, D. (2016). Understanding humanistic management. *Humanistic Management Journal, 1*(1), 33–55; Pirson, M. (2017). *Humanistic management: Protecting dignity and promoting well-being.* Cambridge, UK: Cambridge University Press.

33. Waddock, S. (2017). *Healing the world: Today's shamans as difference makers.* London: Routledge.

34. For one approach to multiple capitals, see Lovins, L. H., Wallis, S., Wijkman, A., & Fullerton, J. (2018). *A finer future: Creating an economy in service to life, A Report to the Club of Rome.* Gabriola Island, BC, Canada: New Society Publishers.

35. Donaldson, T., & Walsh, J. P. (2015). Toward a theory of business. *Research in Organizational Behavior, 35,* 181–207.

36. The ideas in these paragraphs were initially laid out in: Waddock, S. (2016). Foundational memes for a new narrative about the role of business in society. *Humanistic Management Journal, 1,* 91–105.

Section III
Ecologizing Mindsets for Sustainability

How do we move towards rethinking the dualisms discussed in the previous sections as dualities that help us create more integrated—ecologizing—mindsets? That is the focus of this last section on developing ecologizing mindsets for sustainability. To accomplish this task, we consider the implications of adult development theory, as well as ideas about fixed and growth mindsets, so we can understand how mindsets develop and potentially change towards what we label "unchained thinking."

We then consider how mindsets are being shifted by important new frameworks that help us all gain much greater understanding of systems—and of how today's systems are both related to and integrated with the planet as a whole. These new frameworks include ideas about what is known as the Great Acceleration, planetary boundaries, and the ways in which humans are affecting planetary conditions in the new era being called the Anthropocene to reflect that emerging reality. These frameworks help us understand the important impacts and implications of humanity's disconnect from nature—and provide new ways of making connections that have been hard to do in the past.

We argue that by rethinking economics and neoliberalism, we can potentially work our way towards a reconnected, re-integrated future in which all can flourish, and we use the United Nations' aspirational Sustainable Development Goals (SDGs) to help point change makers and, indeed, all of us, in desired directions. In the concluding chapter, we make a case for re-storying and reconnecting us humans with ourselves, with others in community, and with nature, as a way of repairing the broken links in our human chain.

10 Ecological Mindset

Since mindset shift is such an important aspect of moving towards ecologizing and away from economizing, it is important to begin considering what mindsets actually are and how they might change. To do so, we begin with a discussion of adult development theory, as we believe that is important to understanding how people think and why they might believe what they do. Then we briefly move to a discussion of fixed versus growth mindsets, arguing that shifting to ecologizing as a way of being in the world will likely demand fairly high levels of cognitive (and moral) development, along with a growth mindset.

Adult Development Theories

There are numerous theories of adult development, which all argue that adults, like children, go through certain stages of development. One of the pioneers of developmental theory was Jean Piaget, a Swiss developmental psychologist, whose focus was on children.[1] Piaget, in his studies of children, found that they go through four developmental stages, which he termed sensorimotor, preoperational, concrete operational, and formal operational. In the sensorimotor stage, which lasts from birth to 18 to 24 months, the child learns through experiences, particularly through trial and error, but does not necessarily use symbols to understand the world. Preoperational or egocentric thinking occurs from about age two to seven, when memory and imagination begin to develop. At this stage the child mostly sees him- or herself as the center of the world, because their perspective is limited to their own perceptions, with the self at the center of those perceptions.

When children enter the concrete operational stage at around seven to 11 years, they enter what Jesuits call the age of reason. In other words, they are more logical in their thinking and better able to use symbols and ideas to work things through using their thought processes. During this stage, children can begin to reason without necessarily having direct experience of a phenomenon. At the formal operational stage, after age 11 or so, children can begin thinking abstractly, begin to hypothesize about the world based on what they already know, and can manipulate or think about multiple things at once.

Ethicist Lawrence Kohlberg[2] pushed these developmental stages into the moral realm, arguing that there were three main stages of moral reasoning. Pre-conventional reasoning includes early stages of obedience and punishment, and pre-school stages of self-interest. Conventional reasoning, which begins during the school years, includes a stage of conformity and "interpersonal accord," which means that moral reasoning includes getting approval from others, and a later stage that Kohlberg called authority and social order, which orients the person towards the rules of the tribe or society (rather than peers) and maintaining the social order. Kohlberg found that in the men (he only studied men) that he studied, most people remained at conventional levels of moral reasoning. Other studies note that moral reasoning follows cognitive reasoning. In other words, one cannot be at a higher stage of moral than cognitive reasoning.

Kohlberg, building on the work of adult development theorists, also found that adult men can develop through two more stages, which he termed post-conventional stages. In the first post-conventional stage, labeled social contract, which later teens and young adults can (but do not always) enter into, moral reasoning begins to incorporate principles like mutual benefit and reciprocity, as well as utilitarian types of thinking. The last stage Kohlberg described he called that of universal principles, a stage in which moral reasoning is based on principles that go beyond mutual benefit.

Other adult developmental theorists outline related stages of development. For example, Robert Kegan, a psychologist at Harvard, identified five stages of development that occur throughout the lifespan.[3] The first stage is the impulsive mind in early childhood, and the second is the imperial mind most dominant in adolescence plus in 6% of adults. The third stage is the socialized mind, which Kegan said 58% of adults reach. The fourth—and mature—stage is the self-authoring mind, which Kegan claimed only 35% of adults reach. He also identified a fifth stage, self-transforming mind stage, which only reached by 1% of the adult population. In other words, in Kegan's perspective only about 35% of the adult population reach one of the higher stages of development, with the rest kind of "stuck" in an earlier stage of development. At each phase of development, the capacity to incorporate broader ways of thinking and different types of perspectives enlarges.

Other theories of adult development lay out different numbers of stages with different labels. For example, in researching women, Carol Gilligan, also identified three stages, pre-, conventional, and post-conventional development.[4] Gilligan found that pre-conventional individuals emphasize individual survival, essentially selfishness. At the conventional stage, women transitioned from selfish to responsibility for others, where self-sacrifice is viewed as goodness. The post-conventional stage transitions to a perspective of nonviolence, that is, not hurting one's self or others. Gilligan's "ethics of care," then, focuses in on changes in the self in how the self relates to others rather than the more cognitive processes Kohlberg emphasized. Similar processes are evident in Kohlberg's stages as well, for pre-conventional thinkers are self-focused or instrumental in their relations with others, while conventional thinkers can first recognize intentionality (for good or ill) in others and then are able to see that there are abstract normative systems, i.e., social or community-based systems, in the world. Post-conventional thinkers in Kohlberg's stages recognize a contractually based system that provides welfare benefits for others and then are able to engage ideas of mutual respect, seeing how actions impact others.[5]

Another important set of stages was identified in the book *Spiral Dynamics*, based on the work of Clare Graves, written by Don Beck and Christopher Cowan.[6] Using colors to explicate the stages, Beck and Cowan noted that individuals move from "beige," or archaic, instinctive, and automatic thinking, to a "purple" stage of animistic, tribalistic, and magico-mystical thinking. The next stage in spiral dynamics is "red," where people are still egocentric and exploitive (compare to the instrumental orientation of Kohlberg's early pre-conventional thinking, for example), and tend to be impulsive and rebellious. The next "blue" stage emphasizes order, right, and wrong through absolutist thinking, with obedience a dominant characteristic, along with authoritarianism if in a position of power. The "orange" stage is one of autonomy and achievement, characterized by materialism, strategic thinking, ambition, and individualism. The later stage of "green" emphasizes egalitarian values, focused on community approval and equality, tending to be relativistic, sensitive, and pluralistic. Still later stages, "yellow" and "turquoise," which Beck and Cowan note that few people reach, emphasize holistic, global thinking, and the ability to think systemically, conceptualize, and ecologize in flexible ways.

Integral theorist Ken Wilber argues for a similar set of stages, also using colors to indicate stage of development, picking up on work by other theorists. In later stages of development, i.e., teal, turquoise, indigo, violet, and beyond in his framing, people move beyond individualist (green) thinking towards being autonomous (teal), able to think abstractly (turquoise), towards being aware of constructs (turquoise), aware of ego (indigo), and finally towards a transpersonal awareness (violet). As with Gilligan and Kohlberg, from whom he draws, Wilber's integral theory shows people moving from pre-personal stages towards personal, towards transpersonal stages of development, following much along the lines of other developmental theorists.

Kegan ultimately claimed that to avoid the problem of being "in over our heads" in the modern world, many more adults needed to reach at least the fourth stage of development, or the self-authoring mind.[7] As we have seen, each of these theories shows people moving along a similar trajectory of development, despite differences in labeling (and colors), and we could go through a variety of other developmental theories to find similar patterns. Basically, the trajectory, which everyone has to go through as they grow and develop, moves from a self-centric orientation, towards an "other" (my tribe, my society) orientation, towards a more holistic or global, transpersonal orientation in which consideration of multiple (sometimes conflicting or paradoxical) perspectives becomes possible.

Understanding this evolution in reasoning, thinking, and perceptions is why consideration of developmental stage is important in thinking about the shift towards ecologizing. The ecological and social concerns that are paramount today have magnified the complexity of coping in the world successfully for many people, and they have also expanded the need for a more holistic, integrated perspective that comes when people have more fully matured along the adult development spectrum of possibilities. Although no one has tested this idea empirically, it seems likely that moving towards an ecologizing mindset demands that more, perhaps many more, adults be at these higher stages of reasoning—or at least open to thinking about new ways of being in the world.

Fixed and Growth Mindsets

Another way of thinking about shifting the mindset and narrative towards ecologizing, as we argue is needed, is to think about the implications of what psychologist Carol Dweck actually calls mindset theory. In her work, Dweck explores the fundamental beliefs that people have about whether or not they can continue to learn throughout life or have a "fixed" amount of talent and intelligence.[8] People with a fixed mindset tend to believe that they are born with a given amount of intelligence (or talent), a set personality and moral character—and that they are basically incapable of changing those things about themselves. Dweck observes that such people feel a constant need to prove their intelligence throughout their lives, to gain external confirmation that, for example, they are smart, have a great personality, or good character.

In contrast to people with a fixed mindset, stand others who have what Dweck calls a growth mindset. Such people believe that they are capable of learning and change throughout their lives, and that where they began is just a starting point. For such people, individual transformation—and other types of transformation—is not only possible but also desirable. The growth mindset fosters a willingness to work hard, even in the face of obstacles, and to thrive even in difficult circumstances, because working harder or more is seen not only as possible but as the way to overcome obstacles. For growth-minded folks, failure is another challenge, an opportunity to try something new or learn some new things, while for fixed-minded folks, failure defines them. Failure, of course, is painful, according to Dweck, but it need not be definitional—and one can learn from it.

In developing a third way of thinking about mindset, Buchanan and Kern argue that fixed and growth mindsets exist at different levels of maturity—or what we earlier called developmental stages. They use yet another developmental framework, that of Bill Torbert. Torbert argues that mature people move from the developmental logic of being experts (38% of people) to achievers (30% of people) to individualists (10% of people), where they are able to shift from ego to ecosystem awareness. Finally, if they achieve that level—which only about 4% of people do—they become strategists, where they can embrace the tenets of an ecosystem worldview.[9] What these authors term a benefit mindset is aligned with what Rimanoczy calls a sustainability mindset[10] in its ability to grasp the system and its implications, as well as its ecological orientation. People with a benefit mindset, according to Buchanan & Kern, seek to "be well" and also to "do good," by focusing purposefully on why they do what they do, and attempt to contribute meaningfully to opening up new possibilities and opportunities in the future.[11] The key insight here is that developmental maturity and growth is needed, as is implied in all of the adult development models, for people to attain the type of ecological and systemic understandings needed to engage with ecologizing as a new way of being in the world.

Unchained Thinking

Think about the societal transformations that we are arguing are needed to shift towards ecologizing and away from the more simplistic, fixed set of apparent rules inherent in economizing. Ecologizing seems to expect a growth mindset, and the willingness for people to understand or at least accept systems holistically, even at the planetary scale, since physicists tell us now that all is connected. An ecologizing mindset—growth-oriented and having achieved the capacity to reason at postconventional levels both cognitively and morally—is needed because of the inherently paradoxical nature of some of the issues the world is facing. As we try to mend the broken human chain, one thing that we need to consider in doing so is how to move people from wherever they are developmentally towards later stages of more complexly integrated development. In these later stages, people can better understand and "hold" the types of paradoxes discussed earlier simultaneously, they can better accept differences in and multiple perspectives, and still maintain their capacity for seeing the good of the whole. Such an "unchained" mindset can be helpful for helping us envision what is possible if we adopt ecologizing, incorporating the best elements of economizing into it, but expanding it developmentally, much as human cognitive and moral development goes.

Similarly, Dweck's work orients us towards educating people about the nature of learning, and the importance of hard work, effort, and discipline, not just raw talent. If more people had a growth mindset rather than a fixed mindset, then it would become clear that no matter how difficult the obstacles towards creating a better world are, we all have the capacity to move the system forward or make it better in our own ways. Rather than giving up on a broken system—or a broken human chain—a growth mindset helps us achieve what philosopher Ken Wilber calls an integral or integrated mindset and use integral theory.[12]

Integral theory, as developed by Wilber, provides potentially the best lens into developing an integrated or ecological mindset, as alluded to earlier. Wilber draws from many, many sources to develop the integral framework, which outlines the idea that most disciplines function rather narrowly—only in one of four possible domains, part of the left-brain problem that we discussed earlier. Thus, disciplines and understandings tend to be narrowly focused and largely incomplete. Wilber argues that to fully understand any human, societal, or natural phenomenon, we need to use *all four* of the lenses that are available in his four-quadrant matrix. For instance, in considering human knowing or mindsets holistically, one needs to consider the interior individual perspective, upper left (e.g., psychology); the exterior individual perspective, upper right (e.g., brain physiology and chemistry or behavioral psychology). They also need to consider the interior "we" collective experience, lower left (e.g., cultural experience or society from participants' perspectives); and the exterior collective perspective, or lower right (e.g., sociological aspects of human collectives, learning, or experiences that are observable and measurable).

Wilber argues that most of the time, observers are using only one of these lenses, limiting their purview to only one part of the whole. People with the capacity to consider all four quadrants (as Wilber calls them) will gain an integral or holistic perspective that covers much more territory and provides far greater insight—what we label an ecologizing perspective. Of course, to be willing to learn from all four perspectives, or at least consider them, one has to have a growth mindset, in Dweck's terms, because of the enlargement of thinking that is demanded by taking this more integral or integrated mindset. Given the complexities of the world, the tensions and paradoxes outlined earlier, however, we would argue that humanity may have little choice going forward other than to try to understand our world more holistically in these ways. In the final chapters, we begin to explore what adoption of an ecologizing (integrated) mindset looks like and point to some emerging perspectives that offer more integrated frameworks for thinking about humanity's role on the planet in healthier "ecologizing" ways.

Notes

1. See Piaget, J. (1969). *The psychology of the child*. New York: Wiley.
2. Kohlberg lays out these ideas in a variety of places, including: Kohlberg, L. (1973). Stages and aging in moral development—some speculation. *Gerontologists*, *1*, 498–502; Kohlberg, L. (1976). Moral stages and moralization: The cognitive-developmental approach. In T. Lickona, G. Geis, & L. Kohlberg (Eds.), *Moral development and behavior: Theory, research, and social issues*. New York: Holt, Rinehart and Winston.
3. See, e.g., Kegan, R. (1982). *The evolving self: Problem and process in human development*. Cambridge, MA: Harvard University Press; Kegan, R. (1994). *In over our heads: The mental demands of modern life*. Cambridge, MA: Harvard University Press.
4. Gilligan, C. (1982). *In a different voice*. Cambridge, MA: Harvard University Press.
5. Kohlberg, L. (1973). Stages and aging in moral development—some speculation. *Gerontologists*, *1*, 498–502; Kohlberg, L. (1976). Moral stages and moralization: The cognitive-developmental approach. In T. Lickona, G. Geis, & L. Kohlberg (Eds.), *Moral development and behavior: Theory, research, and social issues*. New York: Holt, Rinehart and Winston.
6. Beck, D. E., & Cowan, C. C. (2005). *Spiral dynamics: Mastering values, leadership and change*. Hoboken, NJ: Wiley-Blackwell.
7. Kegan, R. (1994). *In over our heads: The mental demands of modern life*. Cambridge, MA: Harvard University Press.
8. Dweck, C. S. (2008). *Mindset: The new psychology of success*. New York: Random House Digital, Inc.
9. Buchanan, A., & Kern, M. L. (2017). The benefit mindset: The psychology of contribution and everyday leadership. *International Journal of Wellbeing*, *7*(1), 1–11. doi:10.5502/ijw.v7i1.538.
10. Rimanoczy, I. (2014). A matter of being: Developing sustainability-minded leaders. *Journal of Management for Global Sustainabiltiy*, *2*(1), 95–122.
11. Buchanan, A., & Kern, M. L. (2017). The benefit mindset: The psychology of contribution and everyday leadership. *International Journal of Wellbeing*, *7*(1), 1–11. doi:10.5502/ijw.v7i1.538.
12. Wilber sets out integral theory in a long series of books, including Wilber, K. (2014). *The fourth turning: Imagining the evolution of an integral Buddhism*. Boston: Shambhala Publications; Wilber, K. (1995). *Sex, ecology, spirituality: The spirit of evolution*. Boston: Shambhala Publications; Wilber, K. (1996). *A brief history of everything*. Boston: Shambhala Publications; Wilber, K. (1998). *The eye of spirit: An integral vision for a world gone slightly mad*. Boston: Shambhala Publications; Wilber, K. (1998). *The marriage of sense and soul: Integrating science and reason*. New York: Random House; Wilber, K. (2002). *A theory of everything: An integral vision for business, politics, science, and spirituality*. Boston: Shambhala, among others. We draw from these books here.

11 Building an Ecologizing Mindset

Re-Imagining the World

Before we can find solutions to the challenges of human sustainability we need to have a common understanding of the challenges we face collectively on a global or planetary scale and how new thinking and framing of those issues can help us move forward in a constructive way. In other words, we need to begin to "see" the system as it is if we hope to be able to shift it in the direction of a better world. Only then can we begin the mindset shift that we argued in Chapter 10 is so necessary to reframing how we humans relate to our world—and begin to repair the broken links in the human chain. Fortunately, over the past couple of decades, a number of important new ways of thinking about the planet and economies have begun to take hold that provide significant potential for that mindset shift.

Global sustainability highlights the need to move towards flourishing planetary scale phenomena. Sustainability solutions must be inclusive and cover all humans and other species, recognizing not only the dignity and well-being of human beings but of other living creatures as well—not to mention the ecosystems that support all of us. We need a planetary mindset that encourages thinking about providing food, water, energy, shelter, and clothing, to name the very basics, for the more than 10 billion people expected to be on the earth by 2050, unless something can be done about today's almost exponential population growth. Further, we need to accomplish these tasks without further destroying the Earth systems that sustain life and, we hope, finding new innovations that help our ecosystems regenerate.

For one thing, research in the natural sciences has deepened recent understanding of Earth systems. Several international research programs on global environmental change, including the IPCC,[1] document increasing impacts of human beings on natural systems. These impacts have accelerated greatly since the 1950s. They are now breaching essential life supporting planetary boundaries. Indeed, the 2018 IPCC report and numerous reports since argue that a very rapid response is now needed to limit global warming, lest we humans face unprecedented and far-reaching changes throughout our natural ecologies and the societies they support. The 2018 IPCC report, in fact, argues that global warming needs to be limited to 1.5 degrees Celsius, rather than the 2.0 degrees previously thought acceptable. Further, massive societal transformation needs to be well underway by 2030 to avoid the worst outcomes and to ensure a more sustainable, more equitable and just global society.

Equally frightening, the IPBES released a comprehensive report in 2019 that finds that as many as a million plant and animal species on Earth are now threatened with extinction.[2] Calling the situation "ominous," the IPBES chair Sir Robert Watson pointed out the integral linkage between human beings and other species, noting, "The health of ecosystems on which we and all other species depend is deteriorating more rapidly than ever. We are eroding the very foundations of our economies, livelihoods, food security, health and quality of life worldwide."[3] Although the report indicates that it is not too late to make a difference, it also points out that transformation is urgently needed everywhere and at all different scales, even if there is resistance from vested interests. The main author of the report, Sandra Diaz, argued in a press release that "Biodiversity and nature's contributions to people are our common heritage and humanity's most important life-supporting 'safety net.' But our safety net is stretched almost to breaking point."[4] Without using our terminology what Diaz is talking about is what we call the broken human chain.

Clearly, humans need to realign their relationship with the planet, and shift our thinking about how we relate to each other, to other beings, and to the whole, as we have argued throughout this book. We need to re-recognize, as humans, our deep embeddedness with and dependence on Nature. In this chapter we use multiple emerging concepts—the Great Acceleration, Planetary BoundariesSDGs, Doughnut Economics, and the Anthropocene—to examine the evolving relationships between humans and nature. As we explore these frameworks, we also consider how these ideas might help shift many more people towards a more ecologizing mindset.

The Great Acceleration

Steffen et al. (2015), earth scientists at the Stockholm Resilience Center, studied geological records and identified what has come to be called the "great acceleration," or a rapid and dramatic shift in human impacts on a variety of social and ecosystem trends between 1750 and 2010. The resulting charts explain how humans are impacting natural systems (see Figure 11.1).

On the left of these charts are social trends, measured by Population, GDP, Foreign Direct Investment, Primary Energy Use, Large Dams, Water Use, Fertilizer Consumption, Paper Production, Urban Population, Transportation Telecommunication, and International Tourism. Note that they all seem to follow similar patterns. The growth rate of all variables between 1750 and 1950 is slow and steady. From about 1950

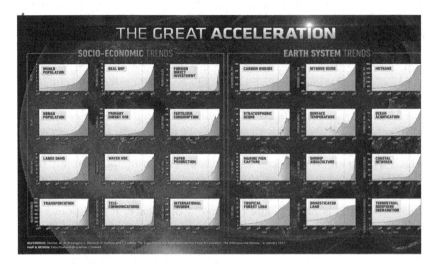

Figure 11.1 The Great Acceleration of Social and Ecosystem Trends Between 1750 and 2010

Printed with permission of publisher from Steffen, W., Broadgate, W., Deutsch, L., Gaffney, O., & Ludwig, C. (2015). The trajectory of the Anthropocene: the great acceleration. The Anthropocene Review, 2(1), 81–98.

Source: Steffen et al. (2015)

onwards, there is an exponential jump in the rate of growth, giving a hockey-stick shape curve to all of these variables. The ecosystems trends during the same period (shown on the right), measured by Carbon Dioxide, Nitrogen Oxide, Methane, Stratospheric Ozone, Earth Surface Temperatures, Ocean Acidification, Marine Fish Capture, Shrimp Aquaculture, Nitrogen to Coastal Zones, Tropical Forest Loss, Domesticated Lands, and Terrestrial Biosphere degradation, mimic the social trends. They grow slowly until about 1950, then much more rapidly in the years after.

The period from about 1950 onwards, in which the next exponential increase of ecological changes evidenced by the hockey stick shape takes place, has been labelled the "Great Acceleration,"[5] a term that describes human impacts on natural ecosystems. The Great Acceleration charts, originally published in 2004 by the International Geosphere–Biosphere Program, were inspired by IGBP Chair Paul Crutzen's observation that humans and the planet seem to have left the relatively stable period known as the Holocene for an epoch in which human activities were actually shaping climate.[6] After this period, that is, from about halfway through the 20th century and continuing till today, human activities are clearly having a dramatic effect on natural systems.

Indeed, human-caused impacts have grown so much that they are running up against fundamental life support boundaries of earth systems, as well as threatening other specials, as noted by the IPBES report discussed above. Partly in response to the observations about the Great Acceleration, Johan Rockström and colleagues (2009),[7] working at the Stockholm Resilience Center, proposed the concept of planetary boundaries, tracking ecosystem performance on nine critical variables that are necessary to sustain life on earth (see Figure 11.2). The idea of planetary boundaries and the diagram are meant to clarify the idea that there are physical

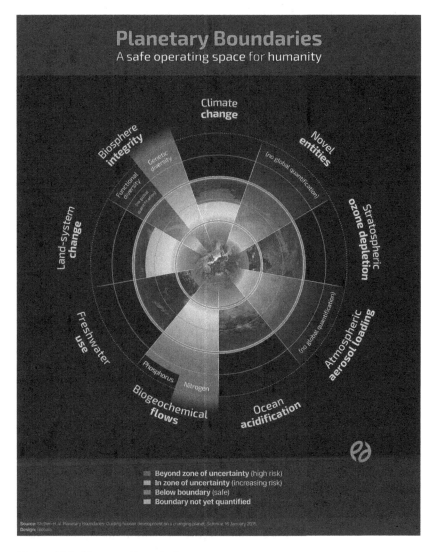

Figure 11.2 Planetary Boundaries

Printed with permission of publisher from Steffen, W., Richardson, K., Rockström, J., Cornell, S. E., Fetzer, I., Bennett, E. M., . . . & Folke, C. (2015). Planetary boundaries: Guiding human development on a changing planet. Science, 347(6223), 1259855.

Source: Rockstrom et al. 2009

limits beyond which the Earth's systems cannot be pushed without risking significant and negative consequences.

Many of the shifts notable in the Great Acceleration charts can be attributed to human population growth as well as to processes of industrialization. Roughly 200 years ago, for example, about a billion people lived on Earth. As of this writing, there are about 7.7 billion people on the planet according to estimates from the United Nations, which helps to explain the exponential curves in the Great Acceleration charts. Earlier population levels of human beings could (and did) affect relatively small geographical regions, but did not, as the human population does today, impact the planetary ecosystem. Although recent population estimates highlight the fact that the growth *rate* is slowing down, population is still growing overall, particularly in developing nations where there is significant demand to raise standards of living—with accompanying ecological costs if business as usual continues. The United Nations estimates that human population will be about 8.5 billion by 2030, 9.7 billion in 2050, and 11.2 billion by 2100.[8] Given the strains that the human populace is already putting on ecosystems, such continued growth, if it occurs and there is no change in the trajectory or how human systems (including production of goods and services and economies as wholes) operate, clearly puts many more ecosystems and the ability of the world's climate to support humans at risk.

Planetary Boundaries

Another framework that can help us humans "see" the planetary system as a whole more clearly is the Planetary Boundaries framework developed by researchers at the Stockholm Resilience Center (see Figure 11.2). The idea of planetary boundaries is that there are environmental limits on physical systems on the Earth that create a set of boundaries for what the authors of the initial report called a "safe operating space for humanity."[9] The Planetary Boundaries framework provides both a dramatic physical image that helps people envision what those boundaries look like and which are important. They provide a ready way of seeing which boundaries have already been transgressed, hence creating an important new meme that can help reshape human beings' relationship to the Earth.

The planetary boundary variables include Climate Change, Novel Entities, Stratospheric Ozone Depletion, Atmospheric Aerosol Loading, Ocean Acidification, Biogeochemical Flows (Phosphorus, Nitrogen), Freshwater Use, Land-System change, and Biosphere Integrity (Genetic Diversity). According to the scientists at the Stockholm Resilience Centre, biogeochemical flows of phosphorus and nitrogen and Genetic Diversity have already gone past safe operating limits as can be seen in the red [or dark] parts of the diagram. For Novel Entities and Atmospheric Aerosol Loading, scientists do not have sufficient data to assess their impacts. For the Climate Change and Land System Change boundaries, the planet is in an uncertainty zone, since no physical limits have yet been determined.

Staying within the limits proposed by the Planetary Boundaries framework would create the envisioned "safe operating space for humanity" geophysically. In a sense this framework with its clearly delineated boundaries provide a foundation for a sustainable—even flourishing—future for humans and other living beings, since it is these physical limits that set boundary conditions for thriving life on Earth as we know. The figure also conveys a dramatic visual image of the reality that the planet's resources are not infinite. What is increasingly clear, however, is that if we continue to operate as we have in the past, that is, with the exponential growth witnessed in the Great Acceleration charts, we humans will breach additional boundaries in coming years, and jeopardize that safe operating environment as well.

The authors of the first and then subsequent Planetary Boundaries reports argued that overstepping even one of these physical boundaries would have serious consequences, including unpredictable, nonlinear, and rapid environmental changes that could take humanity out of its safe zone[10] and even potentially risk civilizational collapse.[11] The 2015 Paris Accord on Climate Change sought to limit carbon emissions into the atmosphere to keep the rise in global temperatures to under 2°C. But as the IPCC report cited above argues, that number may well be too high to keep humanity thriving. Global heating may need to be limited to under 1.5°C to avoid the worst consequences of what is now called the climate emergency or crisis, thus suggesting that our work to change the system is certainly cut out for us all.

The Anthropocene

Given all the human impacts on the natural environment, we are now living in an era that some scientists call the Anthropocene or the age of humans.[12] This nomenclature emphasizes the fact that humans and our activities are now the primary disruptors of natural cycles, impacting atmospheric, geologic, hydrologic, biospheric, and other Earth systems to the extent that the shifts are measurable. The word Anthropocene comes from two ancient Greek words, *anthrop*, which means human, and *cene*, which means new or recent.

Human impacts on nature will worsen as human population rises from 7.2 billion to the estimated 10 billion by mid-century. Simply to address today's wealth inequality across the globe will require lifting up living standards of almost 2 billion people, who are currently living on under $2 per day. Increasing global consumption of food, energy, and other raw materials to accommodate such a shift will further degrade ecosystems. Further, in addition to the projected effects of the climate crisis and species loss, major ecosystems are degrading, as the Planetary Boundaries framework suggests, some potentially to the point of collapse. Unless they can be made more resilient, a few of the ecosystems facing catastrophic losses and even possible collapse include rainforests, fisheries, wildlife habitats, and topsoil. Some oceans are filled with huge swirls of plastic waste that block out marine life in their vicinity and various forms of pollution threaten waterways, seas, and the air in different parts of the world. The human-induced massive biodiversity loss, which some call the Sixth Great Extinction, also poses major threats to human well-being since we depend on what have become known as ecosystem services provided by both plants and animals for our very existence.

The implication of all of these realities is that human consumption and ecosystem destruction are seemingly currently locked in a vicious circle. Changing the dynamics of that cycle means that a significant mindset change is needed to forge new links in the human chain, towards a new way of being and acting in the world, which is what we turn to in the next section.

"Doughnut" Economics

One thing that is clearly needed to bring about the systemic transformation needed is to shift away from the neoliberal narrative discussed earlier towards a new way of thinking about human welfare and economics. To conceptualize what a healthy system in which all humans, not to mention other living beings, can thrive, economist Kate Raworth (2012) articulated an expanded version of the "safe operating space" for humanity. Raworth's framework, so-called Doughnut Economics, emphasizes not just the physical planetary boundaries but also and equally importantly the social boundaries that human systems should not transgress for all humans to be able to meet their fundamental needs within planetary constraints.

Raworth's "doughnut," so labelled because of its torus shape, is shown in the diagram in Figure 1.3, and represents an important and notable effort to have us rethink our approach to economics, physical limitations, and meeting fundamental human needs. Like the Planetary Boundaries framework, it provides a neat visual image that makes explicit and clear a very complex set of realities and constraints—creating, in effect, a new meme that has already rapidly spread throughout the world to help explain where we humans need to think about going. According to Raworth's model, in addition to the nine geophysical limits outlined by the Planetary Boundaries, humans also need a foundation of "goods" to meet the needs of all within the means of the planet. The doughnut model argues for providing adequate food, water, energy, income, education, resilience, voice, jobs, health, gender equality, and social equity for all, in addition to staying within the geophysical boundaries identified by the Planetary Boundaries scientists.

The foundational dimensions of the human system identified in the doughnut model create a sort of "floor" of social justice and equity

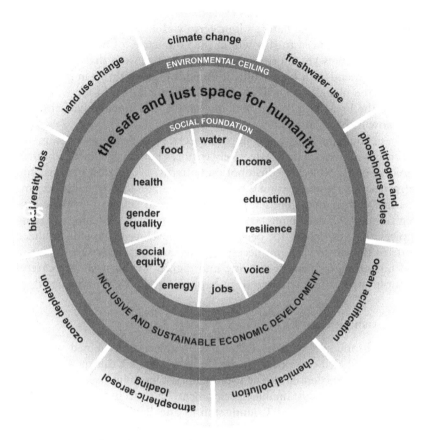

Figure 11.3 A Safe and Just Space for Humanity to Thrive In

Printed with permission of publisher from Raworth, K. (2012). A safe and just space for humanity: can we live within the doughnut. Oxfam Policy and Practice: Climate Change and Resilience, 8(1), 1–26.

Source: Raworth (2012).

below which we should not go, according to Raworth, if people are to meet their needs and if they are to be able to experience dignity and well-being. To do so in a way that promotes flourishing for all, however, we also need to stay within the geophysical planetary boundaries and avert catastrophic climate change, probably while also beginning to figure out ways to reduce human population growth to begin easing the strains on the natural environment. One important way of doing that, according to the United Nations, is to continue to educate women and girls, because educated women can not only help provide for their families but often choose to limit the size of their families, hence Raworth's emphasis on gender equity.

In the "Anthropocene" epoch that we are now in, human activities have a greater impact on nature's cycle than nature itself does, and human choices will determine nature's long-term viability for supporting life as we know it. The need to stay within the boundaries of both parts of the doughnut creates yet another vital paradox or tension that we humans need to contend with successfully if humans hope to thrive in the future. Though the planet itself will continue and some forms of life will likely survive the breaching of various boundaries, it is human civilization as we know it that is at risk.

These boundary constraints impose special responsibilities on humans, because dealing with them effectively requires human agency and human choices about life styles, consumption patterns, production systems, and infrastructures to stay within these limits—changes that arguably become possible with change mindsets and purposes that help to repair the broken human chain. Staying within these limits may well mean making choices that, especially for people in the "developed" or industrialized parts of the world, will not necessarily be easy, but that in the long run can potentially provide well-being and dignity for all if we are careful about how we frame what needs to happen—and how we accomplish it.

A Flourishing Future?

The Anthropocene with its Planetary Boundaries, combined with the foundational elements posed by the Doughnut model, thus pose the possibility of an existential threat to humanity. One solution to this threat lies in the idea of "sustainable development," a concept first put forward by the 1987 Brundtland Commission.[13] The Brundtland Commission defined sustainable development as "meeting the needs of the present without compromising the ability of future generations to meet their own needs." Although sustainability is important, the implied notion of "sustain" is to continue business as usual—a trajectory that our broken human chain suggests is no longer feasible. Instead, while emphasizing that the natural environment needs to be able to sustain humanity (and other living beings, we would argue), we emphasize the idea of a flourishing future of well-being and dignity for all, based on ideas of ecologizing and used with wisdom, that can help move us all forward in healthful directions.

Inherent in the definition of sustainable development is the recognition that there is tension between meeting present needs, particularly in the context of a rapidly growing population, and future needs. Recognizing that tension is particularly important in light of recent evidence about the emergence of the Anthropocene and the increasingly rapid evolution of climate change. Further, the idea of "development" implies continued economic development, but as we have argued earlier, our understandings about what that means and how it is to be achieved may need to shift to accommodate the physical and social realities of the world.

Proponents of sustainable development argue that it is possible to reconcile the tension between meeting today's needs and leaving sufficient capacity for tomorrow's populace by working smarter now and into the future. They also contend that although lifestyle changes may be needed today, that shift does not necessarily need to diminish quality of life for people in more "developed" countries, while it could greatly improve quality of life for people in emerging nations.

Perhaps a wise, if more radical course, would be to redefine what is meant by development in important ways so that it reflects the way nature develops—towards more complexity and abundance, for example, of ideas, of ways of being in the world. And also to deal with what is largely undiscussable—the idea of population control for human beings. That is not to say that any particular population needs to limit its growth, but rather that as a planetary population, we humans need to consider the implications of endless growth seriously and find ways to bring our own growth as a species under control. Otherwise, it is likely that nature will do it for us.

The Sustainable Development Goals (SDGs)

One effort by the world's nations to figure out how to accomplish the potentially conflicting ends identified above, comes in the form of the United Nations' Sustainable Development Goals. They were approved by all the world's nations in 2015 to replace the more limited Millennium Development Goals that had guided economic development activity since the year 2000, though there are inherent conflicts noted above in some of the goals as well, particularly around the idea of economic growth.

To get to the SDGs, some 192 nations of the world agreed on the 17 SDGs (with 169 specific targets), under the United Nations Agenda 2030 (United Nations, 2015). Sometimes called the Global Goals, the SDGs are focused around people, planet, and prosperity for all, and explicitly aim to fight extreme poverty, inequality and injustice, and fix climate change, while recognizing that issues identified in the goals are complexly wicked, interdependent, and interconnected. The SDGs, listed in Table 1.1, are the following: no (extreme) poverty, no hunger, good health, quality education, gender equality, clean water and sanitation, renewable energy, good jobs and economic growth, industry, innovation and infrastructure, reduced inequalities, sustainable cities and communities, responsible consumption, climate action, life below water, life on land, and peace and justice. The 17th goal, partnership for the goals, implicitly recognizes the need to collaborate across multiple boundaries to achieve them, as well as the inherently interconnected nature of many of the issues described by the goals.

The benefit of the SDGs is that they represent a global consensus among nations about what a peaceful, flourishing world looks like. They also provide a unique opportunity to thwart dangerous destabilization

Table 11.1 Sustainable Development Goals

of human-Nature relations. They further serve as a relatively long-term (15 years at their inception) aspirational agenda of economic and social development in the context of climate change oriented towards the year 2030. Many nations, including China, India, Japan, Switzerland, Sweden, and Germany, have translated the SDGs for their respective countries and have established national missions relevant to the goals.

The SDGs now serve as policy framework for provincial level plans in many parts of the world. Further, there is significant support for the SDGs from the business/corporate sector, as many businesses have incorporated one or more of the SDGs into their own agendas, sometimes into business models, and sometimes into their corporate responsibility agenda broadly defined. Leaders of large multinational corporations understand what is at stake with the SDGs and are using them to shape their social responsibility and corporate strategies.

Business Opportunities in Implementing Sustainable Development Goals

The aspirational nature of the SDGs has attracted many businesses, not to mention governments and civil society organizations, to them. Because businesses are the main economic engine of societies, they can and need to play a central, vitally important role in implementation of sustainable development goals. Some businesses are now among the world's most powerful institutions, particularly multi- and transnational firms with their global reach. They are vital players in both setting the agenda for dealing with the SDGs and for playing important roles in achieving those goals, in part because many business practices determine how much the natural environment is affected by human activities. Additionally, the Commission on Sustainable Development and Business (2017) estimates that achieving these goals offers potential market opportunities worth $12 trillion by 2030, which makes achieving them appealing.[14]

But this business will not materialize without some effort. It will require deep innovative restructuring of products/services and business models, along with an emphasis on regenerative business practices in which nature's resources are not depleted beyond their renewal capacity, being adopted. Indeed, successfully achieving the Global Goals may well mean significant revisions in business and the general public's mindsets, transformation of business models, strategies, and operating practices, not to mention purposes.

This transformation needs to be towards redefined visions of growth, and even what it means to be a successful business, away from constant material and financial wealth growth, towards growth in wellbeing for all, or what we discussed earlier as collective value. Talk about a mindset change!

This type of transformation towards wellbeing and dignity for all will require a redefinition of the purpose of business—and, most likely, of governments, too, to really engage with issues of wellbeing. That, in turn, will demand new metrics and assessments, like the Genuine Progress Indicator (GPI) as opposed to GDP. In short, the whole neoliberal narrative needs to be revised away from financial wealth and growth at all costs and shifted to include ideas about well-being, dignity, and flourishing for the whole!

Thus, among the most important changes that need to be made are the ideas around modern corporations as independent, limited-liability, legal entities; maximizing shareholder value; and operating within free capital markets, all of which are the memes promulgated by neoliberalism. The reality is that corporations are dependent on both natural and social resources to thrive. Their liabilities cannot be limited and constantly favoring private accumulation, as compared to collective value or the public good. They must accept liabilities for commons resources that they use or destroy, which means that what economists call externalities— negative byproducts of production, that is, things like pollution, jobs disappearing through automation, or congestion in transportation, will have to be incorporated into the costs of doing business to get to the *real* costs of doing business. And those *real* costs will vary dramatically from today's pricing schemes, most likely

Shareholder value maximization is simply not sufficient as a purpose for business any longer (indeed, it never was actually sufficient). Business purpose, as argued by Donaldson and Walsh[15] among others, must be accompanied with more inclusive value creation for society and the public good, that is value for all stakeholders, including the Earth itself considered as a stakeholder. Traditional corporate driven wealth creation, as discussed earlier, has had far too many unintended consequences for the natural environment and for social and economic equality. Investors and entrepreneurs are now absorbing more risk than ever before. Wealth maximization has led to prosperity and well-being for some—the few, or what the Occupy movement called the 1%—while also creating a highly unequal world that leaves many behind. At this writing, less than 1% of the wealthiest people in the world hold greater (financial) wealth than the bottom 50% of the world's human population combined. Indeed, Oxfam reported that six men (yes, all men) controlled as much wealth as the bottom half of the world's population in 2018. As we have noted earlier, this level of inequality makes for an unstable world at best.

Science, as we see in the discussion of climate change and planetary boundaries above, has provided us a deep understanding of natural and social changes over the past centuries. It also points to the need for solutions that combine science with business logic, and other human values like the need for collaboration, relationships, and community. We need an "Earth systems economics" that is anchored in planetary natural processes and that incorporates other human and natural values like generosity of spirit, altruism, and dignity or valuing each person and living entity for itself. The focus of science in the past has been on observing and analyzing Earth systems, pollution, population, consumption, biodiversity, and biogeochemical trends, among other natural phenomena. Much effort has been spent in specifying problems and measuring earth system conditions. Less attention has been paid to solutions, particularly to holistic solutions that consider the wellbeing of the whole, rather than its fragmented or atomized parts. Indeed, as helpful as science is in understanding natural systems, it desperately needs to be integrated with other human values and, as argued earlier, with more holistic approaches that incorporate the wealth of actual human and natural values articulated by an ecologizing perspective.

Given the dire state of the planet, then, it is urgent to move to transdisciplinary solutions, where the disciplines involved encompass a wide array of expertise, multiple stakeholders from all parts of the system, especially stakeholders whose voice is not frequently heard and whose values might otherwise be lost in translation. Scientific inquiry needs to break out of narrow disciplinary fields and focus on co-creation of solutions with societal stakeholders. The extreme fragmentation of disciplines runs counter to the need for holistic understanding of sustainability on a planetary scale. Transdisciplinary work seeks to co-design and co-produce knowledge with stakeholders with the intention of producing solutions to real world sustainability challenges of the Anthropocene. All of this change involves movement towards an ecologizing mindset and away from the dominant economizing and power aggrandizing mindsets of today.

Indeed, in this context of system change, the idea of sustainability itself needs to be reframed as something that is socially desirable. Ecologizing— becoming actually sustainable—clearly will affect the external and internal identities of a culture, but that can potentially be a very positive thing. It can constructively alter humans' perception of beauty and aesthetics, helping redefine what is beautiful, well-designed, and simultaneously life-enhancing.

To purposely create a sustainable system requires an examination of the ways in which institutions affect cognitive frameworks and behavioral drives (Misangi et al., 2008: 754). New institutional logics generated by both instrumental and aesthetic rationality must be coupled with new guidelines, practices and actions led by institutional entrepreneurs who create change. Otherwise, the status quo is unlikely to be altered in the long-term. The micro-level features of institutional logics influence how individuals understand their own identities (Thornton et al., 2012). Sustainability needs to be perceived as a core part of the organization's functioning through a change of the logics.

Notes

1. IPCC (Intergovernmental Panel on Climate Change), 2018. Global Warming of 1.5 °C: All Chapters, www.ipcc.ch/report/sr15/.
2. Diaz, S., Settele, J., & Brondizio, E. (2019). *Summary for policymakers of the global assessment report on biodiversity and ecosystem services of the intergovernmental science-policy platform on biodiversity and ecosystem services*. Retrieved from: www.ipbes.net/system/tdf/spm_global_unedited_advance.pdf?file=1&type=node&id=35245.
3. IPBES, Media Release. (2019, May 6). Nature's dangerous decline 'Unprecedented'; Species extinction rates 'accelerating.' Retrieved from: www.ipbes.net/news/Media-Release-Global-Assessment.
4. IPBES, Media Release. (2019, May 6). Nature's dangerous decline 'Unprecedented'; Species extinction rates 'accelerating.' Retrieved from: www.ipbes.net/news/Media-Release-Global-Assessment.
5. See, e.g., McNeill, J. R., & Engelke, P. (2016). *The great acceleration.* Harvard University Press; Steffen, W., Broadgate, W., Deutsch, L., Gaffney, O., & Ludwig, C. (2015). The trajectory of the Anthropocene: The great acceleration. *The Anthropocene Review, 2*(1), 81–98.
6. Crutzen, P. J. (2002). Geology of mankind—The Anthropocene. *Nature, 415*, 23.
7. Rockström, J., Steffen, W. L., Noone, K., Persson, Å., Chapin III, F. S., Lambin, E. et al. (2009). Planetary boundaries: Exploring the safe operating space for humanity. *Ecology & Society, 14*(2), 32. Retrieved from: www.ecologyandsociety.org/vol14/iss2/art32/.
8. United Nations. (2015). *World population prospects: Key findings and advance tables.* Geneva, Switzerland: United Nations. Retrieved from: https://esa.un.org/unpd/wpp/Publications/Files/Key_Findings_WPP_2015.pdf.
9. Rockström, J., Steffen, W., Noone, K., Persson, Å., Chapin III, F. S., Lambin, E., . . . Nykvist, B. (2009). Planetary boundaries: Exploring the safe operating space for humanity. *Ecology and Society, 14*(2).
10. Steffen, W., Richardson, K., Rockström, J., Cornell, S. E., Fetzer, I., Bennett, E. M., . . . Folke, C. (2015). Planetary boundaries: Guiding human development on a changing planet. *Science, 347*(6223), 1259855. Also, Rockström, J. (2015). Bounding the planetary future: Why we need a great transition. *Great Transition Initiative, 9*, 1–13.
11. Diamond, J. (2005). *Collapse: How societies choose to fail or succeed.* New York: Penguin.

12. Steffen, W., Perrson, A., Deutsch, L., Zalasiewicz, J., Williams, M., Richardson, K., Crumley, C., Curtzen, P., Folke, C., Gordon, L., Molina, M., Rmaanathan, V., Rockström, J., Scheffer, M., Schellnhuber, H. J., & Svedin, U. (2011). The Anthropocene: From global change to planetary stewardship. *AMBIO: A Journal of the Human Environment, 40*(7), 739–761.
13. Brundtland, G. H. (1987). *Our common future: World commission on environmental development.* Oxford: The Brundtland-Report Oxford University Press.
14. Business & Sustainable Development Commission. (2017). *Better business, better world: Executive summary.* Business & Sustainable Development Commission. Retrieved from: http://report.businesscommission.org/uploads/Executive-Summary.pdf.
15. Donaldson, T., & Walsh, J. P. (2015). Toward a theory of business. *Research in Organizational Behavior, 35,* 181–207.

12 Reconnecting the Human Chain

To reconnect the human chain, we need to begin by re-storying our world. New narratives, and new myths, in a sense, new origin stories that place us humans explicitly into our natural context can help us to reframe the way we think and ultimately how we act and what decisions we make. Some of that thinking already exists, as demonstrated in the last chapter. That is, we need to move towards ecologizing mindsets.

Bringing about a shift to an ecologizing and civilizing mindset, with attendant new behaviors and practices in our institutions, amounts to a major mindset change. It means moving away from humans having (or more accurately thinking they have) dominance over Nature towards balance, harmony, and integration, or embeddedness, with her. This shift involves, as McGilchrist might say,[1] rebalancing the two sides of the brain, the holistic right with the analytic left, in ways that leave the "master," that is, the right brain in control over the more detail-oriented left brain, the emissary, once again. We need, in a sense a unified mind, not a split mind, just as we need to recognize how embedded we humans really are in nature in a both/and logic rather than the either/or one that is more common today. Then we need to act in new ways that are not as destructive as our current ways with respect to nature, and even to each other.

By placing priority on holistic thinking, along with memes that support that way of thinking and orient us all in directions of dignity and well-being for all (in which "all" includes all living beings), perhaps we can as a species begin to understand and honor the primacy of the whole, not just the fragmented and atomized parts of our world. Reconnecting also involves shifting our dominant values, whether in business or more broadly in our societies, away from economizing and technologizing towards ecologizing[2] and civilizing.[3] That might mean that the dominance of businesses over other institutions of the past couple of centuries diminishes in favor of other types of institutions and enterprises, for example, families, communities, and civil society organizations aimed at helping improve conditions for all. Of course, businesses are essential and will always remain vitally important in the world, however, given their historically single-minded orientation towards the pursuit of profits, it may well be important to shift their purposes towards generating some form of collective value. That becomes important in light of the socio-ecological constraints and realities discussed in the last chapter.

Also, in reconnecting the chain, we need to honor the learning and knowledge that has been developed over these many centuries, to honor the understandings that scientific knowledge and industrialization along with technological progress provide. We cannot simply go back to the more-limited understandings that existed before the scientific and industrial revolutions. In other words, reconnecting the human chain means integrating across quantitative and qualitative, scientific and humanistic, empirical and spiritual realities, and human into nature, along with many other splits that have occurred over the years. In a sense, reconnection involves a spiritual journey in which we recognize our oneness with others, self, and perhaps whatever we might call a greater power (or nature) in our universe, rather than emphasizing our separateness from each other, from ourselves and whatever power we might have, and from the world around us.

Reconnecting is an integrated approach that recognizes, as philosopher Ken Wilber does with his "integral" framework,[4] that we need to bring all important perspectives to bear on our living and social systems if we are to begin to understand and fully realize their positive potential. Part of what has happened with the dualisms discussed throughout this book is that more integral or holistic approaches (particularly in Western cultures) have been lost in the dominance of paying attention to only one atomized or fragmented aspect of the "wholes" that make up the world around us. Given the fraught nature of today's world, we humans can no longer afford the disconnects that put us into one or another box: we need holistic conceptualizations of the world around us of the sort that we see emerging that were discussed in the last chapter.

Maybe, in a sense, we need to break out of boxes altogether as we seek reconnection, stepping away from either/or thinking towards both/and thinking. We need, for example, *both* masculine and feminine, *both* long and short term, *both* linearity and cyclicality of thinking, *both* individual and collective, and, ultimately, *both* economizing and ecologizing (along with civilizing) values to make us whole. And we need all these things together, too.

The ecologizing and civilizing frames that we discussed in Chapter 6 are fundamentally important to developing not a one-sided perspective that helps reconnect the chain, but a more balanced, integrated perspective that allows for inherent dualities to exist together, as we have been arguing. Because storytelling and narrative are so vital to us human beings' understanding of our place in the world, beginning with new stories and narratives, built on a shared set of inspirational memes, in this case values, is an important step towards the system change needed to bring about ecologizing mindsets.

If we begin by thinking about how to construct new narratives, perhaps one place to begin is with Donaldson and Dunfee's conception of hypernorms—norms and values that transcend multiple contexts and have a universality to them.[5] These hypernorms represent vital and resonant memes that resonate across cultural differences. Other memes that resonate broadly are also likely to be important in the emergence of a new way of viewing both economies (and, not incidentally, the roles of businesses), and societies when we reconnect the chain. Using this idea, and to the extent that such hypernorms actually exist, we can seek out values that most (if not all) people can resonate to. Dignity, well-being, and flourishing are, we believe, some possibly widely shared memes and potential hypernorms on which most people might agree. Maybe the five core values that Jonathan Haidt uncovered in cultures around the world might also be candidates for relatively universal memes (core units of culture, remember?) out of which new narratives can be constructed: care, fairness or justice, loyalty, authority and respect, and sanctity (and, in some cultures, purity), plus liberty or freedom.[6] These values are important across many cultures and in many different situations, giving them needed heft.

Our disconnections from nature, from each other, and from less tangible aspects of life have taken many forms and a heavy toll on both humans and nature. Staying disconnected for many years has made that disconnection seem more like a normal condition than the recognition that comes in the pan-African notion of *Ubuntu*, "I am because we are," meaning that we humans exist always in a context of community and connectedness. That connectedness is with each other and with Nature. Further, there are enabling social systems and structures that have emerged over the years to support disconnectedness, including the normalizing of exploitation—of nature and other humans, and of separateness from other human beings who are somehow "different" from ourselves (whoever and wherever we might be). Such disconnectedness makes stories like Sergio's—with which this book began, where people live completely disconnected from nature—increasingly common.

Reconnecting the human chain and reintegrating humans and their organizations with nature is the task we have at hand. It requires reimagining and rethinking our beliefs, attitudes and relationships. At the same time, we cannot ignore what has come before—or the values that shaped today's economizing and power-aggrandizing values. These values are powerful reminders of some core human traits and tendencies that need to be respected. Otherwise, they would not be as dominant as they are, which argues for the need to transcend, yet include, those values in the new memes and understandings that underpin our influential, culture-shaping stories into the future.

To move towards an ecologizing mindset imbued with civilizing values that incorporates yet transcends today's economizing and power aggrandizing values, then, we believe we need to start with creating new narratives and stories, built upon resonant memes that can usefully be incorporated into a whole range of narratives. We start, however, with the foundational idea that whatever reconnection might mean, it fundamentally privileges what gives life to our human and natural systems over other values.

Life-Giving/Life-Affirming Systems and Economies

As discussed earlier, there are certain elements of systems that give "life" to them, rather than depleting them or making them feel "dead" in some ways. Healthy living systems have purpose (often to simply survive or even thrive) or intentionality, are bounded in some way that provides for identity, and have interconnectedness and enough diversity to build a sense of abundance. They have to be viewed holistically, lest fragmentation into their parts rip the life from them. In addition, in human systems, the capacity for reflexivity—awareness of intentions and how changes might affect the system—helps guide what changes make sense.

Healthy living systems are based in abundance rather than scarcity, filled with characteristics of "enlivenment," not just the scientific and intellectual components of the Enlightenment, as discussed earlier. In contrast to many of today's systems, which too often (though this reality is changing somewhat) rely on huge monolithic enterprises. Think about the banking system, for example, which in the global financial crisis of 2007–2008 contained several financial institutions that were so big, connected, and impactful that they were considered "too big to fail," lest the whole system collapse. Or think about monoculture crop raising, in which acres and acres of a single species are planted, making the whole system vulnerable to disease, drought, or blight, a reality facing banana growers already. In distinct contrast to these situations, healthy human and natural systems are vigorous in that they include many different species that are constantly interacting, with no one species (or institution) dominating.

In healthy living, socio-economic, and socio-ecological systems, if something happens to one species, there is sufficient resilience in the system that it continues to thrive without that species because nature abhors a vacuum, as the saying goes, and other species can step in to replace on that goes missing. Healthy living systems are like the organic farming described in Michael Pollan's *The Omnivore's Dilemma*, rich with crop and animal rotation, wasting nothing including animal waste, replete with variety, abundance, and diversity, engaged in the production of highly nutritious, delicious, and beautiful food, and satisfied to be doing so meaningfully at a reasonable level of profit and generous productivity.[7]

Today's economic system, in contrast, constantly pushes towards material and financial wealth, forgetting that wealth production is only one form of value (and that money is nothing but a surrogate for value)—and not a value in and of itself that really gives life to the system. Although there are people who desire money and material acquisitions (lots of "stuff") as a primary value, more generally people desire community, belonging, engagement, purpose, connection, and the capacity to be their whole selves in the context of their communities. When we undertake future visioning exercises with our (business) students, for example, few mention making piles of money as what would truly make their lives fulfilling. Rather, they talk about family, friends, thriving communities and natural systems, beauty, the ability to connect and relate to other people through a range of experiences, work that is meaningful and contributes to the world, hobbies that they love, exercise, and other similar types of things.

The whole point of reconnecting the human chain is to bring these features back into our human and socio-ecological systems so that we are no longer disconnected. From the perspective of the economic system, we need to think about how to develop economies that tap into these qualities that give life to systems to create, as ecologist Hunter Lovins says, an economy that serves life[8] (rather than wealth). David Korten, activist and thought leader, similarly talks of building an ecological civilization—what we call ecologizing—moving from phantom wealth (linked to financial wealth) to "real" wealth, which has associations with well-being, as we discuss next. Korten argues for a living economy for a living Earth, noting that we humans are living beings born of that living Earth and that we forget that at our peril.[9] That, in fact, is the goal of reconnecting the human chain. What we need now is to tell stories, based on memes that give life and that help us understand what this transformative approach to the world might look like.

Below we discuss some of the core underpinnings or memes of such a perspective might be to be holistic and encompassing, as well as to tap into the emotions of people living in the system. Drawing from the humanistic management movement, the work of WE-All, Haidt's foundational values, Maslow's hierarchy of needs, Donaldson & Walsh's ideas about collective value, and our own research, we offer several candidates for resonant memes.

We start with the two core values identified by humanistic management scholars, well-being and dignity.[10] Then we expand to incorporate the near-universal values identified by Haidt: equity (justice/fairness), care, loyalty, authority/respect, and sanctity, plus Haidt's sixth proposed value of freedom or liberty (autonomy).[11] We add meaning and belonging, both of which arose in discussions about new narratives we have experienced and are fundamental to human well-being. We end the discussion of memes as values by discussing collective value as a new purpose that can be applied to all of our institutions, especially businesses.

In arguing for a new, expanded set of memes to inform economic, societal, and scientific thinking we do not mean to dismiss existing memes, but rather to include them in new and creative ways that encompass a wide range of values. Thus, we hope to transcend and include older notions with new, more encompassing ideas that can potentially engage us all in repairing our relationships with the world.

Well-Being

Well-being is a state characterized by health, happiness, and prosperity. Definitions of well-being include welfare, health, happiness, security, comfort, safety, good fortune. Interestingly, "well" (as an adjective) comes from the Old English word "*wel*," meaning abundantly, or very, very much, being sure, and having a good reason. Considered as a verb, "well" derives from the Old English *wiellan*, meaning to spring, rise, gush, carrying a meaning of bubbling up from its Germanic roots (and, of course, the noun "well" is a spring of water).

The second half of the term, "being," means to have existence. Thus, the idea of well-being means developing a happy, healthy, and prosperous state of existence. Typically, when we think of well-being, we think of the psychological aspects of it, however, there are also material aspects, that is, the capacity to be safe, secure, and supportive of one's loved ones. Scholar Amartya Sen talks about well-being in terms of capabilities, that is, the ability to "do valuable acts or reach valuable states of being."[12]

Considered as a meme that can inform a new narrative, the idea of well-being potentially provides a framework for helping to move important metrics towards more holistic assessment of the system. For example, the idea of gross national product/domestic product (GNP/GDP) is a measure often used as a surrogate for well-being despite that it merely measures economic activity, whether that activity is helpful or harmful. A focus on metrics that attempt to get at well-being would necessarily be much broader, encompassing both the subjective and more objective aspects of well-being, and taking into account things like care work, which currently goes unmeasured, and also subtracting harmful activities (like clear cutting of forests, for example, or forest fires) from the metric.

One possible alternative metric that attempts to get at a holistic notion of well-being is the GPI. GPI attempts to measure improvement in overall economic welfare by incorporating income-weighted private consumption, the value of non-market services that generate welfare, the cost of deterioration natural resources, and increases in capital and balance of international trade. In an effort to be more inclusive of well-being, GPI includes estimates of the value of voluntary and unpaid work, leisure time, income distribution, the costs of crime, and ecological impact, among other factors.[13] Testament to its potential to assess well-being, the GPI is already being used in a variety of places around the world to attempt to measure well-being rather than simply economic activity.

In a related development, the OECD (Organization for Economic Cooperation and Development) has developed a Better Life index that combines eleven indicators of societal and personal well-being in an effort to move beyond GDP, arguing on the website that "There is more to life than the cold numbers of GDP and economic statistics."[14] The Better Life Index, which includes indicators for housing, income, jobs, community, education, environment, civic engagement, health, life satisfaction, safety, and work-life balance, tries to identify the things that are most important to people around the planet in providing a fulfilling, secure, and healthy life. Like other metrics, the Better Life index can be used to compare countries' in terms of how well they are meeting their citizens' needs.[15]

There are other possible metrics, including Bhutan's Gross National Happiness indicator, the UN's Human Development Index, and the Gross Environmental Sustainability Development Index. Evolving such metrics is vitally important to well-being because, as accountants say, you get what you measure. When you measure (and compare) different attributes, it is those attributes that focus people's attention and shift practices. As more and more criticism of GDP emerges, it is becoming clearer that the world's nations need to adopt one (or more) of these more holistic metrics to begin to push the world towards needed changes and actual well-being for all of humanity.

Dignity/Respect

Dignity, according to author Donna Hicks is the quality or state of intrinsic worth.[16] People, she notes, have such intrinsic worth, no matter what their situation or status in life. At core, dignity means that people need to be treated and honored as valuable and respected for their own sake. Dignity, seen in this way, is an important core ethical principle. Violation of dignity, according to Hicks, who has also been a peace negotiator for many years, for instance being insulted or treated as an object, is at the root of most human conflicts and wars.

Indeed, a fundamental ethical principle, found in virtually all cultures, is some version of the Golden Rule: do unto others as you would have them do unto you. That principle has dignity—and avoiding what Hicks calls dignity violations—at its core. It applies to all human beings, no matter who or where they are.

Perhaps, however, we need to broaden the application and understanding of dignity beyond human beings in our narratives, organizations, attitudes, and practices if we are to truly achieve a better world for all. Consider for a moment whether it is also possible that we might, using a fully realized ecologizing perspective, treat not only all human beings, but also other living beings, as having dignity. For instance, if you have ever seen an elephant or lion in its natural setting, you might readily come to believe that these majestic animals are worthy of being treated with dignity—not simply exploited for human beings' welfare. What about other, smaller (less-majestic) animals or other creatures? Do they not also have their own dignity—intrinsic worth—apart from any possible usefulness they might have for humanity? Might we extend the notion of dignity to other living beings—and possibly stop believing that everything in nature is simply in the world for human exploitation? That reorientation is what ecologizing is fundamentally about.

What about non-animal beings, such as insects and plants? Have you ever seen a majestic tree that in a very real way seems to embody a form of dignity? Might we accord dignity to all living beings—and treat them (as Buddhists do) accordingly? We can even take this idea one step further and argue that manifestations of Nature that are not living in the traditional sense might also have intrinsic worth. Mountains, for example, lakes, streams, oceans, rivers, plains, landscapes, and so on, all exhibit a form of dignity. That is why we sometimes apply the label "majestic" to them. Of course, the implications of this thinking are vast and suggest an entirely revised human relationship with Nature, but it is not necessarily a new relationship.

Indeed, most Indigenous peoples have such an attitude, as articulated by Native American author Four Arrows (aka Donald Trent Jacobs) in his book *Point of Departure*, which lays out Indigenous' perspectives on and relationships with nature.[17] This ecologizing relationship is one in which all of Nature's manifestations are treated with dignity, even while recognizing that we humans need to use some of those resources for our own well-being. The difference in an ecologizing mindset is that even when natural resources are being used, that use is undertaken while still respecting other creatures, other living beings, and other aspects of nature.[18]

Hicks differentiates respect from dignity, arguing that although dignity is inherent and integral to all human beings, respect is something that must be earned through achievements, abilities, or other qualities. Respect is more associated with admiration and esteem for others than is dignity, which simple is because the person exists. In a better-balanced world, both dignity and respect would be afforded to other persons—and, as argued with dignity, potentially to other forms of life as well, moving us humans away from exploitation models of behavior towards more collaborative approaches.

Equity/Fairness/Justice

Equity, justice, and fairness all imply impartial treatment, that is, not either favoring or discriminating against specific people or groups. Fairness is treatment by others or by the bigger system that does not either favor one person or group over others or discriminate against them. A basic sense of fairness seems to be biologically present in human beings, and even in some animals, as biologist Frans de Waal's experiments with capuchin monkeys dramatically illustrate. In videos widely available online,[19] these animals in separate cages are asked to perform the same tasks and are rewarded with cucumbers. When one monkey is then rewarded with grapes, which the animals greatly favor over cucumbers, the disadvantaged monkey throws the cucumber back at the researcher, clearly sensing the unfairness of the reward structure, even though the other monkey still receives cucumbers.

A similar sense of fairness can be found in very young children when they are treated differently by parents or other adults. This sense of fairness also seems to broaden to the next important value to be discussed, that of care or love, with elements of reciprocity, empathy and cooperation also embedded. However, today's dominant human systems, our economies, favor the already wealthy or well-off, who have been becoming richer and richer over decades, while the less well-off struggle. A fairer system would provide equity in terms of opportunity for all, with reasonable distribution of wealth, rather than permitting the accumulation of such vast resources by a very few that eight men, according to Oxfam, are in 2017 were said to control as much wealth as the poorer half of humanity—over 3.5 billion people.[20] As the Oxfam report notes, "Left unchecked, growing inequality threatens to pull our societies apart. It increases crime and insecurity, and undermines the fight to end poverty. It leaves more people living in fear and fewer in hope."[21] The same organization in 2018 noted that the richest 1% in the world captured 82% of the wealth generated in the previous year,[22] indicating that growing inequality, which poses civilizational threats,[23] does not seem to be abating.

Many people view such unequal distribution of the world's financial wealth as inherently unfair and recognize that is how we humans have structured our economic systems that determines how rewards are distributed, not some act of nature. To bring better balance into the world is an imperative of equity and fairness, considered as memes. Not only does today's degree of inequality seem to justify a new story—but presumably, it will also require that actions be taken so that such unequal distribution of wealth no longer occurs, if a move towards an ecologizing mindset and world is to be achieved. At play here on a global scale, are tax policies, income earning potential, distribution and availability of decent work, and paying for "care" work that is now done without financial remuneration. Figuring out how to distribute financial and, importantly, other sources of the "wealth" of nonmaterial resources that lie at the heart of well-being is vitally important to a flourishing future for all.

Ideas about dignity and respect are also related to one of the moral foundation values uncovered by Haidt and his collaborators: sanctity.

Though the idea of sanctity, especially when expressed as "purity," appeals more to conservative than progressive thinkers, it is nonetheless is found in virtually all cultures. Here we relate the idea of sanctity, defined as the state or quality of being holy or sacred, to the idea of sacredness or inviolability—of ourselves as human beings, of our families, of our human enterprises of all sorts, including political and constitutional regimes, and, perhaps most importantly, of nature.

As we consider how to shift our economic and societal narratives towards ecologizing frames, the idea that the world around us—the natural and human world—is sacred, has sanctity, we believe, needs to be given more weight. Shamans, the healers of Indigenous cultures, believed that spirit exists in everything,[24] meaning that the world about us, as well as other people and the institutions they build, are in a sense sacred objects. As such, they are ideally to be treated with dignity, respect, and as if they were inviolable.

Imagine if today we considered the world about us to be sacred, whole and healthy, a living thing in itself that needed to be valued simply because it had its own dignity. What might such a mindset mean for the way we treat the land, our waters, and other living beings? No longer could we exploit them for our own use without regard for their intrinsic worth—dignity. Instead, we might have to devise ways of using—without overusing—what is needed that honor and respect these "others," perhaps in much the same ways that our Indigenous forebears did and that many Indigenous peoples do to this day. This way of thinking brings us to another important set of values out of which new ecologizing narratives might be constructed.

Care/Love/Stewardship

Today's economic and societal systems are all about growth in material and financial wealth, rather than well-being. Our systems are geared towards cutthroat competition through what some call a winner-take-all mentality,[25] which leaves the struggling poor behind while the rich get ever-richer, as we have just seen. There is another way, as cultural historian, systems scientist, and educator Riane Eisler has pointed out for years: building a caring economy. Caring simply means providing what is needed for the health, welfare (well-being), maintenance, and protection of people or, indeed, the world. The idea of caring is also associated with doing things cautiously as opposed to recklessly, developing awareness and paying attention to what is really important, with associations towards stewardship.[26]

We could expand this idea of care to encompass "love," which is typically associated with romantic love. Love, however, also comes to the fore in many spiritual traditions, which argue that love, often expressed as a feeling of oneness with the universe or whatever higher power one believes in, is the highest form of spirituality. Thinking about this notion of oneness as love orients us towards the idea of developing new narratives and systems around inclusiveness, that is, bringing everyone into the benefits and responsibilities of the system in a relatively equitable way, reflecting the values of fairness just discussed. Arguably, the principles discussed earlier in the book that "give life" to systems can also be used to provide a basis of inclusiveness, diversity, and, ultimately, love and care that create a better world for all.

Riane Eisler has articulated a similar set of principles for what she calls a caring economy, an economy that recognizes—in addition to paid work outside the home—the important, yet often unpaid, work of caring for others. Indeed, she argues that the *real* wealth of nations can be found in a caring economics, one that encourages people to achieve their highest potential, be creative, have empathy for others, and work collaboratively in what she calls partnership rather than dominator cultures.

Freedom and Autonomy Set in Community

Freedom is the right or power to speak, act, think as desired without hindrances, that is, without barriers to actions external to an individual's will. Autonomy is the capacity to live one's life according to his or her own lights, not directed by others.[27] Many people value both freedom and autonomy at least to some extent. In fact, Haidt offers the opposites of liberty and oppression as another proposed universal moral foundation to add to the five main ones discussed earlier.[28]

Nobel Prize in Economics awardee Amartya Sen, in fact, defines (human) development as freedom, arguing for what he calls capabilities (substantive human freedoms). According to Sen, human development "requires the removal of major sources of unfreedom: poverty as well as tyranny, poor economic opportunities as well as systematic social deprivation, and neglect of public facilities as well as intolerance or overactivity of repressive states."[29] Sen also argues for positive freedoms, including the basic freedom to survive, access to health care, sanitary arrangements, adequate nutrition, and clean water, plus basic political and civil rights and liberty, economic and other forms of security, all of which he believes essential for people to develop their basic "capabilities." Foundational, in Sen's thinking are political and civil freedoms.[30]

Martha Nussbaum has elaborated Sen's ideas about capabilities and freedom. Nussbaum builds on the fundamental idea of human dignity, discussed above, and argues that freedom manifests in specific capabilities. Core human capabilities, according to Nussbaum, are life (not dying prematurely), bodily health (good health, including reproductive health), and bodily integrity (freedom from violent assault, the ability to move around, opportunities for sexual satisfaction, and choice in reproductive matters). Other core capabilities include senses, imagination, and thought (ability to use senses to imagine, think, and reason); freedom of emotions (attachments to things/people outside of the self); and what Nussbaum terms practical reason (the ability to form a concept of the good and engage in critical reflection). Further, she highlights the importance of affiliation (living with and towards others, along with self-respect), other species (living with concern in relation to other species and beings, as discussed earlier), play (freedom to laugh and play), and control over one's environment (including political participation, material capability to hold property).[31]

The idea of liberty can be carried too far in the context of human societies. Libertarianism expresses freedom in radical form. Libertarianism is a form of extreme individualism that is a collection of political philosophies that upholds liberty as a core principle, and in doing so mixes both liberal and conservative sensibilities. Libertarians emphasize maximum political autonomy (think "keep government off our backs"), freedom of choice, voluntary association, and individual judgment over any sense of the collective or community. In extreme form, libertarians might argue, for example, that any person or company can offer any product or service that people are willing to pay for, no matter what the ethical, social, or ecological impacts, and that relying on markets is the best way to improve lives. In such a context any regulation is viewed as extremely undesirable.

In one study, Haidt and collaborators found that libertarians, in fact, viewed individual liberty as their strongest guiding value or moral foundation, while downplaying the other values commonly found in different cultures. They also expressed a more cognitive versus emotional style, along with less recognition of interdependence and social relatedness to others.[32] This study also demonstrated that "Libertarianism provides an ideological narrative whereby the opposition to high taxes and big government is not just an 'economic' position: it is a *moral* position as well. This narrative provides the basis for principled opposition to a government seen as unfair . . . tyrannical . . . and wasteful."[33] Note here the importance of the particular memes of unfairness, tyranny (because of government's coercive powers), and waste, which have become popular talking points of neoliberalism. Any new ecologizing narrative needs to deal effectively with these memes of libertarianism, which at least in the United States have entered the popular conversation, since in this extreme form, libertarianism opposes concerns for social justice and respect for existing social structures in the overarching interest of promoting and preserving individual liberty.[34]

Freedom, autonomy, or liberty, however, are not absolute in practice, since we human beings are social creatures and we necessarily live in communities of various shapes and sizes. In the context of community, our freedoms are bounded by community norms, values, and acceptable practices. Although ardent advocates of extreme individualism might want to be free from all restraints imposed by communities or by governments, the reality is that this is an impractical solution to the problem of individual freedom.

One of the problems that arises with the neoliberal narrative is that it emphasizes individual liberty and freedom to the exclusion of recognizing that societies and communities exist and have their own values. In a community context, "my" freedom is necessarily restricted to activities that cause no harm to others because, at some level, we really are all in this together, as we are inextricably connected to each other and to the natural environment.

Meaning and Belonging

The need to belong is a very fundamental human trait and one that is also foundational to providing a sense of meaning in life.[35] Yet the neoliberal narrative does not account for these needs, in part because of the belief that (in Margaret Thatcher's words) "there is no such thing as society." To fully reconnect the human chain, we need to realize the importance of people having a sense of belonging and an opportunity to live, from their own perspectives, a meaningful life. The idea of belonging is deeply rooted in the human psyche—and apparently an important aspect of survival, where belonging is associated with the subjective experience that people have of fitting in in a given context.[36] Complemented by Victor Frankl's notion of "will to meaning," or the fundamental need that humans have to find meaning in their lives,[37] some scholars argue that people cannot live if they believe that their lives are meaningless,[38] thus linking these two ideas together.

One of human beings' deep-seated needs is what Baumeister calls the pursuit of a meaningful life. We all, that is, want to live meaningful lives in which we can fulfill our own purposes. Baumeister claims that meaning is driven by four basic human needs: *purpose* in life, *efficacy* or control over one's outcomes, *value* or morally good and correct actions, and *positive self-worth*.[39] He also (with Stillman) concludes that "most human anxiety is focused on issues of belongingness."[40] The need for a place to "belong" became clear to one of the authors of this book at a conference designed to think about new narratives for the future, where it became a major theme, in part because humans are fundamentally social creatures whose survival depends on their relationships with their social group(s), rather than directly from nature.[41] Perhaps that is why issues of inclusiveness and diversity, which are related to the components that give life to systems are so important.

A sense of belonging—affiliation to a place, situation, or community of some sort, thus is as important as is meaning to human well-being. Belonging can be a sense of being "at home" somewhere (place-belongingness) or as part of community of some sort (politics of belonging), both aspects of which are important, according to Antonsich.[42] The need to belong, which has connotations of inclusion, acceptance, loyalty, affinity, attachment, and relationship, seems to be an integral part of the human condition. What Antonsich calls place belonging does not necessarily refer to one's literal home, but rather is an emotional connection to a "symbolic space of familiarity, comfort, security, and emotional attachment."[43] Importantly, place-belongingness seems related to being where one feels safe. The politics of belonging puts the notion of belonging into its social context, that is belonging to a group of people who share language (discourse), perhaps place, and feeling included, providing for a sense of identity.[44]

Obviously, used in this sense, belonging connects us, either to places or to other people, helping to heal the broken human chain, almost literally. People can feel like they belong in a certain place or places, because of the familiarity or resonance of that locality. Belongingness can also be related to feeling part of some sort of social group, like a church, club, or network of like-minded individuals who share situations, experiences, ideas, or interests in common. As new ecologizing narratives that attempt to reconnect the human chain emerge, we believe it is important that issues of meaning and belonging are included in those narratives.

Collective Value

One final value seems to us to be important as part of the foundation for ecologizing narratives that help repair the broken human chain, that of collective value. Businesses are perhaps the world's most important institutions today, yet for the most part their purpose is restricted (in most people's understanding) to the neoliberal maxim of maximizing shareholder wealth or (financial) profits. Some legal scholars (in our view, rightly) question the premise that the only purpose of firms is to maximize wealth for one (already-privileged) group of stakeholders, the shareholders, arguing that the idea is built on flawed legal logic.[45] Others, notably stakeholder theorist R. Edward Freeman, have argued that shareholder and stakeholder values and needs are intrinsically aligned. Stakeholders (whether customers, employees, suppliers, communities, and financiers) are linked by common purpose, and what he terms the "jointness of stakeholder interests, in which the primary purpose of executives is to create the most stakeholder (not just shareholder) value for all."[46]

Taking this thinking one step further towards an ecologizing mindset, in their important paper "Toward a Theory of Business," Thomas Donaldson and James Walsh argued that there has been insufficient attention to actual *business* purpose, beyond the oft-stated corporate purpose of shareholder wealth maximization.[47] Recognizing the importance of economic and business activity to contributing to a better world, these authors emphasize the purpose, accountability, control of businesses, and the nature of what business success actually means. Ultimately, they define the purpose of businesses as creating "collective value,"[48] importantly, absent any (human) dignity violations (though they do give a nod to other living beings as well). They argue that businesses are accountable to their stakeholders (though they do not use that term), whether in the past, present, or future, and that businesses must avoid dignity violations, while attempting to achieve "optimized collective value," as a marker of success.[49]

In this reading of collective value absent dignity violations, we take the idea to mean that businesses and possibly other institutions in a reconnected framework would attempt to do their part, within the context of their expertise and resources, to promote the welfare—well-being—of their various constituents or stakeholders. That wellbeing includes the natural environment viewed as a stakeholder and certainly should also include avoid doing harm in the process of doing business. Such an idea builds on the idea of stakeholder value as articulated by Freeman. Although how collective value is to be measured is still uncertain, the idea broadens our purpose well beyond serving a single stakeholder group towards the collection of stakeholders engaged with a business and also has implications for the broader socio-ecological contexts in which businesses operate. Aligned with more global metrics at the societal or national level, like the GPI, discussed above, the idea of collective value could bring about much-needed reform of how businesses operate with respect to their stakeholders and nature.

Restorying the Human Chain

Our relationships and connectedness, combined with our reflective capacity and a core set of memes that emphasize what gives life to systems and foundational values, means that we can begin to "restory" ourselves as well as important relationships with others and our communities and with nature. What these new stories look like will be up to each person or community, but here we offer some thoughts.

Reconnecting With Self

Reconnecting the human chain has multiple facets to it. We need reconnecting to self, reconnecting to others (community), and reconnecting to nature. Connecting to ourselves is an exercise in developing self-awareness and examining self-identity. Self-awareness and the ability to reflect on what we do and who we are is a social process through which we humans inculcate awareness of ourselves as social beings and our relationships with others and nature. This awareness and resulting identity make us—coming from a certain place (village, town, city), of a certain class (education, economic or social group), following certain beliefs and customs (religion, ideologies, profession)—into who we are as people. We humans define ourselves with such attributes. Sometimes we are a sum of these attributes and at other times we identify with one or another attribute—defining ourselves as lawyers or doctors or through our professional roles. We identify with others of similar characteristics or attributes. They are our "tribe." We distinguish ourselves from other tribes.

Unlike other living beings (that we know of at least), we humans have the capacity to be self-reflective, and to change our minds, our patterns, our behaviors, and the way we approach the world. With this capacity of what is sometimes called reflexivity, we have the ability to change ourselves and our world—hopefully for the better.

Our self-definitions can be a source of our disconnection from self and others. When we choose one attribute to define our self, we reject other competing ones. So if our identity is based on, say, religion, if we are a Christian, we cannot also be a Hindu or a Muslim. If we define our self by place, if we are American, we cannot also be Chinese (dual citizenships notwithstanding). These simplistic dualisms overlook that both/ and of many people's actual lives, in which they experience multiple different facets of themselves, even multiple identities, simultaneously. For example, a woman might be a doctor, a mother, a daughter, a wife, and a musician—or any number of other things that she identifies with. They are all part of her overall personhood, yet she may reveal very different aspects of who she is in each of these roles, depending on the relevant context and audience. More like (multiple) dualities, these different identities peacefully co-exist.

Progressively over the past century, our defining attributes are social, economic, political, professional, and not nature-related. In an increasingly technologized world, self-definition attributes have become more technologized and mediated by technologies. In past centuries one may have self-defined oneself as a "farmer" with overt connections to land and agriculture. Today even farming is largely a highly technological and industrial operation.

Reconnecting With Others

Connection with others is the essence of community. Our connections form into community units of family, neighborhood, towns or cities, and nations. These communities express our shared values and aspirations. Values united families, villages, and regions, giving us a common identity. In the past century, connection to others and formation of community has been deeply influenced by exploding knowledge and technology and by expanding market forces. Knowledge of the world makes us different from others. There is more knowledge and it is easier to acquire knowledge, making us more different as individuals, and less homogenous as groups. We cherish this knowledge; celebrate our differences (uniqueness); and, in some cultures (such as that of America and of many parts of the Western world), we regard individualism as an ideology of progress. In some cultures, collectivism is still valued and some social systems and practices of collective identities remain intact, albeit under tremendous pressure of change and reformation.

In a world where people's identities are tied to their possessions, the acquisition of goods and market forces that enable them have significant impact on how people connect to one another. Goods and possessions are themselves a focus for separating us from others. They absorb our attention and time, taking these things away from others. Our possessions also say a great deal about our availability for connecting with others. Our home, our clothes, and our automobile assign a status identity to us, which others view, compare, and interpret in terms of desirability for connection.

Reconnecting With Nature

The story recounted in the prologue about a man living in Montreal and traveling to Toronto and back, executing his whole workday without ever coming in touch with nature, is symptomatic of many peoples' systemic disconnection with nature, particularly in the "developed" parts of the world. Our isolation from nature is enabled by the social–technical systems within which our lives are embedded. Many if not most of us live in homes and work in offices. That fact alone separates us from nature for much of the day. We may transport ourselves from place to place, by private auto or public transport. Our entertainment options have increasingly moved away from outdoor nature-based entertainment, to indoor organized activities such as movies, restaurants, theatre, and the like. Even sports have moved from being played outdoors to indoor arenas and stadiums. The "infrastructure" of living is largely organized indoors in well-curated denatured specialized environments. So, our options to engage with nature are severely curtailed. And nature activities require special intentionality and effort.

This separation from nature by the venues and organization of our life activities over time normalizes a life without nature. But the primal desire for nature is not entirely lost. To fulfill that desire, there is now an emerging trend of developments/perversions, in which nature is reproduced artificially and in totally controlled ways. Ski slopes routinely run on artificially made snow. There are even covered temperature controlled indoor ski slopes. Fishing in artificially stocked ponds and pay lakes caters to need for convenient and assured catch even for amateur fisher persons. Safaris in controlled state parks guarantee sightings of "wildlife." These staged and managed natural experiences are designed to remove risk and spontaneity in engaging nature, making nature safe for all.

The intense urbanization of the past half century makes nature more and more inaccessible to many people. They may have to travel many miles to reach natural areas. At night urban light pollution in most urban areas precludes residents from experiencing true darkness. In most urban areas, stars are not visible due to light pollution. Over half the people living in urban areas may never see a star in their lifetime.

It is still possible for most of us to access nature. To do that, however, a deliberate choice and effort must be made. Often it also costs a significant amount of money for transport, access, and use of nature facilities. We can make nature a part of our lives by living mindfully and incorporating it deliberately and intentionally into daily practices. Exercising outside, having animals in our lives (pets, farm animals), growing food, gardens, volunteering in and being part of community gardens, trail maintenance, there are many opportunities. But these must be deliberately planned and availed of.

Reconnecting the human chain is also about organizational connections. Organizations connect with each other to further their respective purposes. They resort to trading, information exchange, do business contracts, and network with their stakeholders (clients, customers, competitors, business associates, etc.). These normal connections serve well-understood purposes. But there are benefits to connecting organizationally that go beyond purposive connecting. Connection not directed to fulfilling purpose can create belonging, conviviality, redundancy, and buffers that can build resilience in and among organizations, peoples, and communities at various levels. These connections can activate recovery in unanticipated disasters. As natural disasters become more frequent and devastating under climate change, it is imperative that we build systemic resilience within organizations and systems of organizations. Resilience is the ability of organizations and systems to spring back to functional level after disruption under stress. Resilience comes from a special form of connectivity that enables serendipity, opportunity to act, and fortuity. Complex systems are often opaque or at best only partially visible. Some connectivities are part of the design of complex systems, but others occur unintendedly due to the nature of complexity and the evolving dynamics among its parts. Thoughtful management of connectivities within and across organizations and systems can pay rich dividends in periods of unanticipated disasters.

Notes

1. McGilchrist, I. (2009). *The master and his emissary: The divided brain and the making of the western world*. New Haven: Yale University Press.
2. Frederick, W. C. (1995). *Values, nature, and culture in the American corporation*. Oxford: Oxford University Press.
3. Waddock, S. (2002). *Leading corporate citizens: Vision, values, value-added*. New York: McGraw-Hill.

4. E.g., Wilber, K. (2002). *A theory of everything: An integral vision for business, politics, science, and spirituality*. Boston: Shambhala.
5. Donaldson, T., & Dunfee, T. W. (1999). *Ties that bind: A social contracts approach to business ethics*. Cambridge, MA: Harvard Business Press.
6. Haidt, J. (2012). *The righteous mind: Why good people are divided by politics and religion*. New York: Vintage.
7. Pollan, M. (2006). *The omnivore's dilemma: A natural history of four meals*. New York: Penguin.
8. Lovins, L. H. (2016). Needed: A better story. *Humanistic Management Journal*, 1(1), 75–90.
9. Korten, D. C. (2015). *Change the story, change the future: A living economy for a living Earth*. San Francisco, CA: Berrett-Koehler Publishers; see also, Korten, D. (2017, Fall). Ecological civilization and the new enlightenment. *Tikkun*, 16–23, 70; Korten, D. (2010). *Agenda for a new economy: From phantom wealth to real wealth* (2nd ed.). San Francisco, CA: Berrett-Koehler.
10. E.g., Pirson, M. (2017). *Humanistic management: Protecting dignity and promoting well-being*. Cambridge, UK: Cambridge University Press.
11. Haidt, J. (2012). *The righteous mind: Why good people are divided by politics and religion*. New York: Vintage.
12. Sen, A. (1993). Capability and well-being 73. *The Quality of Life*, 30–53.
13. See, e.g., Ida Kubiszewski et al. (2013). Beyond GDP: Measuring and achieving global genuine progress. *Ecological Economics*, 93.
14. OECD. *How's life?* Retrieved from: www.oecdbetterlifeindex.org/#/11111111111.
15. Check out the Better Life Index yourself, and see where your country stands at: www.oecdbetterlifeindex.org/topics/life-satisfaction/.
16. Hicks, D. (2011). *Dignity: The essential role it plays in resolving conflict*. New Haven: Yale University Press.
17. Arrows, F. (aka Donald Trent Jacobs) (2016). *Point of departure: Returning to our more authentic worldview for education and survival*. Charlotte, NC: IAP.
18. See, e.g., Waddock, S. (2019). Wisdom, sustainability, dignity, and the intellectual shaman. In D. Narvaez, F. Arrows, E. Halton, B. Collier, & G. Enderle (Eds.), *Indigenous sustainable wisdom: First nation know-how for global flourishing* (pp. 244–264). Bern, Switzerland: Peter Lang Publishing Group.
19. One such experiment can be found at: www.ted.com/talks/frans_de_waal_do_animals_have_morals?language=en.
20. Oxfam, An Economy for the 99%, Oxfam.org. (2017). Retrieved from: https://www-cdn.oxfam.org/s3fs-public/file_attachments/bp-economy-for-99-percent-160117-en.pdf.
21. Oxfam. (2017). Retrieved from: https://www-cdn.oxfam.org/s3fs-public/file_attachments/bp-economy-for-99-percent-160117-en.pdf, p. 2.
22. Oxfam. (2018, January 2018). *Reward work, not wealth*. Oxfam Briefing Paper, Retrieved from: https://www-cdn.oxfam.org/s3fs-public/file_attachments/bp-reward-work-not-wealth-220118-en.pdf.
23. Diamond, J. (2005). *Collapse: How societies choose to fail or succeed*. New York: Penguin.
24. Waddock, S. (2017). *Healin the world: Today's shamans as difference makers*. London: Routledge.
25. Giridharadas, A. (2018). *Winners take all: The elite charade of changing the world*. New York: Knopf.
26. *Interdisciplinary Journal of Partnership*, 4(3). Retrieved from: http://pubs.lib.umn.edu/ijps/vol4/iss3/13; also, Eisler, R. (2008). *The real wealth of*

nations: Creating a caring economics. San Francisco, CA: Berrett-Koehler Publishers.

27. Christman, J. (2015). *Autonomy in moral and political philosophy.* Stanford Encyclopedia of Philosophy. Retrieved from: https://plato.stanford.edu/entries/autonomy-moral/.

28. Haidt, J. (2012). *The righteous mind: Why good people are divided by politics and religion.* New York: Vintage.

29. Sen, A. (2011). *Development as freedom.* New York: Anchor. Also, Sen, A. (2014). *Development as freedom.* New York: Anchor; Roberts, J. T., Hite, A. B., & Chorev, N. (1999). *The globalization and development reader: Perspectives on development and global change* (Vol. 2, pp. 525–547), London: Wiley.

30. Sen, A. (2011). *Development as freedom.* New York: Anchor. Also, Sen, A. (2014). *Development as freedom* (pp. 526–528). New York: Anchor.

31. Nussbaum, M. (2003). Capabilities as fundamental entitlements: Sen and social justice. *Feminist Economics, 9*(2–3), 33–59, 41–42.

32. Iyer, R., Kovevena, S., Graham, J., Ditto, P., & Haidt, J. (2010). Understanding libertarian morality: The psychological dispositions of self-identified libertarians. *Plos/One, 7*(8), 1–23. Retrieved August 21 from: https://journals.plos.org/plosone/article?id=10.1371/journal.pone.0042366.

33. Iyer, R., Kovevena, S., Graham, J., Ditto, P., & Haidt, J. (2010). Understanding libertarian morality: The psychological dispositions of self-identified libertarians. *Plos/One, 7*(8), 1–23. Retrieved August 21 from: https://journals.plos.org/plosone/article?id=10.1371/journal.pone.0042366.

34. Iyer et al. (2012). Understanding libertarian morality: The psychological dispositions of self-identified libertarians. *Plos/One, 7*(8), 1–23, 2. Retrieved August 21 from: https://journals.plos.org/plosone/article?id=10.1371/journal.pone.0042366.

35. Lambert, N. M., Stillman, T. F., Hicks, J. A., Kamble, S., Baumeister, R. F., & Fincham, F. D. (2013). To belong is to matter: Sense of belonging enhances meaning in life. *Personality and Social Psychology Bulletin, 39*(11), 1418–1427.

36. Lambert, N. M., Stillman, T. F., Hicks, J. A., Kamble, S., Baumeister, R. F., & Fincham, F. D. (2013). To belong is to matter: Sense of belonging enhances meaning in life. *Personality and Social Psychology Bulletin, 39*(11), 1418.

37. Frankl, V. E. (1984). *Man's search for meaning.* New York: Touchstone.

38. Klinger, E. (1998). The search for meaning in an evolutionary perspective and its clinical implications. In P. Wong & P. Fry (Eds.), *The human quest for meaning: A handbook of psychological research and clinical applications* (pp. 27–50). Mahwah, NJ: Lawrence Erlbaum, cited in Lambert, N. M., Stillman, T. F., Hicks, J. A., Kamble, S., Baumeister, R. F., & Fincham, F. D. (2013). To belong is to matter: Sense of belonging enhances meaning in life. *Personality and Social Psychology Bulletin, 39*(11), 1419.

39. Summarized in: Stillman, T. F., & Baumeister, R. F. (2009). Uncertainty, belongingness, and four needs for meaning. *Psychological Inquiry, 20*(4), 249–251, from Baumeister, R. F. (1991). *Meanings of life.* New York: Guilford Press.

40. Tillman, T. F., & Baumeister, R. F. (2009). Uncertainty, belongingness, and four needs for meaning. *Psychological Inquiry, 20*(4), 249–251.

41. Tillman, T. F., & Baumeister, R. F. (2009). Uncertainty, belongingness, and four needs for meaning. *Psychological Inquiry, 20*(4), 249–251, 250.

42. Antonsich, M. (2010). Searching for belonging—an analytical framework. *Geography Compass, 4*(6), 644–659.

43. Antonsich, M. (2010). Searching for belonging—an analytical framework. *Geography Compass*, 4(6), 646.
44. Antonsich, M. (2010). Searching for belonging—an analytical framework. *Geography Compass*, 4(6), 649.
45. Stout, L. A. (2012). *The shareholder value myth: How putting shareholders first harms investors, corporations, and the public.* San Francisco, CA: Berrett-Koehler Publishers.
46. Freeman, R. E. (2010). Managing for stakeholders: Trade-offs or value creation. *Journal of Business Ethics*, 96(1), 7–9.
47. Donaldson, T., & Walsh, J. P. (2015). Toward a theory of business. *Research in Organizational Behavior*, 35, 181–207.
48. Donaldson, T., & Walsh, J. P. (2015). Toward a theory of business. *Research in Organizational Behavior*, 35, 181–207. They define Collective Value as "the agglomeration of the Business Participants' Benefits, net of any aversive outcomes." (p. 191).
49. Donaldson, T., & Walsh, J. P. (2015). Toward a theory of business. *Research in Organizational Behavior*, 35, 195.

Epilogue

Traveling back to Toronto, we continue to see a city in flux; a grand metropolis trying to reinvent itself in the wake of the Anthropocene Era. Although it is still growing at a faster pace than most North American cities, Toronto faces significant ecological and social challenges, many of which are identified in this book. As this book is being published, the Toronto City Council and the Mayor's Office seek to redevelop the city's vast waterfront on Lake Ontario. For years regarded as an industrial wasteland, Toronto's waterfront remains isolated from the rest of the city. It sits on the south side of the city separated by the massive concrete Gardiner Expressway. One has to cross several lanes of high-speed traffic even to access the water. But the city is interested in redesigning and rethinking its relationship with the lake by redeveloping the area and connecting it more with its inhabitants and visitors.

In 2019, Alphabet Co.'s (of Google fame) Sidewalk Labs has been courting the city and provincial decision makers to design a space on the water. The 12-acre, Quayside property on the eastern waterfront has been the subject of redevelopment for years. It used to house warehouses and factories that served the city during its industrial history. This "dream project" is designed to create a sustainable neighborhood that connects the people of Toronto more closely with their waterfront. It is to provide affordable housing to a variety of socio-economic groups. The property is to achieve climate-positive development for all its buildings and landscape. According to Sidewalk Labs, this innovative new neighborhood would eliminate energy waste through various digital management tools and would generate sustainable energy through a thermal grid district energy system.[1] The smart city infrastructure project claims to be a "living laboratory for the sustainable neighborhoods of the future."[2]

Sounds wonderful, no?

Well, Toronto residents and policymakers have been debating the merits of this economically viable proposal for many months. Concerns center around privacy issues and data collection associated with the "smart" urban development.[3] The plan has aspects of surveillance capitalism.[4] The idea of this form of capitalism relies on technology for the "exploitation of behavioural predictions covertly derived from the surveillance of users".[5] Surveillance capitalism involves collecting mass amounts of data from consumers through the provision of free services in order to monitor individuals' behaviors. So, although affordable housing and a sustainable design of the neighborhood are offered, the cost of better connecting the waterfront to the rest of Toronto is the loss of privacy. This has people all over Ontario worried.

Thus, we have another tension for sustainability. With Sidewalk Labs, we see a good example of organizations trying to help a city ecologize through techno-symbolic advances. The competitive desire for companies to continue to grow economically and expand their influence in the market is rooted in power-aggrandizing values. For someone like Sergio (from the Prologue of this book), if he were to decide to move to the new waterfront neighborhood, he may feel more connected to Lake Ontario, but living there means sacrificing some of his human rights, like privacy. Of course, this tension with big data is not a new story. Businesses large and small have been exploiting individuals' personal data for years, which can itself be argued to be an abuse of power. To economize, businesses innovate through their techno-symbolic values. To ecologize, businesses innovate through these values as well. But does the Sidewalk Labs proposal strike the proper balance we are trying to achieve in this book? We remain skeptical. Ironically, technology can and does make the world feel more "connected." But at the same time, we can feel isolated from ourselves and from our environment. The electronic revolution has indeed generated a plethora of other sets of paradoxes for the human condition.

The 2018 IPCC report on sustainability[6] has called for a great urgency to invoke radical change in order to avoid a non-reversible climate disaster. It advocates for major alterations to how humans live that go beyond current sustainable development discussions. We need new models for interacting with our planet. This requires a greater connection between humans and nature. The Anthropocene mandates that we resolve epistemological challenges in organizational studies regarding the nature/culture dualism.[7] The assumption that humans are separate from nature and the environment needs to be revised,[8] as we have argued in this book.

The organizers of the 35th annual European Group for Organizational Studies Colloquium in 2019 proposed that organizations need to be studied through a cosmological lens that ceases to view business as separate from nature.[9] They refer to Karen Barad's idea of "agential realism" as being necessary for reframing corporate agency as "enactment, a matter of possibilities for reconfiguring entanglements."[10] This view moves away from our current sociomaterial practices in business. Rodolphe Durand proposes an organizing of "worldmaking," which involves reassembling our currently disorganized world that has lost its meaning.[11] Anna Tsing's view of worldmaking, while different from Durand's, involves the "art of noticing" the ruin and destruction of our relationship with the environment.[12] She argues that our current conception of capitalism has caused much of this ruin. One has to think if proposals like the Sidewalk Labs one in Toronto are only proliferating the disconnect and ruin.

Regardless, we feel that such discussions are important developments for reconnecting the human chain. There are stories of hope that can serve as the impetus for meaningful change. Perhaps we are in the midst of a fourth Industrial Revolution, as Klaus Schwab, the founder of the World Economic Forum, has suggested. We now have access to connective technologies that allow us to address these environmental concerns. Despite the worries with big data, the new economy affords society the possibility for revolutionary change. It is just that the technological innovations have to responsibly employed so as not to generate more ruin.

For instance, technology now allows us to have real-time conference meetings that avoid the need for airplane travel to remote locations. Philosopher Walter Sinnott-Armstrong argued in 2005 that we have a moral obligation to reduce our individual carbon footprint.[13] This obligation involves "noticing" each of our roles in affecting the environment. Charles Einstein builds on this notion in his 2018 book, "Climate: A New Story," by calling for a deeper revolution to enable individuals to realize that they *are* nature. By recognizing this fact that humans are part and parcel of our ecological environment, we may be more willing to engage in climate-related lifestyle changes.[14] Are we willing to make individual sacrifices to promote ecologizing values?

As individuals, it is critical for us to "notice" our ecological environment in order to motivate a concern for sustainability. BBC presenter, Ellie Harrison, has argued in her show, "Countryfile," that individuals should be encouraged to engage with wildlife in their natural habitats. To observe other species "living" in the world among us is important to make our place in the world more salient. This is something that Sergio in Toronto needs. By being completely isolated from other living species in his metropolitan existence, Sergio does not have the chance to notice. The Japanese have practiced the art of *shinrin-yoku*, the act of spending meaningful time in the woods, which is believed to improve physical and mental well-being. But it is built on the premise that it is important to have all five human senses engaged with the natural environment.[15] Proponents of *shinrin-yoku* believe that this connection to nature is important for individual health and wellness benefits, like reduced stress and blood pressure. Thus, a connection to nature does not just benefit the planet.

Ana Maria Hernandez, the Chair of the Intergovernmental Science-Policy Platform on Biodiversity and Ecosystem Services, calls for a change from business-as-usual when it comes to the environment too. She argues that complacency is the greatest threat to the natural world.[16] Big changes cannot be made unless people become proactive. Staying in our comfort zones and our current comfortable lifestyles (like Sergio) endangers our ability to make transformative changes. Hernandez is hopeful by the observed greater awareness among young people and thinks this can be a source of optimism for the future of our planet.

Movements at the organizational and industry levels also provide rays of hope for our reconnection with nature. Historic districts and neighborhoods along the East Coast of the United States are increasingly confronted with the likelihood that natural environmental disasters will destroy their communities. Rising sea levels because of the climate crisis and the increased risk of severe weather endanger our historic and modern-day building structures. Currently, architects, city planners, and engineers are rethinking our relationship with nature at the community level by devising new approaches to protecting existing structures.[17] Adaptation design projects are being enacted to allow man-made buildings exist more naturally in their environment. Ideas like allowing water to flow through buildings (much like Frank Lloyd Wright's, Fallingwater, in Pennsylvania), transforming basements into cisterns, and building floatation systems are among some of the efforts. Although reactive to our present predicament, these efforts can inform the design and maintenance of new building structures around the world. Instead of manipulating nature, these initiatives promote "living" with nature.

Motivated by the devastating wildfires ravishing California in recent years, the wine industry is also learning how to change their mindset and adapt to their environment. Residents and winemakers in the Sonoma region are learning how to live with fire and create safer systems for coping and saving lives. Collectives in the area are trying to teach resilience by learning how native oak trees and bay laurels withstand blazes. They are also turning to lessons learned from the first natives who sowed the lands so as to regenerate fire-strewn areas and protect against future disasters. The key to their efforts rests in the community's willingness to "notice" how nature adapts, rebuilds, and survives natural disasters.[18]

We see changes in the fashion industry as well. Overall, the fashion is the second greatest polluting industry in the world with their use of chemicals and a large carbon footprint. But now, partly because of changing stakeholder expectations for sustainable conscious clothing, the industry is adopting a multitude of recycling and clean water initiatives that tap into historic ways of making textiles.[19] Fashion houses like Hermes are working to create a balance between preservation and newness. This company has started practicing corporate social responsibility approaches to their manufacture and distribution of their garments. They maintain old-style craft-making in order to maintain a sustainable future. By turning to the past, wasteful mass production methods are abandoned. This shift from complacency is the result of a growing awareness of the industry's damage to our planet.

Hope doesn't end there. At the systemic level there are a variety of global efforts aimed at fighting our Anthropocene challenges. There is a growing movement for generating climate-oriented public figures in government, despite this Century's swing to populism. Some politicians in the United States are calling for the country to be carbon-neutral by the Year 2050. In Europe, Green parties are expanding their reach and becoming more successful at delivering their message. The European Union elections in the summer of 2019 have seen a significant growth in Green parties influence in Parliament. Green parties won 63 out of 751 seats in Parliament, which is a 47% increase. In Germany, the Greens received over 20% of the vote alone. In France and the U.K., similar increases in those parties' influence can be seen. Southern and Eastern European voters are also speaking out at the ballot boxes by electing more environmentally conscious leaders.[20] This can all be at least partially linked to a growing public awareness for the importance of society's connection with the natural environment. This growth reflects the realization that change cannot happen only by individuals but that social and political systems play a huge role. Pope Francis at the Vatican has also advocated for meaningful change towards sustainability in his 2018 Encyclical, linking social issues like poverty and justice to environmental issues.[21] The Pope advocates counteracting the throwaway culture that inflicts the entire planet and recognizes that changing business behavior is paramount for preserving the lives of current and future generations.

Academic and non-governmental institutions are also making great strides at reconnecting the human chain. Organizations like the Wellbeing Economy Alliance are trying to transform business thinking to create a wellbeing economy, one that emphasizes individual and ecological wellbeing.[22] This group has assembled a global association of organizations, partnerships and social movements designed to connect the economy to the promotion of wellbeing of humans and the environment. Similarly, the SDG Transformations Forum attempts to create radical mindsets with new narratives, capacity development, new evaluation methods, and other approaches for organizing change for our current and future environmental challenges around the UN's Sustainable Development Goals.[23] This Agenda 2030 or so-called Global Goals sets a plan for connecting disparate disciplines and organizations to work together for transformative change. The goal is to integrate existing efforts that are underway separately to accelerate progress for sustainability. This organization also sees individual human issues of justice and human rights to be deeply embedded in environmental issues. Groups like the International Humanistic Management Association (IHMA) partner with these organizations to protect human dignity and promote human flourishing through new business models.[24] IHMA is another global institution that recognizes the interconnectedness of humans with their natural environment.

These movements are just a few examples of numerous other global efforts to reconnect the human chain. But the message here is one of hope. In this book we identify and highlight many tensions at various levels of analysis that we view as generating and perpetuating influences on the sustainability dilemma facing the world. Recognizing these tensions is a critical first step for understanding how to reduce them and create a more sustainable future for this planet. We can restore a balance between our economizing and ecologizing natural tendencies, as illustrated by some of these examples. We allow these tensions to continue only if we fear creating new narratives and changing mindsets. As a species we are capable of innovating and adapting to new challenges as seen throughout our anthropological history. We cannot be complacent with the status quo nor be comfortable with isolating ourselves from the natural world. Individuals, businesses, and systemic institutions all need to take part in enacting change. It will take humility, compassion, and innovative thinking to restore our human links in the environmental chain.

Notes

1. www.sidewalktoronto.ca/innovations/sustainability.
2. Allen, B., & Psaki, N. (2019, August 31). Toronto must take the lead on smart city infrastructure. *Toronto Star*.
3. D'Onfro, J. (2019). Google sibling Sidewalk Labs unveils smart city plans for Toronto waterfront. www.forbes.com/sites/jilliandonfro/2019/06/24/alphabet-google-sidewalk-labs-smart-city-plans-for-toronto-waterfront/.
4. Zuboff, S. (2019). *The age of surveillance capitalism*. Cambridge: Cambridge University Press.
5. www.theguardian.com/technology/2019/jan20/shoshana-zuboff-age-of-surveillance-capitalism-google-facebook.
6. www.ipcc.ch/report/sr15/.
7. Monnin, A., Bonnet, E., & Landivar, D. (2019). What the Anthropocene does to organizations. *35th EGOS Colloquium*, Edinburgh, Scotland.
8. www.technologyreview.com/s/610457/.
9. Monnin, A., Bonnet, E., & Landivar, D. (2019). What the Anthropocene does to organizations. *35th EGOS Colloquium*, Edinburgh, Scotland. See also, Tsing, A. L. (Ed.). (2017). *Arts of living on a damaged planet*. Minneapolis: University of Minnesota Press.
10. Dolphijn, R., & van der Tuin, T. (2012). Interview with Karen Barad. *New Materialism: Interviews & Cartographies Metaphysics*. London: Open Humanities Press.
11. Durand, R. (2014). *Organizations, strategy and society: The orgology of disorganized worlds*. Abingdon-on-Thames, UK: Routledge.
12. Tsing, A. L. (2015). *The mushroom at the end of the world-on the possibility of life in capitalist ruins*. Princeton, NK: Princeton University Press.
13. Skipping a flight might not save the Arctic, but it means you care. *The Guardian,* Saturday, July 20, 2019.
14. Epstein, C. (2018). *Climate: A new story*. Berkeley, CA: North Atlantic Books.
15. Sherwood, H. (2019, June 9). Forest bathing: Can time in the trees help body and soul? *The Observer*.
16. Carrington, D. (2019, June 24). Complacency endangers natural world, warns wildlife expert. *The Guardian*.

17. Dean, C. (2019, July 13–14). A threat to historic neighborhoods. *New York Times International Edition*, p. 5.
18. Bigley, M. (2019, July 7). Sonoma vineyards rebound from a trial by fire. *The New York Times*, p. 8.
19. Brooke, E. (2019, March). Change agents. *Elle*, p. 33.
20. Bennhold, K. (2019, July 16). Greens are the new hope for Europe's center. *New York Times International Edition*, p. 4.
21. Catholic Church. Pope (2013-present), Francis, P. (2015). Encyclical letter Laudato Si of the holy father Francis: On care for our common home.
22. https://wellbeingeconomy.org/.
23. www.transformationsforum.net/.
24. http://humanisticmanagement.international/.

Index

Note: Page numbers in *italic* indicate a figure on the corresponding page.